of society and history . . . a masterclass in the ease with which the writer can blend the contextual and the personal. Perhaps more importantly, *Deep House* is a vivid example of quiet tenderness. It is, indeed, a love letter that details more than a decade's worth of life from first date to marriage. But Mr. Atherton Lin never effuses, never shouts. Love is in the quiet details."

—***Hippocampus Magazine***

"The book pairs backstories of pioneering queer people who pursued marriage equality alongside charged vignettes of passion found in sexual embrace . . . comes at a particularly apt time under the Trump administration's ruthless anti-immigration agenda."

—***The Observer US***

"A riveting hybrid of memoir and socio-cultural interrogation."

—***AnOther Magazine***

"An intellectually and emotionally powerful read today, this book will grow even more valuable in the future; its history lessons are wrapped in relatable passions." —***Passport Magazine***

"Sublime, sensual . . . Atherton Lin's descriptive powers, salty and sultry, prove inexhaustible . . . Some pages you can smell, others you can hear." — ***The New Yorker***

"The fact that this is often a deeply hilarious book doesn't detract from the seriousness of its subject matter, and Atherton Lin's unique voice is irresistible." —**NPR**

"It'll scratch the itch for anyone who wants a sexy and sweet story of young love, but it has plenty to teach about the culture wars and bureaucratic hurdles that have made living and loving so difficult for LGBTQ and immigrant communities, too." —**NBC News**

"A dreamy queer romance...*Deep House* is an incisive blend of memoir and cultural history, tracing the evolution of his decades-long relationship with his British partner against the backdrop of queer legal progress." —***Dazed***

"The book merges memoir with history, giving it a crackle of humour amongst the pathos. It's also a gorgeous portrait of how gay relationships form, and where we find the time and space to insert people we love into our lives" —***i-D***

"Messy and sexy, touching and enlightening, *Deep House* is a necessary addition to the queer literary canon." —***Crosscurrent***

"Humorous, elegant, and intelligent...An inspiring and deeply affecting read." —***Cha Journal***

"Jeremy Atherton Lin's memoir is a tribute to home. Part memoir, part history of the fight for marriage equality...a delightful rejection of traditional genre...encapsulates the deep need for human connection denied by the law." —***Wallpaper***

"For anyone with even a passing interest in queer history, it's a seductive approach, and a testament to Atherton Lin's talents as a writer that he pulls it off." —***The Face***

"Questions gay marriage as an object of queer liberation through historical case studies and [Atherton Lin's] own tender, but acerbic lens." —***Electric Lit***

DEEP HOUSE

Also by Jeremy Atherton Lin

Gay Bar

DEEP HOUSE

The Gayest Love Story Ever Told

Jeremy Atherton Lin

LITTLE, BROWN AND COMPANY
New York Boston London

While every effort has been made to maintain historical accuracy, this creative work is not intended to be taken as definitive nor to imply official affiliation with depicted individuals or institutions.

Autobiographical aspects of this book have been fictionalized; some names and identifying characteristics have been changed and some individuals are composites.

Some passages have been previously published in very different forms, as detailed in the endnotes.

Little, Brown and Company
Hachette Book Group
1290 Avenue of the Americas, New York, NY 10104
littlebrown.com

Originally published in hardcover by Little, Brown and Company, June 2025
First trade paperback edition, June 2026

ISBN 9780316545792 (hc) / 9780316546072 (pb)
Library of Congress Control Number: 2025934638

Printing 1, 2026

LSC-C

Printed in the United States of America

and my windows might be dirty
but it's my house
and if i can't see out sometimes
they can't see in   either

—from "My House,"
Nikki Giovanni

CONTENTS

1
SHUT THE FRONT DOOR

It's the pulsing I remember, not the spunk.

The first time wasn't triumphant, pornographic. We moved like streams. I can't recall the who-first, or how, or even if we came at all. We were impassioned but had been holding out for hours. Such a long bus ride back to your place in East London. We were sleepy. Your bedroom, wet and wallpapered, might have been quaint if it belonged to a grandma but seemed squalid occupied by a twenty-year-old with a saturnine smile. You were all elbows and knees, and ears that weren't big but stuck out so that you looked like not just a cherub but a cartoon monkey. So skinny you were only as wide face-on as I was in profile.

You said you'd always liked the name Jeremy, at least since the Pearl Jam song. You enjoyed that our first names are alike. We'd each entertained the delightfully narcissistic fantasy of a boyfriend with the same name. We'd both been to the Jean-Michel Basquiat exhibition at the Serpentine, where we bought the same postcard: the artist with a Siamese cat on his lap. The Velvet Underground poster that hung on your wall was the exact one I had in my bungalow back in Los Angeles, where I'd been living before graduating college and traveling the Old World by train. London was the trip's bookend; my friend Xuan and I landed several weeks earlier and were back for a few nights before the return flight.

I wasn't looking for you. I had been—as you'd later put it when people asked how we met—*fucking my way around Europe.* I was looking for fun. And for affirmation that I qualified as fun to other young men.

Back in Los Angeles, I'd been looking for *older.* Seeking my own history in the form of a more mature man. On some preconscious level, I'd been searching for big gay brothers. So many of them were dead. Theorist Michael Warner has described it as 'the most painfully instructed generation.' He sets forth how, with the decimation from AIDS, queer cultural memory, already obscured, became violently redacted.

And I didn't want just to pick their brains, I wanted to touch their bodies.

The search would appear in my mind, and still does to this day, as a dark hallway with no discernible end. The walls are black like in a cruise club or bathhouse. Unknown men avert their eyes and disappear behind doors. I sense these open onto intergalactic space. I do not hold the keys. Some doors are left ajar, so I'm not necessarily prevented from entering. It's just that I'm not able to move down the hallway.

This could be diagnosed as bathophobia, a fear of depths, being pulled into a hallway (or cave, lake, well, tunnel . . .) and consumed by a bottomless abyss. But my hallway does not make me fearful, exactly. Harrowing, but it isn't all about absence. I have described the image to a therapist who reminded me that a hallway also connects, so contains possibilities—of encounter, for one thing.

Now I'd found someone who seemed even more guileless than I was. Not an anonymous hunk with the guidebook, but a hormonal lad who couldn't stop grinning. I *was* looking for you; I just wouldn't allow myself to hope for it. You were sheepish, you slouched, but that face, with its helpless optimism, could not hide itself.

Still, I could not be sure what color your eyes were. They kept rolling back in your head. On the dance floor, this had been a coy gesture, at once mocking and angelic. The first words you said to me, or mouthed while the music pounded, were: *I'm so embarrassed*. When you were supine beneath me, your lids fluttered and there went your pupils again. I figured you felt safe enough with me to let go. Or was the upward motion defensive, like an optical cremaster reflex, an involuntary act of protecting the blue?

Of course we opened up in the afterglow, but it was embers. We were spent. Saturday morning had dug itself out from the fathoms of Friday night. I didn't bring up the chimerical hallway. I hadn't yet articulated it to myself. We whispered of rooms we once lived in, like my weird little place on the wrong side of West Hollywood where I'd tacked up the identical poster—THE VELVET UNDERGROUND & NICO PRODUCED BY ANDY WARHOL—that hung across from your bed. We murmured the beginning of stories we would continue to tell, with more detail and further distance, over the following months, then decades.

THERE WAS PUBIC HAIR in the wall paint. Or, I preferred to think while rolling a strand free with my fingertip, just bristles from a brush. But I kept returning to the image of a hirsute house painter, stripped-down and shedding as he hurried along with vehement strokes.

The bungalow was the first—and remains the only—time I lived alone. An unusual move for an undergrad to make: extravagant, and emotional, as if I could rewrite *lonely* as *independent.* I took the place I thought I deserved: tiny, leaking gas, with those wiry pubes clinging to the walls like the rim of a toilet. I encountered a cockroach so enormous I took it for a rat. Kids played handball in the adjacent parking lot, bouncing on the wall I slept against. I tried not to let it bother me. Waking to the insistent *boing* on weekend mornings was a bit like having company.

I never dealt directly with the landlord, Freddie. I later wondered if it was he who was forwarding my details on to an identity theft ring. Initially I passed over the forms and a check to a woman at a desk positioned like a barricade at the very front of an undecorated apartment. I imagined smoke-filled meetings behind the bedroom doors. It did not seem to be a space without at least one gun.

This "office" was in a different apartment building, somewhere in Hollywood—a dingbat, one of those two-story structures teetering on stilts over its parking spaces, with a name on the facade like La Traviata or Lido Capri. I knew dingbats. In one, I snorted lines of crystal meth off the floor while a hooker crouched low in the empty kitchen, anticipating an imminent police raid. Then I moved into a dingbat with Xuan, considerably more salubrious but still faintly depressed.

Xuan graduated early and moved to New York City. That didn't last long, but while she was away, I decided to look for a cheap place of my own. At a dingbat near Crescent Heights, the key was handed to me by a manager in a turban with lipstick on her teeth. A Maine Coon wandered in and out of the folds of her muumuu. Her demeanor telegraphed: *I could've been somebody.* What happened? The apartment was a shithole, so I didn't stick around to hear. Apartment hunting on a budget was the opposite of following a Hollywood star map—a free tour of other people's broken dreams. Prestige was presented in the past tense. One unit, I was told, had been rented by a young Mary Tyler Moore. Apparently Charlie Chaplin had lived in several of the available properties.

The place I did wind up taking, a couple blocks north of Melrose, was slummy and small, but the many windows brought in decent light. It was one of eight or ten in a bungalow court. Each poky unit opened onto a neglected central walkway, directly facing another like strangers across the table at a dinner party. It's said that non-native palm trees were first planted in Los Angeles by Franciscan missionaries in the eighteenth century to simulate a biblical landscape, and bungalow courts possibly had pious origins, too; it's been suggested that their design was based on groupings of cottages built in the nineteenth century on Protestant campgrounds, a communal form of architecture.

The neighbors and I were generally not communal. Several did leave their front doors open because there was no air-conditioning. An old dude hoarded newspapers in stressfully tall stacks. An actress always dressed in exercise gear kept trying to get off the phone to keep the line open for news of a callback. I was vaguely fond of the guy in the unit next to mine, a skinny young brunet in a trilby with a dodgy, horny vibe who graffitied his walls, apparently resolved to never get his deposit returned.

Bungalow courts, whether built in Spanish Colonial, Tudor,

Islamic or "Japo-Swiss" style, aspired to an ideal of California living. Because each front door opens directly onto the world, perhaps by way of a small porch, the courts could be construed as mini suburbs. In Southern California they served as luxury rentals to vacationers from colder parts of America before being taken over by low-income residents, whose permanence lowered the tone. A hospice for high hopes.

I was telling you about the place because I wanted to tell you about the man. He must have been waiting in the adjacent parking lot, where the kids played on other evenings, but not this one.

That afternoon I'd driven Xuan around to the usual vintage clothing stores. Then we came back to mine to plan our trek through Europe after I finished my degree. We smoked pot. We agreed that Prague was a priority. Xuan promised a spreadsheet. She perched uncomfortably on the edge of my futon, then moved to the folding chair at my desk, impatiently leafing through an issue of *i-D* magazine that featured a London nightclub full of cute boys like you—and where indeed we would meet.

It was dinnertime, and she wanted to see her ex-boyfriend, with whom I was hopelessly in love. He could not just breakdance; he could vogue. I'd give her a lift back to her nicer, cleaner place.

Night came slowly, like waiting out unknown opening bands in a near-empty club. It was balmy, though September had come and gone.

I paid no mind to the loitering figure.

Hello, he hollered, a little too loud, as I locked the door.

Without actually looking, I got the impression he wore coveralls—one of Freddie's lackeys fixing pipes or the washing machine.

I gave a chipper *hey* as Xuan and I walked to my car. I dropped her off at a Spanish Revival in Miracle Mile. She rented a place there with high ceilings and actual tableware, not just a pizza box for a plate. I drove home listening to "You Gotta Be" by Des'ree.

Back at mine, I took a couple more tokes. Figured I'd masturbate to get to sleep. Put Jane's Addiction on the boom box, skipping ahead to "Summertime Rolls." Switched off the blue porch light, then the bedside lamp. Between the sheets, I became more aware of my body, of being inside flesh, thick and sun-baked.

A knock at the door startled me slightly. Mostly, I was annoyed. Naked, with a semi from the weed, I wasn't in the mood to be cooperative and helpful. I gathered myself in a blanket woven with the image of Van Gogh's *The Starry Night.*

What is it?

Something-something. Have to.

Maintenance, I presumed. Pulling aside the tablecloth I'd hung as a curtain, I discerned the fidgety shape of the guy from earlier. I switched on the blue porch light.

He kept up with the prattling. I cracked the door. *The Starry Night* fell off my shoulders like a gown.

The man looked relieved. *I'm supposed to meet somebody here?* he panted.

I wouldn't know.

A guy?

I don't know, I repeated, starting to get it.

Bisexual?

No—I don't know, I said in a tone at once arch and butching up.

...I come in?, he said, sharper.

I tried to close the door, but he wedged it with his foot.

Want me to suck your dick? he said, almost angrily.

I laughed at that, which slackened my control of the door. I shook my head broadly, smiling without teeth. *No,* I said roundly.

You want to suck MY dick?

Uh! No! I barked.

He began to force the door. I planted my weight and pushed back.

The blanket slipped down my hips.

Did I gather it back up too slowly? Was I shamefully parading my happy trail and cum gutters, the routes into me?

I can't believe, I thought, I'm about to do what they taught the girls sophomore year in high school. Then I went for it:

NO! I commanded. *GO. AWAY. NOW.*

I managed the door shut; *The Starry Night* fell to the floor as I locked and latched. Scooped it up and crouched below the sightline of windows—so many windows—reaching up to twist the blinds shut.

I was too young to be laying down roots, and what's more, unsure of the soil where I found myself standing. What world had I entered, inhabited by such desperate men? I went to bed as lonely as he was.

I'd remain low that night, and jumpy for days. I'd wonder if blue lightbulbs are *a thing*, giving off a signal of wanton availability. I'd fret that I courted the attention, presented as alluring to sex pests. My wide mouth, the unmade black hair. A descendant of abuse, but I did not know—did anyone then?—that such trauma could be wired into me.

A surprising thought had come to me at the door: Because he had arrived, then waited, had made all that effort, was I obliged to let the man in? Being gay, was that what I signed up for? Could his brusqueness and greed force me to finally feel *something?* Because the big brother I'd been waiting for, the one armed with the instructions, was clearly not on his way.

The man was older, a little ugly. He had "an accent." I was

inexperienced and awkward. And while I may have been white-passing, I was non-white enough to be exiled from the gay scene. All in all, I probably had more in common with this creep than the men on Santa Monica Boulevard who fell into each other's arms without shoving. Most of those clones were probably no more aware than me of the full extent of the collective trauma we'd inherited. But we were scorched by the residual traces. It was a part of what made such a disparate bunch into a "we," though sometimes it seemed what I experienced most from them was hostility.

Maybe the man didn't identify as gay, even bi. Maybe he had a wife and kids, and I represented some form of relief on the side. Maybe what he actually wanted was other than sex, and the proposition was just a ruse for another form of invasion.

But what if I'd been more passive? What if I'd been so swayed by an eagerness to please that I forgot about the boundaries that, come to think of it, nobody had taught me? Would I have let him in?

The truth is, I was flattered. Which only added to the fear—made it both stickier and less adept.

It could have been, something in me shrugged, a *learning experience.* I would've at least gotten head. That could have been the rule. Only receiving. In which case, he'd still receive what he wanted. I had my dick to give. Maybe I *was* learning something about my desires, then.

A couple days later, watching MTV, I became angry about the scanty outfits worn by Salt-N-Pepa in the video for "Shoop." A woman can have a weakness *(MEN!)*, the song goes, and that does not make her a *ho.* I'd known every word by heart since it came out a few years back. But suddenly I disapproved. They *did* look like hos, leaning against a topless convertible. Was I becoming moralistic? I decided I felt closer solidarity with Queen Latifah's hands-off anthem "U.N.I.T.Y." The song's narrator wore shorts, but only because it was *CRAZY HOT!* Latifah herself was swaddled—in blazers, turbans, sashes, baggy basketball jerseys. I should wear more clothes, I thought. Then there was "Waterfalls" by TLC, a candidate for most cautionary R&B track ever. I'd always been slightly uneasy about the lyrics and the video. It seemed to me the aspirational, impatient, waterfall-chasing characters were held responsible for their own deaths by gun violence and AIDS. Now I found the message comforting: I had a choice not to chase an ungraspable flow. I could stay behind locked doors.

Really, though, I craved attention. I found myself biding my time, waiting for it.

Then this man's aggression turned me prudish. Not only did I consider covering myself up—turtlenecks, no shorts—I joked to a friend that if I attacked my own face with acid, I could be sure that I wasn't going around asking for it.

I'd been lightly harassed on the street before. On my doorstep, the man had me actually scared. And ashamed. He described my sexuality back to me as a potential site of violence. By forcing himself onto me, he also incriminated my gay identity.

He *saw* me, I feared, the *real* me, in other words, *the slut.* He saw an orgasm addict, a wolf cub with no pack, listening to sleazy rock, stoned, marked out by a blue lightbulb.

What kind of person would allow the thought to even cross their mind: Should I let this random man in and allow him to taste me?

It was the way he'd put it as a question. As if granting me agency, suggesting it was possible I could want it.

Because he put it as a question, saying no meant I was left to inspect its shadow, the unticked yes.

When he tried to force his way in, I closed the door. Ended an encounter I might have otherwise allowed open for longer. Out of—what? Something like empathy; at least not wanting to pass judgment where a connection might exist. Instead, I latched the door and hid.

Soon enough, I moved out. I would be given the key to other doors.

THE LANDLORD KEEPS A small room above, you told me.

It was a cupboard, basically, on the landing between floors, his refuge from wherever home was. You and your flatmate Pauley had sat there with him to arrange the lease, clocking the shelves of his smutty VHS tapes from your perch on the vinyl bench. The landlord spilled Baileys Irish Cream on a well-thumbed magazine, then held it up and licked the cover boy's smooth midriff clean.

Could he be peeping now?

You guffawed. You seemed to be forgiving of creeps. This made me want to become one myself and handle you roughly.

You'd only just moved to London from Bath. There, you had managed to find yourself an avuncular figure. Several years older. Regaled you with tales of piss and socks. The idea of him made your dad nervous. It made me possessive just hearing about this guy, and I'd only known you for a matter of hours. But he never touched you. Maybe you were a better listener than me, so you found a better speaker.

You seemed more innocent but also somehow more broken-in than I was. You were so quiet, so nice. The type of boy that someone will always take under their wing. In a crowd, the one who is nearly overlooked, then identified as the best. As it had been with me. You made me the subject. You were so clearly the object. I had no doubt that men saw you as prey, and themselves as both predator and protector.

At twenty, you were barely legal. The age of consent had been lowered from twenty-one to eighteen just a year and a half before. I was twenty-one, so I guess if the law hadn't changed I'd be committing an offense. Another reason why being naked together had a naughty, conspiratorial halo. We were half innocent and obscene. We'd been infantilized by our governments—our twink years prolonged. The scent from beneath your foreskin was practically an illicit substance.

The vague vice of "buggery" had been illegal in England for over four centuries when sex between two men was partially decriminalized in 1967, and then there were plenty of stipulations (no groups, not in public). The minimum age of twenty-one was far above that of straights, which had been set at sixteen (no anal, though) in 1885. Weirdly, when the age of gay consent was brought down to eighteen in 1994, it was a part of the Criminal Justice and Public Order Act, mostly known (and reviled) for its clampdown on raves. (The act also, as if in a spirit of equality, legalized anal sex between heteros over the age of eighteen.) It wouldn't be until the new millennium that the age minimum for male homosex was adjusted once more to finally match the straight age of consent of sixteen.

In certain places in America, anal and/or oral sex were still crimes no matter the age of the participants. And while such laws could also apply to straights, they had the effect of solidifying a perception of gays as a criminal class. It was seldom, though, that the cops kicked down a door to enforce them.

Not long before we met, your own front door came off its hinges. This was back in Bath, where you had been living alone, too, in a studio flat in a Georgian town house. You stained the carpet with red wine. You attempted to "stain" a shelf in tasteful green. Other than the couch, which your mum had upholstered in patchwork at some point, you kept it minimalist. An Oasis poster hung above the mantel of a fireplace that did not work. You never turned on the hot water. The river Avon flowed past, hidden by trees.

On the night in question you were sleeping at the flat of your gay mentor, who was lending you a room to be with some boy.

Your ex-girlfriend sometimes crashed at your place but did not have the key. When she arrived and you weren't home, she took the door down.

How?

Sheer fury. You laughed. *Shoulders.*

It seemed like more than the need to enter. She was angry. You didn't seem the type to enrage people, except for that very quality. You were inoffensive, which people find infuriating.

You and I separated for a day and a night; then, for my last sleep before departing the country, I somehow found my way back to your flat. I had a sore throat. Nothing much more than the scratch from too many cigarettes, but when I griped about it, you showed concern. You weren't yet used to us Americans, with our nonstop updates.

I explained how when I got back, I planned to move to San Francisco, first crashing at my parents' place an hour's drive south of the city. I wrote their address on a Hugo Boss cologne ad torn from *The Face,* featuring a Juergen Teller photograph of a model who resembled James Dean. The copy read:

THE WORLD IS GETTING SMALLER. SMELL BETTER.

THE DAY BEFORE I met you, the *New York Times* reported that members of the United States government were plotting to keep us apart.

On page 15 of section B, just before the obituaries, in the Thursday, May 9, 1996, edition: 'State-by-state skirmishes over prospective marriage rights for lesbians and gay men escalated into a national battle today.'

That week, Bob Barr (R-GA) introduced H.R. 3396—the Defense of Marriage Act, or DOMA—in the House of Representatives. DOMA would amend the United States judicial code so that no state or territory was required to recognize a same-sex marriage solemnized in another jurisdiction.

Barr was one of eighty-four Republican freshmen who'd entered Congress in a wave referred to as the Republican Revolution. Barr was highly caffeinated and ambitious. Just after being sworn in to Congress in January 1995, contrary to the usual protocol of sitting back during early sessions, he proposed a repeal of Clinton's ban on assault weapons. He was a thrice-married, mustachioed, suspender-hoisted man who was seen, while a candidate for the Senate in 1992, 'licking whipped cream from the chests [or 'neckline,' as other observers attested] of two buxom women' at a Leukemia Society fundraising luncheon.

During his first summer on the job, Barr's office received an article clipped from the *New Republic* and circulated to select colleagues by a fellow congressman, a Mormon convert from Oklahoma, regarding potential ramifications of the situation in Oahu. By then, the prospect of same-sex marriage had been hot-potatoing around courts on the island for years.

The Hawaii Marriage Issue, as it became known in Barr's office, started with a stunt. In December 1990 three same-sex couples, egged on by a highly divisive local activist, walked into the health department headquarters in Honolulu, trailed by reporters, and applied for marriage licenses. Upon rejection, they took it to court, where they lost the first round. Then in 1993, Hawaii's supreme court vacated that decision. There'd be a final hearing, but gay marriage was a distinct possibility.

The *New Republic* article was entitled "No Fantasy Island." Law professor Andrew Koppelman wrote that gay marriage on the Pacific archipelago could not play out in isolation: 'As a general rule, most states honor each other's marriage laws. That's why a heterosexual couple can get married during their vacation in Reno and have their marriage recognized back home in Atlanta.' An exception can be made when nuptials performed in another jurisdiction contravene a specific policy of the home state. In the case of same-sex marriage, Koppelman speculated, objections 'will be stronger in states that criminalize sodomy than it will be in states that prohibit anti-gay discrimination, but the issue will have to be litigated anew in each state. And marriage is also significant for some federal purposes, such as Social Security, military pensions and immigration.'

The notion of gay marriage may have seemed unthinkable—an oxymoron. But, Koppelman noted, the state of Hawaii was half a billion dollars in deficit. And the only proposal for solving that was based on a study, published in the *Southern California Law Review,* regarding the potential tourist revenue that would result from same-sex marriage.

Watchful conservatives, perceiving an impending "threat," devised the Defense of Marriage Act as a preventative to keep it from proliferating elsewhere.

It also made a pretty great wedge issue in a presidential election year. Bill Clinton, the incumbent, had a wishy-washy track record on gay rights. Now he needed to hold on to gay and lesbian votes without appearing to be in their perverted pockets. Republicans had him in a no-win situation.

A couple weeks back, on the 18th of April, the *Washington Times* had run the headline CLINTON OFFERS NEW PROMISES TO GAYS: HINTS HE'LL PUSH LEGAL "MARRIAGES."

This was apparently intended to alarm a conservative readership. 'President Clinton,' according to the lead paragraph, 'is wooing homosexual voters and AIDS activists, who were angered by his handling of their issues earlier in his term, by making new promises to consider expanded civil rights—including same-sex "marriages."'

Never mind that the article went on to quote a White House aide on same-sex marriage: 'Not something we intend to espouse.' The administration vowed to 'do everything we can to support' traditional straight marriage. Senior adviser George Stephanopoulos would later reiterate that the president was 'against same-sex marriage.' It would've only been in private that Stephanopoulos might suggest his boss need not rush into a staunch position.

But the *Washington Times* leaned on some off-script lip service from Marsha Scott, a straight woman who occupied the unprecedented full-time White House position of liaison to the lesbians and gays. At a private address to 'a homosexual group' in Boston, Scott commented that the government should 'find ways to ensure that those of you in these loving, long-term and committed relationships can enjoy all the same benefits' as straight couples, going on to specify that marriage may not be the right 'vehicle' to achieve equal status.

Still, there were enough woolly words to spin into a misleading headline that put the Clinton administration on the back foot. According to journalist Sasha Issenberg, who has extensively chronicled the issue in his tome *The Engagement: America's Quarter-Century Struggle over Same-Sex Marriage*, Senator Don Nickles (R-OK) picked up on the article right away, emailing his staff: 'Interesting story in the *Washington Times* today.' To which a member of his staff replied, 'Sounds like an opportunity for us.' Meaning the Republicans could instrumentalize the mere specter of gay marriage to force Clinton to take a position, potentially alienating a core of gay supporters or swaths of heteronormative undecideds.

While Representative Barr was drafting DOMA, Senator Nickles worked on his own bill, called the Meaning of Marriage Act, or MOMA. In the space of a brief dictionary entry, it established a federal definition of *marriage* as the legal union between one man and one woman, and *spouse* as a husband or wife of the opposite sex. Nickles had advanced this notion as early as 1993, when he persuaded sponsors of the Family and Medical Leave Act to limit the definition of *spouse* so that employers would not be forced to grant unpaid leave to gay and lesbian workers caring for their domestic partners.

Republicans orchestrated a merging of the drafts across the two chambers of Congress, so that in its final form, DOMA absorbed Nickles's federal definitions. This made it more consequential: the legitimacy of gay marriage would not only vary across state lines, it would be plainly invalid at the federal level. On May 8th, the day after DOMA was brought forth in the House, Nickles introduced an identical bill in the Senate. 'An Act,' it trumpeted, 'to define and protect the institution of marriage.'

DOMA, Representative Barr insisted to the press, would not altogether outlaw same-sex marriage at the state level. Yet through its rigid definitions, the bill would deny gay and lesbian couples federal rights and privileges, including immigration. When the world appears to be getting smaller, politicians find ways to draw up borders.

A lot of queers, of course, didn't want in on the historically proprietary and patriarchal institution in the first place. But marriage affords privileges, including mobility across borders. Marriage is, among other things, a passport.

When we met, same-sex marriage did not exist anywhere, not in any meaningful legal sense. There was no civil or domestic partnership across the UK, where I found you, nor the US, where I'm from. It wasn't against the law for us to fall in love. But if we were to forge a commitment, there didn't seem to be any place to take it.

How was I to anticipate that if, on that Friday night in London, I happened to glance, right then, across the room, and spot you, and if you were to see me back, and feel it too, a lurch, overwhelming, and if we were to give in, it would mean we had found each other but become lost?

ON THE FLIGHT BACK to California, I wondered if I should still be pining for Piero, my pickup in Rome.

Piero had taken me back to the apartment he was subletting from an actress, where I'd somewhat lost my anal virginity to him, if you count half an inch in. He'd been gentlemanly about the stains on the sheets.

No, Xuan said as we buckled up. *London is the one.*

I reminded myself that it's the reduced oxygen that makes people tear up on the plane. I'd long thought this would mark the point when I moved to San Francisco to begin my independent adult life. Now I found myself reluctant to admit that the plane was not headed toward my future, but away from you.

While we were up in the air, White House press secretary Michael D. McCurry was asked why President Clinton opposed same-sex marriage.

'He believes this is a time when we need to do things to strengthen the American family,' McCurry responded, 'and that's the reason why he's taken this position.' This didn't deviate much from an Oval Office–approved script, but the emphasis seemed off, a little too close to the conservative battle cry of "family values."

Soon after, David Mixner, gay rights advocate and friend of Bill Clinton's, would state, 'I don't think there's any question that the statement was extraordinarily political in nature, because no one in the White House can make a cogent argument about how gay people committing themselves to a lifelong relationship threatens the American family.' Mixner concluded, 'It is a ridiculous statement.'

But Clinton was never going to be the gay marriage president. As the vulnerable incumbent, he needed to maintain a traditionalist image. Around the time of that damaging *Washington*

Times headline, Monica Lewinsky, a young staffer in the White House Office of Legislative Affairs, was spotted in the West Wing after hours by a Secret Service officer. He reported this to the deputy chief of staff, and within days Lewinsky was reassigned to a junior role at the Pentagon based on 'immature and inappropriate behavior.' The *Post* later disclosed, 'White House officials say they engineered the move because Lewinsky appeared to be infatuated with Clinton.' It's thought their affair began in 1995. Though the scandal hadn't broken, one might suspect such indiscretions put him on guard.

Political adviser Dick Morris counseled the president to embrace a 'values agenda' and brought on author Naomi Wolf as an unpaid consultant to help connect with women voters. Clinton needed 'an overarching, pre-emptive metaphor,' went a leaked memo attributed to Wolf. The memo offered this one: 'The Good Father,' with a narrative of 'building a house together—the American house.' That way, Clinton could state that he was willing to 'negotiate about the shape of the house we are building; the design; the details; but I will not let anyone or anything touch the bedrock. I will DEFEND/PROTECT the foundation.'

I LEFT BEHIND A stick of deodorant at your place. You held it to your nose while you masturbated. We were about to begin disclosing intimacies like that—some unknowable mix of missing and imagining the other—in countless long letters. We'd reckon with absence through language. Madly proclaim and confess. In a way, I'm still writing a love letter now.

I'm also writing on the trails of those who went before us, though we had few means of knowing who they were back then. I want to learn how we arrived here together and find out who traveled first, as well as something about those who obstructed their way. Allow me to shuffle the cards that were stacked against us. But the learning does not put an end to the wanting. The wanting must be kept on like a pilot light.

Our first few years would be defined by apartness. To say *feels like forever* only sounds childishly impatient to others—at best, an abstraction—but that is how we would move through the next period of months and years. Eventually, we would form—*force*—a life in one place. It was outside the law but full and real, lived in a succession of rented apartments.

All words are just an abstraction, but my memories of us amount to *home*—some shapeless notion of hearth, as well as the material details. When anyone asks about the history of us, my mind goes to locations. Our love is a house.

I think of poet Robert Duncan, who married mononymic artist Jess in a 1951 ceremony in San Francisco, which of course bore no legal significance. They dubbed themselves *householders*. Jess referred to himself as a *housewaif*. Curator Tara McDowell has found in Robert Duncan's notebooks his description of their domestic sphere as

> *a lone holding in an alien forest-world, as a campfire about which we gatherd in an era of cold and night—a made-up thing in*

which participating we have had the medium of a life together.

I find myself returning to this line often. I'd been sure it was the image of the campfire that drew me back until I realized it is as much the phrase *a made-up thing*.

While it can feel safe inside a household of our own making, there is always the threat of invasion. I'm writing the threshold. And the terror of having made a thing worth protecting.

2

BETWEEN TWO FAGGOTS

In a *Tonight Show* monologue broadcast in the spring of 1975, Johnny Carson mentioned a man who approached the county courthouse in Boulder, Colorado, with his horse Dolly. Incensed at the news that the office had begun issuing marriage licenses to same-sex couples, he intended to make a point by applying to marry his horse. 'Now, you can make up your own jokes,' Carson said. (He did offer up a few, such as: 'Y'know, this could be the first time that a husband will ride his wife to the wedding reception.')

The initial gay marriage in the mountain state was between two men both named Dave. In Colorado Springs, where they tried first, the Daves were told they'd have a better chance in Boulder. Two years before, the Boulder City Council had passed one of the country's first declarations protecting gays and lesbians from discrimination (though it had since been repealed by voters). The newly elected county clerk, Clela Rorex, wore her hair long and her skirts short. Her campaign brochure unfolded like a piece of origami. She was low-key in nature but used the newfangled honorific *Ms.* She drove a car with the license plate MS1 and a YES! EQUAL RIGHTS bumper sticker.

The hopeful couple arrived at her office in late March 1975. Clela was careful about procedure. Her father had been a county clerk, too, and her mother was a teacher. She made the relevant inquiries and was told by the assistant district attorney that nothing in the Colorado marriage code specifically prohibited providing a license to two women or two men. It was her call. On the 26th of March, Clela issued the two Daves a license, and they wed the next day.

A few more queers showed up, prompting the *New York Times* to dub Colorado 'a mini-Nevada for homosexual couples.'

Clela began to suffer migraines as she was attacked with hateful phone calls. She was a single mother, and her young son sometimes answered the phone, only to be exposed to indiscriminate vitriol.

Then came the guy with the horse. 'He had a line all prepared,' Clela recounted to documentarian Thomas Miller. *'If a man can marry a man, and a woman can marry a woman, why can't a tired old cowboy like me marry his best friend Dolly?'*

Clela was at a loss—until she came to the question of Dolly's age and the man replied that she was eight. She laid down her pen and said, *'I'm sorry. Dolly is underage.'*

TONY SULLIVAN AND RICHARD Adams were watching *The Tonight Show* at their place in Tujunga, a neighborhood in the foothills of the Angeles National Forest. The couple had read a brief report on Boulder's same-sex weddings in *The Advocate* but dismissed it. How long could that possibly go on? Now that the situation had been brought up on national television, they realized that licenses had been issued openly and unimpeded for nearly a month. Maybe this *was* the moment they'd been waiting for.

Tony and Richard met on Cinco de Mayo 1971 at a Los Angeles gay bar called The Closet. They made a date to rendezvous the next day at Greta Garbo's star on Hollywood Boulevard. Tony was a globe-trotting Australian passing through on his way to England. The next year, he returned to California, and continued to form a deeper love with mild-mannered Richard, who was born in Manila and was a naturalized US citizen.

With no recourse in the States, they planned to move together to Australia, where a flamboyant young Tony had been brought up in a privileged yet troubled household. In Thomas Miller's documentary *Limited Partnership*, Tony recalls his mother planning to have him lobotomized.

Tony went to the Australian embassy in Los Angeles to apply for a visa for Richard. 'Everything was going along blissfully fine until I happened to mention he was born in the Philippines,' Tony later told on the history podcast *Lost Highways*.

The consulate rep declared that if Richard was Filipino, his visa would not be approved. Though the White Australia Policy, a group of rules obstructing the immigration of nonwhite people, had recently ended, the bureaucrat took it upon himself to continue its enforcement.

'And then he said, *Filipinos shouldn't complain. They're the worst of the lot.*'

Tony got hitched to a female friend two days before his visa expired in January 1974, but flubbed the green card interview by refusing to pretend their marriage had been consummated. It was annulled.

He developed the routine of going to Mexico and back every three months, though by 1975 he and Richard were wary about the accumulation of stamps in his passport, an obvious sign that he'd found a workaround to prolong his stay in the States. In March the two were wed at the gay-affirming Metropolitan Community Church, for whatever that was worth.

The pair didn't want just a symbolic exchange of rings; they needed a legal loophole. So after *The Tonight Show* bit aired, Tony and Richard flew to Colorado, with two MCC ministers in tow, and showed up at Clela's office.

On the 21st of April they received their license, wed on the spot in the corridor outside the office, and returned immediately for their certificate. They later held a ceremony in Denver, wearing open-collared white shirts. They went back to their hotel room, then emerged for a press conference to declare that this time the marriage had indeed been consummated. Like other gays before them, they made the most of secondary gains.

After all the scheming, adrenaline, and publicity, it was only when they were back home in Tujunga that it sank in. As his husband put the key in the lock of their front door, Tony realized that they were actually married.

Along with Annice and Violet—who received their license the same day—they were among the last of six same-sex couples to be married before the Colorado attorney general ordered the licenses to cease. These half dozen marriages were declared invalid, but slipped into a strange limbo, never specifically nullified by the state.

THOSE WERE NOT THE first same-sex marriage licenses issued in the United States, nor the first to enter into an indefinite state of uncertainty.

In the most famous story, Jack Baker met Michael McConnell on the weekend before Halloween 1966 at a barn party held near the college town of Norman, Oklahoma. The place was jumping with young gay men, many of them students at the university. Jack and Michael were introduced by a mutual friend, as if rolling two socks together from a pile of fresh laundry. They were both twenty-four years old and blue-eyed, stood right around six feet tall, wore the same shoe size. A 'matched pair,' Michael later wrote, like 'salt and pepper shakers.' Or salt and salt. Side by side, they look like a dictionary image of the prefix *homo*. But in the early days Jack had a neat flattop, making Michael, whose own hair fell across his brow, suspicious he was a *suit*—a repressed married man with a secret penchant for the gay college scene. Jack soon loosened up his look.

On his twenty-fifth birthday, Jack asked Michael to move in with him. To become *lovers*, in the parlance of the time, meaning to set up home together. Michael agreed, with the stipulation that they get married. 'Legally.' Since his playground days, he'd shared the dream of the two girls he counted as his best friends: 'a sparkling new house with a handsome husband.' Jack and Michael had a traditionalist streak, a belief in doing things the right way—albeit with bending. 'We outfoxed them,' Jack told the *New York Times* years later. 'That's what lawyers do: make the law work for them.'

The pair moved to Minneapolis, where Jack enrolled in law school at the University of Minnesota and Michael accepted an appointment as head of cataloging at the campus library. It was there that they realized the state law's definition of marriage did not mention the sex of the spouses. In 1970 they applied for a marriage license, commonly considered to be the first such request by a same-sex couple in the United States. The Hennepin County clerk denied their application. (Two months later a pair of women applied for a license under pseudonyms in Kentucky, also unsuccessfully.)

In light of the press coverage, the university regents refused to proceed with Michael's hiring. He sued, won, then faced the regents' appeal. Meanwhile the pair battled through the state court system in pursuit of their marriage license. Their photographs appeared in *Look* magazine, alongside text like 'Not all homosexual life is a series of one-night stands in bathhouses, public toilets or gay bars (those queer, mirror images of the swinging-singles straight scene). Some homosexuals—a minority—live together in stable, often long-lasting relationships, like Baker's and McConnell's.'

The editors apparently failed to recognize that a happy home life and free love are not mutually exclusive. Jack and Michael's engagement was not a whim, but neither was it a cage. 'We love each other; we don't own each other,' as Michael has put it. They sometimes slept with other men. Michael knew gay bars and bathhouses where sex was 'usually the evening's entertainment.' Some visitors, he noted, sweetly judgment-free, 'just enjoyed feasting their eyes on all those good-looking male bodies.'

As their case wound its way to the Minnesota Supreme Court, Michael adopted Jack—a not unheard-of means for a gay couple to qualify for inheritance rights and tax benefits. Hurling yet another wrench into the system, Jack changed his name to the gender-ambiguous Pat Lyn McConnell. Then in August 1971, staying with friends in Blue Earth County, Michael applied for a marriage license again, this time stating his intent to wed *Pat*

Lyn. A clerk in the town of Mankato granted the license; Michael recalls she was 'just as friendly as she could be.' In early September they held a seven-minute ceremony with a few pals present. Both had grown their hair out and donned lacy white headbands. They looked earthy and wholesome. When they kissed, they really went for it.

Weeks later, in the oral argument of the 1971 Minnesota Supreme Court case *Baker v. Nelson,* one of the justices rotated his chair—literally turning his back on Jack and Michael's lawyer (and housemate) Mike Wetherbee, a bright mind associated with the Minnesota Civil Liberties Union. The justice needn't have been so performative. The court's decision ruled unanimously against the couple on the grounds of a 'sensible reading' of marriage law, citing references to gender-specific language elsewhere in state law and describing marriage as the sole provenance of a man and woman to be 'as old as the book of Genesis'—in which Jacob marries Leah and her sister Rachel, too.

Jack and Michael advanced their appeal to the Supreme Court of the United States. Meanwhile, Michael's job discrimination victory was reversed, putting an end to his agonizing bid to keep his eleven-thousand-dollar-per-annum job. They later discovered the university had spent twenty-five thousand dollars to keep him from working there. A half year later their marriage case, *Baker v. Nelson*—a breakthrough in gay legal proceedings, as journalists Joyce Murdoch and Deb Price have observed, in that it was 'about love, not sex,' and the first to stake a claim for equal citizenship rather than respond to an allegation or punishment—was dismissed by SCOTUS for failing to bring a substantial federal question.

Michael took to calling it a 'landmark indecision.'

What precedent had the Supreme Court established, exactly?

By turning away Jack and Michael's case, it sustained the Minnesota decision that the two had no claim to a marriage license. Yet the highest court in the land didn't take the opportunity to codify such restrictions. So even as SCOTUS denied Jack and Michael, it had not erected a broader obstruction on the legal path to gay marriage.

In 1977 the Minnesota statutes were amended, adding to the definition Jack had found on the books—'Marriage, so far as its validity in law is concerned, is a civil contract'—the words 'between a man and a woman.'

But *Baker v. Nelson* specifically addressed the pair's initial license rejection in Hennepin County. In Blue Earth County, local bureaucrats might have balked at Jack and Michael's marriage certificate—it was never officially recorded—but the pencil pushers never bothered to have their license annulled. As with Richard and Tony's marriage four years later, the license remained in limbo. In 2018 their 1971 marriage would finally be declared by court order to be 'in all respects valid.'

AMID THE MEDIA HUBBUB surrounding the wave of gay marriages in Colorado, news of Richard and Tony's nuptials wasn't met only with felicitations. Richard was fired from his job. Tony was disinherited. A letter from his mother in Australia read:

> *I can endure no more. Perversion is bad enough but public display never.*

Richard immediately requested spousal classification from the Immigration and Naturalization Service, who had begun deportation proceedings against Tony. When they learned that their INS interview was, weirdly, to include FBI and CIA agents, they refused to attend.

The INS wrote their decision that day. When it arrived in the post, Tony opened the letter on the spot. Because he couldn't believe his eyes, he asked the mailman to also take a look. The denial read:

> YOU HAVE FAILED TO ESTABLISH THAT A BONA FIDE MARITAL RELATIONSHIP CAN EXIST BETWEEN TWO FAGGOTS.

A revised letter refrained from dropping the f-bomb, but stated explicitly that two males cannot be considered married because neither 'can perform the female functions in marriage.'

Tony was told by an activist friend that, though his comrades loved him, a push for old-fashioned marriage wasn't a part of their revolution. It wasn't the couple's chosen cause, either. 'Right from the beginning, Richard and I were opposed to the discrimination brought about by marriage laws,' Tony has made clear.

'When people get married in the US, they become officially special' is how author Bella DePaulo has put it. 'With their marriage certificate in hand, they automatically qualify for the benefits and protections of more than one thousand laws—and that's just counting the ones at the federal level.[1]

Richard and Tony opposed this systemically while also objecting to their exclusion from those laws. After their matrimony was ruled invalid by the Board of Immigration Appeals, the pair went to US district court; *Adams v. Howerton* marked the first lawsuit seeking recognition of a same-sex marriage by the federal government. In 1979, armed with their marriage certificate and the aid of constitutional lawyer David M. Brown, they filed suit against the acting district director of the INS. (The pair found Brown through the American Civil Liberties Union, whose willingness to invest in gay causes had been arguably inconstant.) Richard and Tony lost in district court in 1980 as well as in another round at the Ninth Circuit Court of Appeals in 1982. Significantly, the latter opinion held that, in respect to immigration law, the term 'spouse' indicates an opposite-sex partner in a heterosexual marriage.

Unable to afford the funds to get their case to SCOTUS, Tony and Richard each filed a pauper's affidavit. Richard put down his total estate at a hundred dollars and a Peugeot nearly two decades old. Tony claimed his worth to be seventy bucks plus his old Ford. With that, they sent their petition to SCOTUS in the spring of 1982.

The Supreme Court justices hadn't heard oral arguments in a gay-related case for fifteen years. In the last instance—the 1967 case *Boutilier v. Immigration and Naturalization Service*—the majority decided that a Canadian man could be booted out of the country because being a homosexual is equivalent to being psychopathic. When *Adams* arrived at SCOTUS, the justices declined to hear it, as they had with *Baker*.

Meanwhile, the pair also fought Tony's deportation on the

basis that the separation would qualify as an emotional hardship. An INS court ruling disagreed and declared Tony deportable. *Sullivan v. INS* ultimately made its way to future SCOTUS justice Anthony Kennedy, then at the Ninth Circuit Court of Appeals. In a 2–1 decision authored by Kennedy in 1985, the court decided there was no 'extreme hardship' in dividing the two lovers, because the Board of Immigration Appeals had established that Tony was not 'a qualifying relative' to Richard.

A month before Christmas 1985, Richard and Tony flew to Heathrow Airport in London. They drifted around the continent using a Eurail pass gifted by a friend, traveling in the coldest temperatures recorded so far that century. They ended up in Ireland, living in a damp abandoned house just below the border with Northern Ireland. They didn't have much money. They felt somehow dead.

In October 1986, figuring they'd rather be back in Los Angeles, illegal but warm, they reentered the States via Mexico. Their friend Jeremy drove Tony through the border inspection station. Tony was unshaven and sported 'a cap like someone from Bakersfield would wear.' He held a can of Coke as the finishing touch. The officer peered into the car, then waved the men through based on their all-American look.

Or could it be, as Tony long suspected, that the officer was gay, knew exactly who he was and opted to be complicit in their reentry?

With that, Tony was back home—albeit now completely, even notoriously, illegal.

AIDS was ravishing their friend group. Their lawyer David succumbed. So did Jeremy, who told the couple before his death that driving Tony through border control had been the proudest moment of his life.

Tony was now unable to leave the country for fear he would

not get back in so easily the next time. He and Richard set up house together in Los Angeles again. They painted, cooked and bickered. They smoked too many cigarettes. They would go on to watch the same-sex marriage debate unfold on TV news.

They would see the Defense of Marriage Act implemented, followed by a mind-boggling number of state and federal battles through the early years of the new century. In California a majority would vote against gay marriage on more than one occasion. Renegade weddings would take place in San Francisco around Valentine's Day 2004, and marriage laws would relentlessly flip-flop in the wake. In December 2012, Richard would die of cancer. The following year two gay-related Supreme Court opinions would be announced on the same day: one legalizing same-sex marriage in California and the other striking down Section 3 of DOMA, the federal definition of marriage as between a man and a woman. Finally, in 2015, the decision in *Obergefell v. Hodges* would require all states to issue licenses to consenting same-sex couples.

The deciding vote in *Obergefell* would be from Justice Anthony Kennedy, the very same who ruled in 1985 that it would cause no extreme hardship to tear Tony and Richard asunder. Perhaps he never forgot that. Kennedy authored the majority opinion in *Obergefell*. 'The nature of injustice,' he wrote, 'is that we may not always see it in our own times.' But I'd be loath to call this redemption when other people *do* see the injustice, and are dealt it.

After *Obergefell* Tony would write to President Obama, seeking an apology for the faggot letter sent four decades before. The head of the US Citizenship and Immigration Services would duly issue a formal apology for that hateful language and offer condolences on the loss of Richard. In 2016 Tony would finally receive his green card on compassionate terms, as the widower of a deceased American spouse. That decision was dated the

21st of April, suggesting that immigration officials were deliberately marking the forty-first anniversary of his marriage to Richard.

Tony would die in 2020. Clela Rorex, who took the risk of issuing their license, would pass away in 2022, while I was writing this.

3

HOMOSTUPID

It was becoming a whole thing. By the time I landed back in America, gay marriage was a huge political story, due less to impetus from gay activists than to Republicans who thought they had President Clinton cornered. In addition to the Defense of Marriage Act, several states were debating bills to inscribe a definition of marriage as between one man and one woman. May 1996, the month that we met, turned out to be a pivotal period, setting the course for two decades of war over same-sex marriage.

Two days after my return, the 15th of May, was an especially eventful date in national politics.

Majority leader Bob Dole (R-KS) announced his resignation from the Senate, where he'd served since 1969, to devote his energies to his campaign against Clinton. Dole's colleague William J. Bennett, author of *The Book of Virtues* and *The Moral Compass,* urged him to highlight his role as cosponsor of the Defense of Marriage Act: 'Presidential election years are the time to talk about big issues, and this is a more important issue than the gas tax.'

Lawyers for Clinton filed a Supreme Court appeal to delay the sexual harassment suit against him by his former clerical employee Paula Jones, who was seeking seventy thousand dollars in damages, alleging that Clinton, then governor of Arkansas, made 'crude sexual advances' toward her in a Little Rock hotel room in 1991.

And the House Judiciary Subcommittee on the Constitution held its hearing on the Defense of Marriage Act. A dozen witnesses for both sides of the argument—local legislators, journalists, activists, scholars, lawyers—had been rushed to the capital from across the nation to testify in three rounds before House members ensconced on a platform like judges. The bill's author, Bob Barr, reasserted that the proposed legislation was an act of defense. Specifically, DOMA would fortify the mainland against the Hawaiian court system and its 'frontal attack on the institution of marriage.'

What was he protecting, exactly? Marriage rates in the United States were in decline. (Between 1970 and the time of my writing, by some sixty percent.) Households—including those of "straight" people—were made up of an ever-expanding number of arrangements.

Early on in the hearing, Barney Frank (D-MA), the first member of Congress to voluntarily come out, described the defense of marriage as an 'elephant stick.' If you inquire, the person carrying it will explain that it wards off elephants. If you point out there aren't any elephants in sight, they can proclaim: *See, my stick worked.*

It would be a day of rhetorical gymnastics. There were many shaggy dog stories as well as rabbinical jokes, puns, symbolic props, exasperation, self-deprecation, earnest pleas, *What about the children?* crescendos and a lot of conjecture about polygamy.

'Aloha,' began Terrance Tom, a Democratic Hawaii state representative, lawyer and occasional pianist at the Paradise Lounge of the Hilton Hawaiian Village. He passionately read from a braille script about the actions he'd undertaken to legislate against same-sex marriage. Public opposition to gay marriage, he explained, had only grown as the state appeared poised to legalize it. 'The people of Hawaii are not speaking out of ignorance or uncertainty,' he asserted, citing a poll in which seventy-one percent believed marriage licenses should only be issued to different-sex couples.

Tom and other members of the state legislature were proposing a statewide ban, thereby rejecting audacious judicial activism. In their book *Courting Justice: Gay Men and Lesbians v. the Supreme Court,* Joyce Murdoch and Deb Price identify the term *judicial activism* as a conservative grievance when individual rights have been read into laws where they haven't been explicitly laid out; the irony is that a form of activism actually occurs when judges 'uphold an anti-gay status quo by discovering homophobic restrictions in laws that make no mention of gay people.'

Among the day's most flamboyant characters, Hadley Arkes, a professor at Amherst, introduced a new audience to his ongoing philosophical propositions, in which he was prone to using the phrase 'the N word' to indicate what he saw as the increasing unsayability of the word *nature*—specifically, an encroaching contempt for 'the nature of things.'

To Arkes, marriage was an institution 'for the begetting and nurturance of children.' (This despite the fact that, for instance, being postmenopausal or sterile is not disqualifying.) He proposed floridly that if the institution were to detach from 'the natural teleology of the body,' there'd be nothing to prevent its expansion beyond just same-sex pairs: 'On what ground would the law say *no* to people who professed that their love is not confined to a coupling, but woven together in a larger ensemble of three or four?'

During questions, Arkes referred to a nineteen-year-old son and his mother, banned by the state of Virginia from living as husband and wife. 'I suppose people could argue that their presence wasn't going to disintegrate the institution of marriage,' he said, and yet the example brought him to what he called his 'melancholy point': changes to the institution would erode 'that special kind of significance that makes it an object right now of such craving.'

In subsequent years and decades, as with others present that day, Arkes would continue to concern himself publicly with the issue of same-sex marriage. He'd put the word *homosexuality* in disquieting proximity to not only incest and group marriage but bestiality. He'd put forward takes on abortion and 'the transgendered'—the stuff I guess he considers contrary to nature's plan.

There was palpable relief when journalist Andrew Sullivan—a British-born Catholic, openly gay and openly conservative—began his plainspoken testimony. A muscular, Oxford-educated Englishman abroad, Sullivan spoke eloquently against the bill, his voice sometimes quivering. 'We do not seek equality in marriage because we despise the institution of marriage,' he said, 'but because we believe in it and cherish it and want to support it.'

Sullivan's landmark article "Here Comes the Groom: A (Conservative) Case for Gay Marriage" had been published by the *New Republic* in 1989. 'As it has become more acceptable for gay people to acknowledge their loves publicly,' he wrote, 'more and more have committed themselves to one another for life in full view of their families and their friends. A law institutionalizing gay marriage would merely reinforce a healthy social trend. It would also, in the wake of AIDS, qualify as a genuine public health measure.'

Shamefully, this resembles a combination of thoughts I entertained as a teenager. I bought into this kind of rhetoric about being "acceptable" and making a public commitment. Moms back then had a tendency to say they just didn't want a life of unhappiness for their gay sons. Wouldn't marriage help reassure them? Wouldn't two grooms be cute? I was also convinced that to deny marriage to gays amounted to withholding a form of inoculation in the midst of an epidemic. In a hastily scribed pontification I self-published in a xeroxed zine, I described this as 'the current conspiracy by our government to make our community self-destruct.' I should have known better. I was familiar with the 1987 slogan SILENCE = DEATH. But on some level I fearfully replaced the word *silence* with *sex*.

Legal scholar William Eskridge, in his 1996 book, *The Case for Same-Sex Marriage: From Sexual Liberty to Civilized Commitment*, described a 'self-civilization' among gay men that includes 'an insistence on the right to marry.' Gay men, he averred, were becoming more dignified and 'lesbian-like' after disco fatigue and the AIDS crisis. 'Never mind that many gay men have developed their own sense of what "civilizing themselves" means,' countered theorist Michael Warner, 'or that nonmarital sex or nonmarital intimacies have been crucial parts of their alternatives.' He pointed out that 'it was precisely because of their virulent hatred of gay sex that so many straight Americans did nothing about AIDS and still continue to impede its prevention.'

I never took a single queer theory class. And yet everything was theoretical; I was a virgin. By the time of the day's debate, I had become more ambivalent about marriage. I certainly had disentangled myself from the prudish conviction that marriage was morally correct because it was a container. What I'd come to believe in was an image of Hawaii. I believed that we weirdos deserved horizons, too. We deserved horizons *more*.

The next witness at the hearing was Dennis Prager, an effortlessly offensive right-wing radio host who began by patronizingly complimenting Sullivan's presentation before embarking on one of the most bewilderingly circuitous arguments of the day. He referred to the conclusion of a UCLA professor of psychiatry that human nature is largely bisexual, and Judeo-Christian civilization has been unique in prescribing it be narrowed to monogamous heterosexual marriage. Prager's take was that the very uniqueness of this project—'to channel the polymorphous sexual urge'—was something to be admired and preserved. He became increasingly heated, like he was sweating out manifest destiny. 'Does my heart go out to those who cannot love sexually a member of the opposite sex? Yes it does. My heart goes out to anyone who cannot fulfill a standard that society sets for its good. But I will not drop the standard.'

Prager's use of the term *society* has echoes of the definition by Hannah Arendt; differentiated from the political, the realm of open debate in antiquity, society follows the model of the private family household. In the *polis*, or city-state, in ancient Greece, Arendt argued, 'everything was decided through words and persuasion,' whereas the *oikos*, or family home, was a site 'where the household head ruled with uncontested, despotic powers.' The patriarch could be tyrannical. A layman who did not participate in politics or public life was known as an *idiōtēs*. The emergence of society meant a population ultimately governed by bureaucracy and facing group pressure to conform. In *The Human Condition*, Arendt wrote of how 'society always demands that its members act as though they were members of one enormous family which has only one opinion and one interest. Before the modern disintegration of the family, this common interest and single opinion was represented by the household head who ruled in accordance with it and prevented possible disunity among family members. The striking coincidence of the rise of society with the decline of the family indicates clearly that what actually took place was the absorption of the family unit into corresponding social groups.'

In this sense, the day's debate seemed to be all about *society*. Prager kept summoning it, while it also provided the basis of the opposite argument made by Andrew Sullivan. Including gays in the institution of marriage, or 'a deeper and harder-to-extract-yourself-from commitment to another human being,' Sullivan wrote in his 1989 op-ed, would offer 'social approval' and 'foster social cohesion.' He reasoned that 'even the most hardened conservatives recognize that gays are a permanent minority and aren't likely to go away. Since persecution is not an option in a civilized society, why not coax gays into traditional values rather than rail incoherently against them?'

Dennis Prager climaxed chaotically as he ended his testimony. 'I am a talk show host. Stutterers cannot be. It's not fair to them. But I will not drop the standard that you have to be able to articulate in certain ways to be one. You're all lucky,' he said to the members of the subcommittee. 'You have your faculties; you could be congresspeople. There are people who cannot be. It is not fair. But we don't lower standards in order to allow everybody to do something.'

As Barney Frank and other liberal-ish members of the committee looked on in weary bafflement, Prager dissolved into a directionless rant about being called a *bigot*, squeaking on the word as he built up to *What about the children?* His theory was that teenagers would be even more tempted to experiment with homosexuality if same-sex unions were accepted as a social norm and sanctified by the government. Frank was skeptical. 'Boy you've got a different set of teenagers in mind,' he quipped.

Then came Nancy McDonald from Tulsa, Oklahoma, with a mushroom haircut and gigantic spectacles. She regretted that her only unmarried child was her lesbian daughter. 'We live in a house divided. My three heterosexual children share in equal rights and responsibilities of American citizenship. My lesbian daughter does not enjoy those rights. If you pass this bill, you are telling me that the state of affairs in America is OK. You are telling me now that it is OK to treat the members of my family differently.'

McDonald, the vice president of Parents, Families, and Friends of Lesbians and Gays, saw the repercussions as fundamental. 'The bill tells me that the federal government does not consider all Americans equal. The bill tells me that ultimately it is OK to beat up on gay and lesbians.' She urged, 'I am asking you to understand that lives that are *perceived* to be of lesser value are at risk.'

Her son, Jason—*'this is my straight son'*—had been misidentified as gay and beaten in a grocery store parking lot, landing him in the emergency room. Intolerance can be determined not only by how people self-identify but by how they are read. As Jason reminded his mother, *'no one* is safe from anti-gay violence.'

McDonald attempted to keep calm under subsequent questioning by Bob Inglis (R-SC), who had by then come up with a new hypothetical—that under an inclusive new definition of marriage, a bisexual person could only ever be satisfied by marrying both a man and a woman. He set about asserting this in slightly different ways, going in on McDonald like a bratty child imitating his domineering father. The PFLAG vice president couldn't get a word in edgewise. She smiled politely, incredulously, looking as if what she should really do is send Bob Inglis up to his room without dinner.

'Let's tell the truth about this legislation,' Elizabeth Birch of the Human Rights Campaign commanded. 'This is nothing more than a campaign ploy to rip apart this country, divide, and to scapegoat one group of Americans. The political climate is marked by demagoguery, hatred, ignorance, and upheaval, with the scapegoating of gay Americans on the rise. The public overwhelmingly rejects that kind of scapegoating.'

Her group, the HRC, with no mention of lesbians or gays in its name, has been considered emblematic of a transformed approach, away from democratic organizing that encourages liberatory, even utopian, thinking and toward a professionalized lobby that pushes for specific gains rather than challenges overall structural inequalities.

Birch gave an intense performance, throughout which she seemed not to blink. 'We are continuously accused of lacking stability and the deepest kind of commitment in our relationships,' she soared. 'Well, let me assure all of you, our relationships are nothing short of miracles given all that tears at them.'

Inglis acted indignant when Birch compared the plight to racial segregation. 'It offends me tremendously to have homosexuals compare themselves to the historic struggle for civil rights among Black people,' said Inglis, who is white.

'Why?' asked an undaunted Birch.

'Because Black people were economically disenfranchised and cut out of this society whereas homosexuals, by most studies that I'm aware of, have a higher standard of living than heterosexuals.'

It's a familiar tactic—portraying the scapegoat as wearing a cashmere sweater. Yes, there are high-end gays. There are also poor ones. Some gay people have the means to patch together the legal standings that come automatically with marriage, but that takes more time and much more money. 'A full set of documents necessary to approximate the protections provided by marriage could cost several thousand dollars,' historian George Chauncey pointed out in 2004; 'a marriage license might cost $25.'

A broad 'higher standard of living' argument is a sham. Take the fact that within the lifetime of those present in the room, there'd been a ban on homosexuals serving in the federal government. This was first instituted by Eisenhower in 1953. At the peak of the McCarthy era, more homos than Communists were dismissed from government posts. Restrictions on access to national security based on sexual orientation had not been overturned until the year before the hearing.

'Erasing the history of gay political disenfranchisement,' Chauncey has written, 'makes it easier to vilify gay people as a powerful, conspiratorial class whose struggle for equality threatens the American dream instead of fulfilling it.'

Historian Lisa Duggan has reminded us to frame the marriage debate within the context of neoliberal economics, with the married household held up as a site of mutual support while social programs diminish. Marriage is therefore 'seen as the proper place for the provision of private caretaking in the absence of adequate incomes, benefits, and services.'

So in fact, economic conservatives would be wise to "allow" more individuals into this privatizing institution, lest they encourage inventive and unwealthy queers to mobilize instead for the return of public forms of mutual care and shared accountability. By transforming us into contented dyads, marriage chips away at a larger *us* worthy of universal rights and benefits. Duggan has called this 'the loss of the plural statuses that we already had.'

Nonetheless, excluding people from forming tiny alliances—whether because they are of "different" races or of the "same" sex—can be no small thing. 'Marriage bans,' Chauncey wrote, 'play an integral role in reinforcing broader patterns of inequality.'

In one sense the Republican interlocutor Bob Inglis, disingenuous as he may be, had a point. It's wise to resist vague equivalences when discussing historical inequalities, as with gay marriage and miscegenation. Chauncey has drawn attention to how 'between the late nineteenth century and the 1950s, hundreds of Black men who violated or were suspected of violating the ban on marriage or sex with white women paid a penalty of death at the hands of lynch mobs. Claiming the two experiences have been the same does no justice to history and no service to the gay cause.'

Three and a half hours into the subcommittee hearing on the Defense of Marriage Act, Inglis continued swallowing his "question" time by reiterating how offended he was.

'The fact is...' he finally spewed, 'that is not a choice, to be Black. But it is a choice—I know you don't like this—but it is *obviously* a choice to be homosexual.' He held his thumb and index close, as if pinching his point.

'*Wrong,*' Birch blasted. She wagered he didn't know the first thing about the struggles of civil rights movements.

'I know,' he scolded, 'because you are the head victim. You're in charge of victims...'

It was probably inevitable that the day's circus would culminate in a conservative accusing a liberal of playing the victim. Elizabeth Birch's word *scapegoat* seems more relevant.

There are two kid goats in the ancient rituals of Yom Kippur. Lots are drawn, allocating one to be sacrificed as an offering to the Lord, and the other, the scapegoat, to be cast away into the wilderness, carrying on its back the sins of the people.

Depending on the scholar who tells it, the scapegoat perishes out there on its own or is driven over a precipice to fall to its death. Such ambiguities open up myriad variations in the significance of the ubiquitous proverb. But either way, the scapegoat is meant to depart and disappear. The scapegoat is not meant to be in the room, let alone express a point of view. But what about those of us who clawed our way back? What did we face out there in the wilderness—what demons, what sublime? What did we learn there? What have we brought back with us?

'What would the world be like if all people were adapted?' Carl Jung wrote. 'It would be boring beyond endurance. There must be some people who behave in the wrong way; they act as scapegoats and objects of interest for the normal ones.'

But then the scapegoat must keep silent. The normal ones speak about and over the wrongly behaved. They don't want to yield the floor to someone who's been cast out and returned. The normal ones don't want to actually listen to someone who has seen what their house looks like from a distance.

16th May '96
Dalloway House Hotel

Dearest Jeremy,

It's five past twelve on Thursday morning. I'm just starting the Nightshift, and I thought I'd write a bit before I have to start my usual night-time routine.

So here is letter number one—the first installment of what I think is going to be a fantastic correspondence. I tried ringing tonight again but there wasn't anybody in. I think it would of been about 3:00 pm across the pond there. The first time I called I got through to an answering machine, but the second and third time there wasn't one—so maybe I got the wrong number—good job I didn't leave a message then.

I hope you're getting better. It doesn't seem like I've contracted anything—touch wood. I can't believe how much I'm missing you. If one of my friends was in this situation I'd tell them they were more in love (and for my own sanity I'm convincing myself that I'm using the term without it's full implications) with the idea than the reality. However I know this to be untrue. I think we romantic scynics ('scuse spelling) must always be the ones to be hit hardest.

The wise words of my friends have generally revolved around the all too predictable "...life goes on..." type. Ce la vie? (my french ends there).

I hope my writing's legible, I've got the most inconsistant scrawl. I should get a type-writter.

My letters have become my diaries in recent times, so I get a bit carried away sometimes. I do feel able to say alot more in writing though. Unfortunately they become muddled ramblings rather than the sort of beautifully written letter that famous people tend to get published—not that I'm famous (yet).

I WAS FINALLY THERE to pick up. An expensive call, especially for a poor boy like you. The line was somehow damp and dark, as if you were phoning from a Mike Leigh film. I was at the end of a Silicon Valley cul-de-sac with a Spanish name, in the house where I grew up — the stone rabbit on the front step, the wooden playhouse, the elm tree. I was crashing there as I began to look for a room to rent in the city.

It wasn't just the bad connection. Your accent. The mumbling and smoking. You sounded atmospheric; I couldn't make out the words.

I'm on... think... seventh page... my letter to you, you whispered. Then you rushed through a life update which let slip that you were saving up to come to California.

I can't really understand what you're saying, I said.

Eh? I'll turn the telly down.

This kid, I thought — watching TV while on the phone like a teenager. You were a teenager only a few months before.

I love television, you said.

I supposed you meant it in an Andy Warhol kind of way.

I'm going to get at least a rocket liftoff...! my sister reported from the floor as the Tetris blocks dropped faster and faster. Jenny nearly always managed at least a rocket liftoff. Sometimes a whole cathedral ascended. We all agreed she'd place high in a championship. *C'mon, cathedral!* she shouted.

What? I barked into the phone.

Just — television, you said, then doubted yourself. *I don't know.*

Uh-huh. What did you say before that?

I teased out that you'd met some lawyer — obviously lustful — out clubbing and he arranged through a real estate pal for you to view a rental in Soho before it was announced. It was beyond your means already—and now that you were *saving up to visit California,* it seemed out of the question.

Was I keeping you from this cool new life in Soho? Or saving you from being indebted to a lecherous lawyer? And what were you keeping or saving me from?

Meanwhile you'd entered into banter with your flatmate Pauley, who'd put on the American accent that's a stupid hick voice. He was teasing you so that you could in turn make a show of being annoyed—a way to signal that you liked me.

...because I'd love to come to San Francis-co, you said.

I hadn't exactly invited you.

...in Californ-I-ay! Pauley hollered in something like a Texan drawl.

So we'll see each other soon! you chirped.

You told me you were finishing your letter—*the first,* as you put it.

I told you to include a secret.

I knew what I was doing. A boy like you wanted a boy like me to extract something private—to open the cage in your chest and watch the thing fluttering inside take to the air.

We did the *you hang up—no you hang up* thing. You were laughing with Pauley again. And, Jesus, I thought: Is the kid also *eating?*

I thumbed the switch hook, released it and listened to the dial tone like it was the sound of you sleeping.

WHAT THE FUCK. I was just about to start living the way that I wanted. As a slut in San Francisco.

I emerged into the heat on the back patio, where Mom joined me.

He seems a little—don't you think—assertive? she offered.

I was supine on a recliner that needed replacing. She sat in a precarious garden chair. Our family had been here for a while; things had rusted.

You don't seem—maybe—ready for this?

A part of her couldn't shake the old notion that whoever your gay son is dating is grooming.

Yeah... I said. *He's enthusiastic. But you're not picturing him correctly. He's not a creep. He's younger than me. He looks like Christopher Robin. He looks like he's waiting for Mary Poppins to take him up a chimney.*

Defending you put things into perspective. You were, after all, adorable. You just also happened to be inconvenient. The timing wasn't great for you either. The reason you'd moved to London was to begin an art degree, which would start in September.

But you weren't inclined to think of something new—like me—as *not a part of the plan*. You wanted to take detours. You wanted the baggage.

What did you see in me? I suspected something *exotic*. I feared you'd found yourself an *opportunity*. But what was really so wrong with that? I think that I—despite my black hair, twisted into short soft spikes with thick wax, despite the nagging cough and complaints—struck you as sunny. Why wouldn't you cross to my side of the street? You have bony Victorian fingers and toes that require warming.

Were you naive? Adventurous?

If I had asked you why you were coming, you'd probably have

said: *I can't explain*. It's something you'd go on to say regularly. It is the beauty of you, it's where the art is.

If someone were to ask me today: *What is it about him?*, and I were to reply, *I can't explain*, it would not mean *not sure* or *don't know*. It would refer to this aspect of you, this inexplicable way of being.

17th of May 00.20
Dalloway House Hotel

morning darling. sorry this letter is such a mess. i feel embarrassed to send it.

i spoke to you on the phone again this evening. how are you really feeling, is it the same as me, or am i living in a fantasy at the moment? This isn't like me, living in a fantasy is, but i hardly ever urge to reveal an infatuation, a dependance. maybe the situation has just never really arisen before. i remain coy though, terrified my words may scare you.

i'm determined to come to california before i start university. god only knows how though.

time for night-time things again. i'll try and think of a secret as promised.

ON THE 20TH OF May, the Supreme Court issued its opinion in *Romer v. Evans* (1996), invalidating Colorado Amendment 2, which would have prevented municipalities from enacting protected status for people of 'homosexual, lesbian or bisexual orientation, conduct, practices or relationships.' Apparently, while a majority of Colorado residents were averse to discrimination based on sexual orientation, people voted according to the perceived threat of another form of affirmative action. After Amendment 2 passed, noted George Chauncey, 'Conservative activists in nine states promptly announced their intention to seek similar constitutional amendments.'

In the majority opinion that prevented the law from taking effect, Justice Anthony Kennedy wrote that 'the amendment seems inexplicable by anything but animus toward the class that it affects' and that a state cannot 'deem a class of persons a stranger to its laws.'

'Gay activists seem to understand,' Hadley Arkes wrote in a subsequent essay, 'that their interests will not be secured as long as there persists in the public a residual moral sense that there is something about homosexuality that is not quite right. Hence, the need to seek more and more occasions for inducing the public first to tolerate, and then, in small steps, to endorse or approve. And now, with *Romer v. Evans,* the Court has handed the activists a powerful new device for advancing the movement ever further.'

On the 22nd of May, a dozen days after we met, White House staff received the memo: the president had committed to signing DOMA if it passed through Congress.

The next day, at the president's news conference with Chancellor Helmut Kohl of Germany in Milwaukee, Wisconsin, Clinton made his first definitive public statement on the matter.

'Mr. President,' a journalist asked, 'yesterday your Press Secretary said that you would sign a bill banning recognition of same-sex marriages. What do you say to those who feel that this discriminates against gays and lesbians? And how do you respond to the many gays who supported you who now feel betrayed?'

Clinton naively or misleadingly depicted the bill as defining marriage between a man and a woman but having the singular consequence—'as I understand it, the only legal effect of the bill'—of allowing a state to deny gay marriages granted in another. 'And if that's all it does, then I will sign it.' Characterizing himself as a champion of gay freedom, he added, 'We all know why this is in Washington now,' and proclaimed, 'I am going to do everything I can to stop this election from degenerating into an attempt to pit one group of Americans against another. Every time we do that, the American people make a mistake.' To mark the end of the matter, he asked, 'Who else is there? Chancellor, do you want to call on somebody?'

The president figured that downplaying the stakes would make the whole thing go away. Instead, Clinton had become, as Sasha Issenberg later observed, the first of three consecutive sitting presidents whose campaign for a second term was 'molded by its handling of gay marriage.'

Stories don't really have beginnings and endings, do they?

You wrote this on the ninth page of that first letter, probably in the wee hours, cigarette smoldering on the front desk of the Dalloway House Hotel. Desperate to tell me everything, you began to detail your childhood in coastal South Africa:

> *i remember my homelife as being incredibly happy and i'm not sure that it particularly bothered me that i walked the playground on my own. it must of—it pains me to admit it but i am dependant on company. solitude is appealing only when it is an option.*

When you eventually made friends, it turned out you were bossy. You orchestrated pretend fights. Never real scuffles. But of the writhing, you wrote:

> *i realise now this is one of my earliest memories of sexual pleasure.*

I described who I was by listing my cultural influences, like a kid thrusting forward their toys. The band Unwound. The song "Unwind" by Sonic Youth. The Jon Moritsugu movie *Mod Fuck Explosion,* with its soundtrack by Unrest. About the things you hadn't heard of, you wrote back: *I'm such a philistine.* But I didn't know what the word meant.

A *NEW YORK TIMES* headline on the 29th of May—"Weary Aide Is Buffeted in Gay-Marriage Storm"—suggested that fatigue over the topic was already setting in. Bob Hattoy, White House liaison to the Interior Department (and 'unofficial envoy to the homosexual community') saw fit to caution that 'people should not expect such a complex cultural issue to be settled in the flash of a Presidential campaign.'

'Living with AIDS and addicted to politics,' wrote *Times* journalist Francis X. Clines, Hattoy was witness to newly polarized social circles. Lately, Hattoy told Clines, every cocktail party he attended was 'like the gay '90s,' meaning not that life's a scream but that the marriage issue had taken over, with everyone offering a hot take.

Meanwhile the Republicans had cleverly baited Clinton into using their terms, like *traditional.* It was a losing issue, Hattoy surmised, and one he swore had never been a priority among his gay and lesbian friends. Anyway, gay voters weren't going to abandon the incumbent in significant numbers. Sometimes they just had 'a bad Clinton week.'

Still, he opined, the administration should probably stop cribbing their opponents' "family values" jargon. 'I just wish the straight white boys at the White House would educate themselves a little more. It's not that they're homophobic—they're homostupid, and they don't know that the buzzwords they're using are the buzzwords the right wing uses as terrorist dividing tactics.'

4
THE APHOTIC ZONE

By mid-June, you were sending your letters to San Francisco. I'd taken a summer sublet in the smallest bedroom of a railroad apartment above a liquor shop on 16th Street between Valencia and Guerrero. Local stores sold used clothes by the pound, first-edition Black Sparrow paperbacks, lucha libre masks, ingredients for a hex.

I'd only ever visited San Francisco, staying with my pal Naya in each of the dilapidated Victorians she rented. Naya was the polar opposite to Xuan, my best friend down at UCLA. Whereas Xuan was elegant and irritable, a refugee from Vietnam who'd cultivated sophistication as armor in relentlessly square Orange County, Naya was a hot mess, bursting with talent and reeking of patchouli. She could be painfully shy. Like me, she had a Chinese father; we referred to ourselves as *half,* as if incomplete. Maybe we saw our identity as pasted together, a collage in which the glue was visible and sticky. Naya produced creepy zines and hatched distasteful schemes but always remained endearing. She saw no reason to be sophisticated.

It was Naya who took me to the dive bar where I met the first guy to plant his face in my ass. His zeal made me reconsider myself as delicious. The city was affirming in such ways. It saw—smelled—the best in me. In Los Angeles, I felt like a shadow. In San Francisco, I could be a star. The standards were lower.

It was also a "city" city, dense with pedestrians. Out my window: the rumble and clack of skaters, the preachers, the taggers, laughter, near-collisions, the intricate improvisations of what urbanist Jane Jacobs described as 'the ballet of the good city sidewalk.' And yet Naya and I, like immature audience members, hurled water balloons through my window at passersby as they headed to Poncho Villa for a Super Veggie Burrito or filed out of the Roxy Cinema where *Nico Icon* was playing.

During term time three San Francisco State students occupied the apartment. Only one chose to stay in town that summer. She was a hippie who mostly slept at her boyfriend's place while her voracious rabbit chewed the big red dictionary in which I looked up the word *philistine.*

The other subletter wore feathered slippers and kept driving home to Malibu to top up her tan. I never met the dude whose bedroom I borrowed, a philosophy undergrad back in Orange County for the summer. I wished he'd never come back. Surely, being gay, I was more entitled to citizenship of this city.

I took my dirty socks and undies to a laundromat on Guerrero and sat on the curb outside, stoned yet hyperactive from a Jarritos Mandarin. It was hard to imagine then that doing the laundry would one day mean both of our clothes.

Naya and I were ambling toward Poncho Villa one evening

when we picked up on the commotion on Capp Street. A crowd was gathering amid spotlights and epic music. We became part of a scruffy audience, everyone in beanies and puffer vests, the sartorial standbys of mercurial San Francisco summer nights. We craned our necks at a half dozen harnessed dancers who leaped from the side of a building, twirled, formed combinations, touched the wall and bounded into the air again.

It was magical. I now thought in the past tense, always writing my next letter to you. *The whole of the city seemed to gather to watch.*

I longed to see everything through two pairs of eyes. Without you, the present was never complete. I drafted sentences: *The fog arrives in the evenings like a dragon awakened. The fog monster. When I get lost, I look for the Sutro Tower on Twin Peaks to orient myself, but if it's too soupy, I scan lower in the sky to spot the Safeway sign on Market Street. Safeway is the name of a huge supermarket chain, but the big red S makes for another unintentional monument, as meaningful to me as the Golden Gate.*

I hugged myself, lit up a cigarette, lifted my face to exhale over the crowd.

I'm sorry you missed the dancers. I hope something else like that will happen when you're here. It's impossible to force serendipity. But I have a feeling we'll both be open to it.

How could I truly describe the constant sense of occasion, the perpetual contact high?

Then I worried you'd find the city mawkish, and here I was presenting myself as at one with the place.

THAT JUNE, THE ASSOCIATED Press reported that when San Francisco mayor Willie Brown was asked by White House planners what sort of event they should organize for Bill Clinton's upcoming visit, he replied, 'Don't come.' Brown knew how fed-up gays can lash out in his sparkling city.

The Advocate published an interview with Clinton. 'I remain opposed to same-sex marriage,' he said. Then repeated: 'I am opposed to same-sex marriage. If Congress sends me the Defense of Marriage Act in the form now being considered, I will sign it.'

The *New York Times* ran a piece about gays annoyed that an unwinnable fight had been picked for them. It cited a poll in which eighty-two percent of nearly ninety thousand census respondents affirmed that they 'would like to be legally married to someone of their own gender,' but then again, that majority existed among the type of gays who self-select to fill in a gay census. And it didn't mean marriage was their top priority. Activists persuasively argued that there were more urgent issues at stake: battling against AIDS and for women's health, defeating antisodomy laws, preventing hate crimes and workplace discrimination.

'Why should three couples in Hawaii drive the entire gay rights movement?' asked the director of a Los Angeles nonprofit called Spectrum Institute, which proposed a new secular form of domestic partnerships instead.

'Mad vow disease,' comedian Kate Clinton quipped.

Professor Nancy Polikoff proffered, 'One thing our community can stand for is a principle that expands the definition of family and does not place a monogamous relationship with one partner at the pinnacle of all human relationships.'

By contrast, campaigners against the Defense of Marriage

Act came across as jingoistic or fusty. The Human Rights Campaign spokesperson: 'We're going to fight it tooth and nail to the bitter end.' A man about to tie the knot in a Manhattan synagogue: 'We want it defined under God. Besides, we are tired of living in sin.'

ON THE 12TH OF July, the House held its vote on the Defense of Marriage Act, which Nancy Pelosi (D-CA) called 'ill-named.' The report submitted by the judiciary committee recommended the passage of DOMA, based in part on 'moral disapproval of homosexuality' and 'conviction that heterosexuality better comports with traditional (especially Judeo-Christian) morality.'

John Lewis (D-GA) suggested that DOMA should be renamed the 'Defense of Mean-Spirited Bigots Act.' He built his arguments up, then soared: 'Why do you want to destroy the love they hold in their hearts? Why do you want to crush their hopes, their dreams, their longings, their aspirations?' He climaxed: 'We're moving toward the 21st century. Let us come together and create one nation, one people, one family, one house, the American house, the American family, the American nation.'

The vote went: YEAS 342, NAYS 67, PRESENT 2 and NOT VOTING 22.

The bill would next go to the Senate before landing on Clinton's desk.

YOU DID IT: SAVED up, bought a ticket for a three-week visit from late July, even arranging to stay a night in New York City on the way.

Magical, you concurred on your first glimpse of San Francisco from the 101.

We left your massive borrowed suitcase in the hall and sat, nervous all over again, on my borrowed bed.

You had landed in America at night and, on the bus into Manhattan, were offered the unsolicited advice to get off a couple stops before Grand Central Station. When the man's suggested stop arrived—in some forsaken, unlit zone—he insisted it was the place to alight, but you made the sound decision to stay on until the end. I felt protective at the thought that this guy could have led you down some alley. Once again, coming together seemed to involve escaping other men.

I'd asked Ben to put you up at his place in the East Village. Ben lived with a buttoned-up roommate he met during the two semesters he got through at Parsons School of Design. They got on each other's nerves, being very different types of gays. Ben slept in an alcove accessed by a ladder. I asked where you bunked.

With him.

In his hole in the wall?

Yeah.

I didn't know two could fit.

Yeah. Sorry.

Why?

It just happened.

What?

I don't know. I just rolled over, into his hand, and came.

I was complimented as well as annoyed. As long as we'd been friends, Ben went for sexy, unreachable white guys, mostly straight. He'd obviously decided you made the grade. Only your unreachability wasn't your sexual orientation but your devotion to me. His move weirdly affirmed your value. I resolved not to mention the incident to him.

We hadn't made any sort of commitment. Since we were together in London, I'd been blown by two different boys. I met both of them at Baby Judy's, the Wednesday-night club on Valencia Street. The first was the most wholesome-looking gay there. Amid a bunch of rodent-like thrift store fops, he had a blond crew cut and short-sleeved shirt, looking like he was fresh out of the military in the fifties. When he poked me in the back, he could have been proselytizing.

He even took me on an actual date. At Puerto Alegre, he ordered the margarita pitcher. A very *top* thing to do. But back at the sublet, he made clear his intention. He held my dick at the base like a cock ring, allowing the rest of my shaft to bulk up and support its gargantuan head. I had maybe never been as engorged as I was in his mouth. I'd formerly treated my junk as a kind of sensory zone where information was received and processed—a *crotch* more than the kind of cock-and-balls doodled on a bathroom wall. I'd been too shy, maybe ashamed, to look down with attention, to really coax it into confidence, allow it to stand proudly, be a dick. This boy teased out something more figurative, less abstract. Both servile and alpha, he provided me with an enveloping orgasm, like being pulled under a crashing wave.

Then I fumbled to reciprocate.

Don't worry. He grabbed his shaft and started jerking. *I want to cum on you.* He touched my chest. *Here.*

The next boy—a man, really, several years older, though still boyish—was so hung he nearly put my newfound confidence back in its place. Yet, an artist and former goth, he seemed to transcend the merely corporeal. He was adoring. He asked if he could take my picture, so when we got together a second time, it was a photo shoot. Me in a black T-shirt I was too coy to take off.

I was coy about everything, looking through his spooky music (a lot of both Coil and This Mortal Coil) and absorbing his tales of growing up in the weird Deep South. He was erudite. He has been and will be, I concluded, somebody else's obsession.

There was no official reason that either encounter constituted a betrayal. One boy had coaxed my penis out of a darkened auditorium, brought it up onstage. The other had seen something photogenic in me, not just in my face, but *behind* it. He called me elegant. Two blow jobs, each from a very different boy, each not just relieving but *improving* me. I couldn't help but see them as preparing me to be better for you.

You promised, you said, *that you'd take me to Chinatown.*

In the hall, you opened the suitcase that was too huge for my tiny room. I rifled through your clothes. You'd packed kitschy vintage shirts with big collars.

I don't like all this polyester, I declared. *All these patterns.*

You just smiled. This American boy with his opinions.

Shall we go? you said, buttoning up one of those eyesores.

Chinatown was like a pinball machine before the quarters are dropped in; neon lights glinted and buzzed routinely, but nobody was knocking about in the damp night.

The best Chinese food I've had, you enthused.

There's better, I said, at once apologizing for the place I brought you and judging your approval.

I ordered youtiao, long sticks of deep-fried bread, crispy on the outside with a stretchy, aerated interior. *Good, right?*

Delicious. Like a savory doughnut. Which is a real treat for me because, you know, I can't eat anything sweet.

Nothing?

At all.

No fruit?

A strawberry, maybe. A slice of watermelon.

No honey?

Gawd, no.

No sugar substitutes?

They can be worse. It's the taste of sweetness that makes me sick.

Too sweet already, a friend later put it. I didn't come up with the line at the time. In fact, the intolerance struck me as a little annoying.

For Easter, my parents gave me an avocado instead of a chocolate egg.

Adorable, I said. And, I thought, a little pathetic.

I really looked forward to it.

This gentle kid. He spoke like a bedtime story. I was compelled to lock his adorableness away before any more men noticed. *Have you been diagnosed?* I asked.

No.

Right, I thought. It was a very American question. *I've never heard of the condition before,* I said, sounding like the Chinese side of my family, to whom things were taxonomical, established, institutional. The rubric of any situation one entered into had been decided long ago.

Yeah—I've never met anyone else with the same thing. I'm weird.

When did it start?

According to your family, you did nibble some fruit when very little. But you knew your aversion from a young age. You told your Cub Scout leader you couldn't eat the pineapple in the packed lunch. Incredulous, she forced you to eat it in front of the group.

I hope you . . .

Threw up all over the place.

Good. What she deserved.

So, that was the first time it was—identified.

Or else you were just sick that day anyway. And ever since, the trauma of the wrong kind of attention has made your body steer clear.

Maybe, you said, unconvinced.

Maybe you could be hypnotized.

Oh, gawd! Maybe. Dunno.

I'm sorry.

Eh?

For commenting on your shirts.

You smiled sadly. You were starting twentysomething days in my company wearing shirts I loathed.

We'll just have to get you naked, I said, attempting to be like the boy who seduced me over margaritas.

You glanced at the roast ducks hanging in the window.

SOME DAYS LATER—between ingesting magic mushrooms and vomiting—we decided we were in love.

Who said it first? Maybe me, but it seemed that we both arrived there together, relieved. We were at the top of Dolores Park, having stolen away from Naya and the others, who were scattered about inspecting blades of grass and turning supine to gaze at infinity through floating dewdrops and wavy branches.

Of the rooftops in the middle distance, you said, *I'm sure I've seen this exact view in a dream.*

The word *love,* on shrooms, arrived with a hippie vibe. We were always going to find the first utterance embarrassing, but it got to be in an "everything is blowing my mind" way, not a sickly rom-com way. Although truthfully, even vibrating on psilocybin, I was feeling pretty rom-com.

I took you home so you could barf. We made ourselves into a pretzel underneath a blanket and awaited the return of my friends, sure they would walk in and instantly recognize our love. When they got back, what they saw was that we'd figured out what they already knew.

After that, we became defined by impossibility. It was our shared identity. It lent us charisma, in that it gave people something to root for. Which made us feel held. We might also have been a little high off the separation that loomed.

I taught you how to rip from the giant bong by standing on the couch while I sat on the floor, firing up the bowl. I put your first 40-ouncer into your hands. Mickey's, not the harshest brand of malt liquor, and with the adorably pugnacious bee mascot on the cap. A 40-ouncer is meant to be guzzled on a front stoop, but the stairwell to my walk-up sublet was narrow and enclosed, so I took you out back instead.

We squeezed through the kitchen window. You found it very American, the way the apartments backed onto one another with a crosshatch of fire escapes. The backstage of a city. *We should be on a front stoop,* I apologized. There were no passersby to check out.

My annoying instinct was to show people The Best Of a place—the coolest, most bustling sites, to construct impressive experiences, the music video version of living. It betrayed an insecurity, the way I overidentified with the city, exploited its edge, appropriated its urbanity. It was like showboating by presenting the ocean. Look—I reside in an amazing place, ergo I am amazing myself.

That's OK, you said, lashes fluttering. *I like it here.*

You understood what it is to be somehow near the center, but at a slight remove, in orbit, where we discover not a hard border but periphery after periphery, shadow then penumbra then unknown. To set ourselves apart, nearly lost but within range. Remote, but not so far out that there is no radio signal. That's where we found a place we could dwell—or the idea of a place, anyway.

THE DEFENSE OF MARRIAGE was headed to the Senate. It would pass there, and Clinton would sign it into law. So even if and when we could get hitched in Hawaii, that would not provide the grounds from which to petition for your visa. We'd only be "husbands" adrift in the Pacific, still in scare quotes. The notion of the *aloha*—sometimes *rainbow*—state as a safe haven for gays and lesbians was a quickly invented then swiftly outmoded shibboleth. Still, we needed a symbol, and the word *island* has connoted awayness from its earliest use.

Instead of Hawaii, we might have chosen the island of Nosy Boraha as our gay marriage metonym. In 1699 the mutineer Robert Culliford and his 'great consort,' little-known pirate John Swann, were living together off the coast of Madagascar on Nosy Boraha, also known as Île Sainte-Marie or, according to a map from 1733, 'the island of pirates.' Their actual domestic life could have looked like many different things. And though I may hear the word *consort* and think spouse or fuck buddy, the term also then indicated a group of allied ships sailing together, leading many pirate historians to argue that the pair were merely being described as especially loyal members of the same fleet. Nevertheless, tales of Culliford and Swann stir the imagination: these two invading assholes sipping rum al fresco while horny humpback whales slapped the surface of the sea.

A contract formed by two pirates during the seventeenth and eighteenth centuries was known as *matelotage*—French for seamanship. This often occurred across rank, echoing ancient, nonegalitarian arrangements such as the claim an emperor made over a boy in servitude. The notion that matelotage marked a romantic or sexual relationship remains an outlying take. There may be broader consensus that a given pair would enter into matelotage as a practical arrangement, not only to protect each other in a scuffle but also to share income and claim property inheritance, with the partner potentially entitled to a larger share than the widow back on shore. But I'm prone to read between the lines of, say, an alluring cabin boy swiftly promoted to first mate, having found himself a convenient form of both financial security and bodily protection.

Apparently rings were sometimes exchanged, and if one pirate switched to a different ship, their matelot followed. It also says something about the implications of this setup that it was disdained by colonial landlubbers. In 1645 the governor of Tortuga, Haiti, a hot spot for matelotage ceremonies, brought in nearly two thousand female prostitutes from Paris in an attempt to help bring the practice to an end. (Some of the ladies subsequently found themselves shared by two male mates.)

Matelotage offers another image of people choosing to form a private commitment articulated publicly, though it doesn't inherently demonstrate some idyllic departure from the status quo. Pirate life in the Caribbean overlapped with imperial violence more broadly. It's just intriguing to me that within nearly all-male company, in a greedy society, amid the dogs of war, some pirates took their stab at self-protection through a bond with another human being.

Till death do us part certainly has a different ring when it involves interlopers wielding swords and pistols on the high seas. Then again. The AIDS crisis. This violent world. The inaccessibility of American medical care. And whether loved up or not, people do get hitched for the practical stuff, like filing taxes. When in 1987 at the Second National March on Washington for

Lesbian and Gay Rights, two thousand queer couples petitioned for same-sex marriage by holding a mass wedding, the spectacle was staged in front of the IRS Building.

I don't necessarily find such pragmatism unromantic. It's rather lovely to think of someone willing to do the admin with you.

BRING HIM ALONG! CHIRPED the artist with the gargantuan penis who had taken the not-topless pictures of me. The images came out flattering, though obviously would have been better without the T-shirt, which made me appear store-bought rather than heaven-sent. I showed you the contact sheets, and you didn't see the same me that you would have photographed. I looked slick.

I figured taking you to the dinner party of an older guy whom I'd slept with was very Gay Liberation of me. He and his housemates lived on the ground floor of a shaky Victorian conversion. What would have once been a wealthy family's boot room was now the kitchen, where ravenous gossip was exchanged over bubbling sauces that made me think *toil and trouble.* The crockery was mismatched, and the girls did not shave their legs.

The cooks brought vegetarian dishes to the dining table, where we sat with people in their twenties, maybe thirties, who appeared to be wearing every item of clothing they owned at once. They spilled wine as they gabbed about Throbbing Gristle and BDSM and go-go dancing. The posters on the wall related to these topics. *Foucault? God let's not with him anymore.* Pasolini. Wojnarowicz. I brought up my favorite story of that summer, the plague of chupacabras, some kind of bat-alien-dog creature, chewing up cows in Mexico. This went down with mild success, though the conversation soon returned to *Discipline and Punish.*

I wanted you to think it was all very convivial, very *Tales of the City,* a book I'd insisted you read before coming. But maybe San Francisco had hardened since the seventies. Its bohemians seemed more likely to close ranks than open arms. It was hard to shake the sense that we were outside of a clique. Everyone knew one another's names. Everyone was called a genius or saint, and thought to be the devil. What did we do to deserve an invitation?

Surely we were seen as having less depth. I thought we were probably there because we looked like sex. You, so skinny you could be broken in two with a caress, and that little upended nose; *piggy*, you called it. My ass, a thick slice of cake.

Sometimes a fag would glance at us skeptically; sometimes a girl would slip us a smile of solidarity. Maybe some of them had seen those photographs of me. Maybe some of them thought I should have moved to San Francisco and become one of them, not arrive with this baggage from London. I looked at you in your hopeless patterned shirt. In their eyes, you may have appeared too mannered, too pretty. People said they were a choreographer or a writer. How did they have jobs like that?

One of the fags turned to you, as if obligated: *And what do you do?* He was as tall as a bad year is long, with a face like a magistrate.

An artist?, he repeated incredulously, tapping a cigarette. *Whose work do you like, then?*

The room went silent, of course, and I winced as you forgot the name of every artist.

I like . . . Francis Bacon? you said.

He snorted. *And what do you like about Francis Bacon's work?*

You squirmed.

I wish I could have helped you, announced that those paintings look like a howl, and you were still so young, a howl is what you carried inside. Those paintings look like a cum shot, and you were still so young, that's what you needed to release. His paintings have an aggression, a cruddiness, that resonates with someone growing into adulthood filled with desire and unable to quite clean up their own mess. You made a fist under the table, holding it in the other hand, then dug your thumb into the cradling palm. If you were going to be hurt, let it be you who applied the pressure. Or maybe the gesture was like pressing a button that would make you disappear.

I was sick of gay men who located an insecurity and exposed it as if yanking a cat from its hiding place under the bed. I was mortified, but also fretful that I was embarrassed as much for you as for him. Was I complicit?

An upbeat choreographer announced that everyone should try the chili, and chatter resumed.

I couldn't help but think that the most upsetting thing to you was that I had brought you there. I detected that while you may have been more vulnerable with me than with anyone else, you also found it particularly unbearable to show weakness in my presence.

I was itchy and found it hard to eat. I looked around the room. Did I want to fuck any of them? Not really. Maybe one, a guy with a fauxhawk who took the photo on the wall of a caravan at Burning Man, filled with people who looked like extras from *Mad Max Beyond Thunderdome.* I imagined that when he didn't shower for days in the desert, he smelled the way an ostentatious, bourbon-fueled guitar solo sounds. That was enough to make me consider those parts of his body I might huff or lick. Did I want you to think that was a possibility? Maybe. But what fun is it to keep a boy on his toes when he's drowning?

We walked home past the Victorian houses lining each foggy street.

Tell me about Francis Bacon, I said.

Oh gawd, you said. *I dunno. Let's please not talk about it.*

I kind of dropped it but, bad habit, didn't: I told you about a student in the art department at UCLA. From what I heard, the graduating class was gathered for his final presentation. He'd constructed a piñata of himself and asked the student who'd become his nemesis—an art jock—to take the stage. He handed the guy a baseball bat. *Typical passive-aggressive behavior, we thought,* someone who was there told me. The art jock began to decimate the effigy. When it broke, instead of candy spilling out, dozens of butterflies filled the room.

Isn't that beautiful? I asked, and glanced at you.

Your brow raised slightly. Your silence was enough to make me see my nation as I think you saw it: proclaiming its wonder by violently pulling back a curtain, taking pride in a tenderness it took pulverizing to achieve. America was a master calling its captives resilient. I didn't have to ask what you were thinking, which was: What about the butterflies?

WE FUCKED. MY FIRST time fully inside another, and taking another fully inside me. I was born into the era of AIDS, injected with fear and penetrated by hate. I fumbled the few opportunities I was given: the drug dealer who commanded, *Fuck me, do it without a rubber,* but I was too spun out on the crystal meth that he'd supplied me. The obsessive to whom I found myself saying, *I just need some sleep.* The redheaded girl, when there were still girls, who sat on the edge of my dorm-room bed in a Thelonious Monk T-shirt, making me feel like another cultural experience, like she was waiting to get a foot tattoo in Thailand.

Among other gay boys of my age, we were seldom willing to discuss our phobias of poop, shredding, limp dicks, virus, pain, farts. The snippets of information came with long lonely roads between. I learned the phrase *tossing the salad,* then didn't hear it again for ages. Fingers inside hurt. A tongue was more my thing. *Toss the salad*—why was it called that, again? Someone said because all the shit and blood were like ingredients and dressing, as if a rim job was a massacre.

I got through the gang bang scene in *Hustler White,* but that was way too advanced for me. I required the 101. Safer sex education seemed to be predicated on the safety, skipping over the sex. Connection remained more an idea than a reality. When I did make contact, what I relished was the attendant depravity—the way my unwashed ass made a guy's face stink. I liked the transgression, the thought of who I'd tell later, and of his roommate smelling it on his face. In other words, I did not leave society behind. I was, even with a tongue up my asshole, not yet internal.

Perhaps I already grasped how penetration precedes an inevitable separation. It would take longer to understand the act of slowing down time, sex as the suspension of humdrum deadlines and daily demands, sex as present tense. It required a new patience. I had been rushing—to finish university one term ahead of schedule, to acquire this or that signifier, to derive opinions. Then you arrived and brought stillness. It oriented me.

We paused time by fucking. The scent from inside you filled the room, sweet and clammy. You could work your tight buns. You worked them. I held your legs up in the air. Your eyes did not just roll back. You looked at me. You closed your eyes as your butt opened. I gave you my penis. It was centering; you were staked. Yours was pale, wide and leaky. A Bel Ami dick. I hadn't noticed in London. I was too enchanted by your aura. You seemed like a seraph. Now I saw your potential for high-end pornography.

Your penis was Bert to my Ernie, even if our personalities went the other way. My pits screamed out a fierce masculinity. Our soles and discarded undies also fragranced the room. You grabbed the mattress. We were not procreating. We weren't producing.

We warped time. We were outside it, above the pedestrians on 16th Street, sharing the same air, yet apart.

You cannot attack me, Republicans or evangelists. I'm away.

And slowness is not a weapon, but may be a form of happiness. And happiness is not a weapon, but in its vapor trail, there may be revenge.

By surrendering to you, and through that to myself, I saw how not to surrender to them.

A slow fuck is an act of resistance. It was our enlightenment—now outside society, together in that sublet, discovering intimacy. But could we form something other than the private household that Hannah Arendt spoke of—that tyrannical site of violence and force? Could we play house without a patriarch? Yes, we could try; maybe it's there in how you call me daddy.

Inside the sublet bedroom, inside each other, there were no

mediators or pundits. We tried to speak to each other, to listen and find silent ways to agree. We climaxed together, or as close as it gets, and it was like coming up with the same idea, or laughing at the same joke.

We squelched. Listened not just *to* but *in* each other. And the exquisite rush of trying not to make a noise if anyone else was home, of almost-silent bursting. You were so quiet in the world, but getting fucked, it turned out, you could be a banshee, unconsciously loud, as with when you slam doors.

Our surrender to each other was our accusers' defeat. Why not find ecstatic peace away from their rapid-fire, hypocritical rhetoric, the noise they create, which bamboozles and distracts, designed to make it impossible to pay attention? It's not impossible to pay attention. I'd gaze at the creases of your asshole. Wonder at its whorl. Attend to it slowly, like your butthole was my wrinkle in time. Rimming on the edge of a sublime abyss. *The Wanderer Above the Sea of Fog* by Caspar David Friedrich? He was rimming! The pink whisper of it. If I go out into the world smelling of you, and us, I take their power, dismantle it, and find my own status—less about power than potential. It's about opening. They're afraid of the open. They close down the conversation. If they seek to divide, I slip inside you and we combine. A slow fuck is a small revolution because it is our time together, so far away from their quick, cruel tantrums and their sharp, hard rules.

Coming inside you, I could be totally present and yet someplace else. You were in both places at once, too. My rubbery flesh, your round mouth like a starlet's.

The term *power bottom* amuses me, but with you it was not a matter of one-up, one-down. Leo Bersani wrote in that big juicy essay "Is the Rectum a Grave?": 'It may, finally, be in the gay man's rectum that he demolishes his own perhaps otherwise uncontrollable identification with a murderous judgment against him.'

We made "A Groovy Kind of Love." *Groove*: a word I'd shamelessly enjoyed since I was something like fourteen. I wore it across my chest on a T-shirt. *Groove*, as in pit, ditch, mine, hole. So near to the word *grave*. "Groove Is in the Heart"—and the butt. Your ass, so skinny the hole announces itself like a front door that's right on the sidewalk. Because of this, years later, when we began to experiment with other boys, in threes and fours, making our intimacy expansive, you would earn the nickname Easy Access.

I'm not saying that homosexuals are special or extraordinary. Plenty of homosexuals suck. And, alarmingly and excitingly, non-homos find new ways of rethinking themselves through intimacy, too. That is what the churches and congressmen were afraid of: we were contagious not just with disease but with *notions*. And it doesn't need to be penetrative. One thing fags and dykes excel at is how to flow in other ways. Neither is it dependent on having the "right" parts. One of the things that queer and trans people know is that anatomies are not tool kits. We can be a more pliable kind of puzzle.

The word *perversion* derives from Latin *pervertere*—to turn around. Maggie Nelson has helpfully differentiated the word from *subversion* and *transgression*, with their respective etymological roots in overthrow and crossing, as in 'a line or a law.' Perversion is an alteration, she wrote: 'perversion enacts a sort of alchemy.' This could be considered a humbler ambition; as Maggie put it, 'perversion has no serious designs on upending the power structures that be'—and yet: 'the pervert's alchemical aspirations and activities have a special largesse, insofar as they threaten to become godlike.' In *The Argonauts*, Maggie wrote of Harry: 'Why did it take me so long to find someone with whom my perversities were not only compatible, but perfectly matched?'

You fucked me, the first penis to go all the way in, and even then, not really. Being gently impaled felt uncomfortable, not in a totally bad way, kind of like swallowing a drink "down the wrong pipe" and enjoying the discomfort. I'd tense, seizing up from the small of my back to my toes, as if I was one tight tendon that couldn't unfurl. The closest I came to experiencing pleasure that way was akin to how the itchy ache of a fever almost feels nice. But I never exactly trembled, just got stuck in the shudder. My prostate seemed uninterested, or you were too big.

I thought being inside you would cement my notion that we are the same, bring us into one. Instead, witnessing the pleasure it gave you, very different from my sensations in the "active" position, I saw you as someone else, completely your own. Was it I who completed you? You did seem needy. I found it beguiling.

It was a worthwhile experiment, the bottoming. But my body wasn't receptive. We both wanted it the other way: me inside you. Somehow, that still felt like you inside me.

It was as if I'd been given an award or something. *I'm a top!* As suitable as any identity. And as contingent. It was not a power grab. It was not following the ancient model of pederasty where the younger or poorer submits to the socially dominant body. Sure, we'd role-play that later. But we arrived at our sex together, as if both facing forward before entangling. To any politician conceiving of us as a dick and an ass, they'd be leaving out a whole lot of other body parts. I wasn't pulling my car into your garage to park it. We were uncontained, like swimming in the ocean, diving and surfacing, seeing each other anew at different levels of submersion. In other words, sensation told me that I could be a top, yet constantly *opening onto.*

We returned, like disembarking from a roller coaster still airborne. As composure arrived, we played no music, just felt the breeze through the window and heard the city again. We took up the chat. What was the name of your teddy? Your pet? We traced the histories of our sameness and difference. *My hamster exploded,* you remembered. It seems that line would come close to breaking the spell, but really the magic was all about those kinds of disclosures. *I was in love with Xuan's boyfriend,* I confided. *I think*... you said, when I probed about the girl who brought down your door, *I've always just kind of floated along.*

I was going to want to spend a lot of time in bedrooms with you. It was our way to extend duration. We had such limited time left. Fewer and fewer days. Sorry, world. Sorry, friends and obligations. Sorry, work. (I quit my job as a buyer at a used clothing store, ostensibly in solidarity with a mistreated friend, but also so we could drive to Los Angeles.) Sorry, tourism: no more parks or museums. The time in those places isn't prolonged enough. The time there is too orderly. We needed fuck time, which is a longer sort of time. There was so little we could navigate, let alone master or beat. But when we were in that room together, we departed society. We made a home out of little more than twenty fingers and twenty toes.

It was not just the shrooms when I said I love you. Let me tell you through fucking. It doesn't have to be in the butt. You can put my thickness in your palm. You take me into your throat. It doesn't have to involve penetration at all. We can rub like polishing. But I want my dick everywhere, all over you. I want you to reek of it later, on your innocent little face, in public, detectable to some, to those fellow perverts (which means fellow time travelers). In San Francisco, there were quite a few. *Had we become fellow gay men?*

Then out there in the city I'd be a part of other people again, and not nearly as resentful or alienated or insecure, if always slightly out of place. Yes, we were both out of place, but we had arrived. In the vinyl booths of diners, on boulders, sandy shores and carousel horses, in front of an aquarium or some friend of a friend's TV. And anyone who paid attention could just *tell* about us.

Love, Hannah Arendt wrote, 'is killed, or rather extinguished, the moment it is displayed in public.' Love, she declared, is inherently *worldless,* and 'can only become false and perverted when it is used for political purposes such as the change or salvation of the world.'

But it seemed to me it was only now, because of love, that I was a part of everything. Maybe not politics. But *landscapes.*

Your eyes, I was now sure, are the blue of a sky just before it clouds over and grays. You were so skinny you didn't even have an ass yet, just a rear end. You would, years later, I don't know when exactly, get your butt, among other lovely deliveries.

YOU LEFT, WHICH FELT like being a kid and getting "the wind knocked out" of me when coming up against the interlinked forearms in a hardcore round of *Red Rover Red Rover Send Jeremy Right Over!* The sensation of breathlessness that will not end.

In San Francisco without you, the MUNI subway stations were more like hospital corridors, wipe-clean, barely populated. Each routine announcement was a foreboding echo against walls that contained me while keeping you out.

The city was colder. Rockabilly zombies roamed the fetid streets. The fog was crisscrossed with wires powering streetcars and trolley buses. Sometimes the pole that connects a bus would dislodge, and all the passengers waited while the driver danced around trying to hook it back in, like casting a fishing rod into the starless sky.

5

LOST WEEKEND

On the 10th of September 1996, the Hawaii same-sex marriage case was finally back in the courtroom. Journalist Sasha Issenberg has relayed that, in response to a series of threats, extra-tight security measures were enacted, including the installation of a metal detector and the use of assumed names by witnesses. In the Hawaiian supreme court decision three years prior, representatives of the state had been tasked with demonstrating a compelling state interest to exclude gays and lesbians from marriage. Hence the fervor around "defending" the rest of the nation from the perhaps inevitable legalization of same-sex marriage in Hawaii, because on some level Republicans intuited: What "compelling" reason could state officials possibly come up with to discriminate?

Especially considering how a Hawaii deputy attorney general had gone out of her way to clarify that while the state should not allow same-sex marriage, it was making no claims that homosexuality was socially unacceptable. The state supreme court rested its majority decision on the premise that restricting marriage to male-female couples amounted to a form of sex-based discrimination. 'A male and a male walk in and want a license...' as one justice put it, as if opening a joke, 'you won't give it to them. You are discriminating against them.' The deputy attorney general awkwardly responded that this was 'permissible discrimination.' She'd given the state the onerous task of justifying the exclusion of homosexuals while refusing to classify homosexuality as, in Hadley Arkes's terms, 'not quite right.'

It wasn't yet nine in the morning when Judge Kevin Chang gaveled the case to order at the First Circuit Court in Oahu, and it became clear within hours that the best that state lawyers had come up with was to make a spurious claim that gay and lesbian couples do not make ideal parents. The headline of the afternoon edition of the *Honolulu Star-Bulletin* read STATE: KIDS NEED MOM, DAD.

The same day, the US Senate voted on the Defense of Marriage Act. As in the House, the outcome was resounding: YEAS 85; NAYS 14; NOT VOTING 1.

The total number of out gay or lesbian senators in 1996 was zero. Perhaps it could be claimed there'd been one the previous term, but Harris Wofford (D-PA) was married to a woman during his four years in the Senate and wouldn't come out until 2016 at the age of ninety. Even then, while he announced his pending nuptials to a man (fifty years his junior), he stated, 'I don't categorize myself based on the gender of those I love.' Which means that, at the time of my writing, there has never been a self-identified gay man in the Senate. The first out lesbian wouldn't arrive until 2013.

In late September, a few weeks after you returned to London, Bill Clinton signed DOMA into law. The document was waiting on his desk when he arrived back at the White House after campaigning in six states over four days. It's been said Clinton was reluctant—he'd rather have gone to bed—but staff got the pen in his paw. They strategized that he should sign under the cover of night. 'He signed the bill in the wee hours of the morning,' the Associated Press stated frankly, 'in hopes of minimizing news coverage.'

In December, the exclusion of same-sex couples from marriage was ruled unlawful in Hawaii. This would be immediately challenged, plus the state legislature was on the way to passing its constitutional amendment banning same-sex marriage; it's been reported that the Church of Latter-Day Saints donated some six hundred thousand dollars in support of the amendment campaign. Anyway, whatever the oscillations there, Clinton's signature resolutely ensured that gay and lesbian spouses would not be entitled to federal recognition for purposes including immigration.

In the space of four months, we'd already seen a dream dashed; nonetheless, or maybe because of that, Hawaii remained our symbol. You mailed me a foldout *National Geographic* map of the archipelago, on which you'd drawn our barefoot figures. We are childlike but huge compared with land and sea, as if two giants who formed volcanoes and valleys by splashing in the waves. I look like a bad influence, and you wear a corruptible grin. You placed funny creatures at our feet and floated silly objects in the bays. A dragon head surfaced; some miles away, his hump, and farther still, tail. You added a motto in a leaky ink scrawl: *Let's just move to Hawaii.* But that was no longer an option, just a fantasy.

On the heels of the Defense of Marriage Act, the Illegal Immigration Reform and Immigrant Responsibility Act (IIRIRA) was also voted through both chambers of Congress, with slightly less overwhelming majorities, and signed into law by Clinton that September. IIRIRA expedited the deportation process. It lowered the bar for the types of crimes that qualified to give an undocumented person the boot, while setting a higher standard (and capping numbers) for cancellation of removal—the avenue through which a noncitizen could stay in the States based on their continued presence in the country, good moral character, and the hardship that would be incurred if separated from their family. Someone who overstayed by a single day became ineligible to apply for a new visa. Those who overstayed for a year or longer were banned from reentering the States for a decade. If caught attempting to return, a further decade was tacked on.

Taken together, it could seem as if these new laws rewrote our real experience as fiction. We were aliens in each other's countries because in our own we remained second-class citizens.

Then on the 16th of December, in perhaps the final big gay news in a year full of it, the *Washington Post* ran the optimistic headline: GAYS' CASES HELP TO EXPAND IMMIGRATION RIGHTS.

The article told of successful asylum claims by sixty queer or HIV-positive people over the past year and a half. Deemed to be in danger of persecution in their country of origin, they included twenty-three-year-old provocateur Slava Mogutin, who'd been accused of 'malicious hooliganism with exceptional cynicism and extreme insolence' in Russia, where he was the country's sole out gay journalist.

The gays amounted to only a minuscule percentage of the more than thirty-three thousand asylum grantees in that period. But their success, building on the 1994 decision by Attorney General Janet Reno that persecution based on sexuality could be considered grounds for asylum, marked a significant change in policy for a nation where homosexuality had been cause for exclusion or expulsion just a few years prior. The *Post* heralded 'a new area of immigration law, helping to expand the definition of who is eligible to seek refuge in the United States.' The article made no mention of the potential impact of the new set of rules known as IIRIRA.

The article clarified that two men, from Togo and Brazil, had been granted asylum for demonstrating they were members of a 'particular social group' not based on their sexuality but because they would be ostracized and denied health care if deported to their countries of origin due to their HIV-positive status. This despite the fact that Clinton's push to overturn the Reagan-era HIV travel ban, in which authorities could refuse entry to someone living with AIDS or HIV, had backfired: in 1993 Congress retaliated by passing a law that *mandated* the inadmissibility of people with these diagnoses, whether they were coming to live and work or just traveling.

'We're telling HIV-positive people that you're not allowed to come to the US,' griped a representative of the pro-border-control group Center for Immigration Studies, 'but if you manage to sneak in, we'll give you asylum based on the characteristic that would have made you excludable.'

He wasn't wrong that there was an apparent contradiction between policies. The thing is, crossing borders and finding refuge often entail feeling around for loopholes in the tangled red tape.

IT USED TO BE that we were not merely treated as second-class citizens but classified as psychopaths.

For nearly four decades until 1990, noncitizens were excludable and removable from the country based on homosexuality. The ban was established by the Immigration and Nationality Act of 1952, which closed borders to several categories of "aliens," including the feeble-minded and insane (or those who once had an attack of insanity), beggars, vagrants, prostitutes, and polygamists. The gays were considered to be included in Section 212:

> (4) Aliens afflicted with psychopathic personality, epilepsy, or a mental defect;

The terms *homosexuals* and *sex perverts* had been spelled out in the bill's original draft, but at some point the words were deemed unnecessary, as it was safe to conclude that homos and pervs fell under the psychopathic umbrella. Also in 1952, the American Psychiatric Association published the first edition of its *Diagnostic and Statistical Manual of Mental Disorders,* in which homosexuality was classified as a 'sociopathic personality disturbance.' The Public Health Service advised that *psychopathic personality* or *mental defect* was sufficient to mean gays. But just to leave no room for doubt, when Congress passed a revised immigration act in 1965, it included the term *sexual deviation.*

What to do, then, in the case of Clive Michael Boutilier—whose circumstances came to light in between the ambiguous 1952 law and more specific 1965 prohibition?

Clive was a slim young Canadian, six feet tall with hazel eyes, a devilish brow and a self-conscious grin. His Hollywood hair was combed back like a calm ocean ripple. In 1963, just as he turned thirty, Clive applied to become a US citizen. He'd been living in Brooklyn, having migrated in 1955 along with his mother and siblings.

In his citizenship application, Clive disclosed that he had faced a sodomy charge four years prior. Clive had sporadically been with other men from a young age, sometimes in public places. In the single instance he was apprehended, it was with a seventeen-year-old. The charge was reduced to simple assault, then dropped altogether because the boy (or 'complainant') did not show up in court. But because Clive had declared the arrest, he was brought in to be interviewed in January 1964.

'I am an officer of the United States Immigration and Naturalization Service,' the investigator began, 'and I desire to question you under oath regarding your homosexual activities.' Their initial exchange established that Clive was born in Sheet Harbour, Nova Scotia, and now resided with a roommate in a Brooklyn apartment, in the same building as his mother and stepfather. His father had passed away back in Canada. The officer moved on to the matter at hand.

Q: THIS CHARGE OF SODOMY, WHAT DID IT INVOLVE?
A: I INSERTED MY PENIS IN HIS RECTUM AND HAD AN ORGASM.

Q: DID ANYTHING ELSE HAPPEN BESIDES THAT?
A: YES, LATER I PUT MY PENIS IN HIS MOUTH AND HAD A BLOWJOB.

Q: WAS THIS VOLUNTARY ON THE PART OF THE PERSON WITH WHOM YOU WERE DOING THESE ACTS?
A: YES.

Q: WAS IT VOLUNTARY ON YOUR PART?
A: YES.

Q: DO YOU REMEMBER THE NAME OF THIS PERSON?
A: NO. I DON'T RECALL THE NAME.

Q: WAS THIS A MAN THAT YOU PERFORMED THESE ACTS WITH?
A: YES.

Q: WHAT DO YOU MEAN BY AN ORGASM?
A: EJACULATE.

Q: WHAT DO YOU MEAN BY EJACULATE?
A: I HAD MY SEX MYSELF.

Q: CAN YOU BE MORE SPECIFIC BY WHAT YOU MEAN BY ORGASM?
A: A FLOW OF SPERM CAME FROM MY PENIS.

Clive stated that his first sexual encounter was at fourteen, with a much older man, around forty. On a hunting trip, he stayed the night in the bed of this guy, whose wife was away. The man didn't manage to complete anal sex, but 'a flow of sperm came from his penis on my clothing.' Some two years later, Clive had a consensual encounter in a park in Halifax.

Q: WHEN YOU SAY A BLOWJOB, WHAT DO YOU MEAN BY A BLOWJOB?
A: I PUT MY PENIS IN HIS MOUTH AND A FLOW OF SPERM CAME FROM MY PENIS.

Teenage Clive was sucked off by men three or four times a year, and was intimate with girls, too, over the six or seven years before his relocation to the States at the age of twenty-one in 1955. In New York, he continued to hook up with anonymous men and on occasion with his male roommate.

The line of questioning specifically set Clive up to not only be denied citizenship but removed from the country based on the 1952 law. If taken to entail homosexuality, the psychopathic personality exclusion meant he should have been refused entry into the country on a permanent residency visa in the first place.

Clive was asked if he had registered with selective service in the United States. He said that he'd been classified as 4-F, not qualified for military service. Could he explain why?

A: I'M HOMOSEXUAL.
Q: DID THEY JUST ACCEPT YOUR STATEMENT THAT YOU'RE A HOMOSEXUAL?

In his book *Sexual Injustice,* an assiduous survey of Supreme Court cases with a rare emphasis on that of Clive Boutilier, law historian Marc Stein considered how, by inserting the article—*a* homosexual—the investigator shifted from adjective to noun. The implication is considerable, repositioning a proclivity as an essential identity. Clive was also fixed in language as an alien. Four days later, without meeting him, two doctors from the US Public Health Service Hospital on Staten Island looked over the interview transcript and declared that 'the alien was afflicted with a class A condition, namely, psychopathic personality, sexual deviate, at the time of his admission to the United States for permanent residence on June 22nd, 1955.'

Within months, at the suggestion of Robert Brown, the attorney who'd previously represented him on the assault charge,

Clive went to see a psychiatrist directly. In March 1964, the unfortunately named Dr. Falsey concluded, 'He is not psychotic.' In Falsey's opinion, Clive was intelligent. Prior to his current job as a building maintenance worker, he'd been the responsible attendant and companion to a mentally ill man. Clive saw himself as having a psychosexual problem, but Falsey believed he was not a lost cause; just attending the session demonstrated he had indeed begun treatment. Clive was neurotic, he surmised, but did not demonstrate 'potential for frank criminal activity.' There now existed a declaration that Clive was not psychotic by a medical professional who'd actually examined him in person.

Maybe he could make a case. As pointed out by Marc Stein, probably the preeminent authority on the subject, Clive presented as a respectable employee and honest citizen, not to mention masculine, Christian and white. Clive additionally retained the services of lawyer Blanch Freedman. She was a lefty with ties to the American Committee for the Protection of the Foreign Born, therefore considered a scourge by Red Scare types. But, Stein has observed, as a middle-aged straight woman, she could also help normalize her client. Her presence might telegraph that Clive was somebody's son.

At Freedman's recommendation, Clive also went to see Montague Ullman, the director of psychiatric services at Maimonides Hospital in Brooklyn and a professor of psychiatry at the State University of New York. According to his report, written at the end of March 1965, Clive was cooperative but anxious, his eyes sometimes brimming with tears. The first time he broke down—what Ullman calls his 'initial spontaneous outburst'—was over the financial burden the proceedings had incurred. He'd taken out bank loans for the first time in his life. At the conclusion of his INS interview, Clive had commented that he planned to seek medical help, and that the reason he hadn't already was due to budget. He was not wealthy.

Clive told Ullman about how he worked from a very young age. Everyone in the family did, maintaining their small farm. He was the second eldest. By the age of thirteen, his schooling was interrupted so that he could better support the family. When his mom and dad fought, he took his mother's side.

'What emerged out of the interview,' Ullman wrote, 'was not a picture of a psychopath but that of a dependent, immature young man with a conscience, an awareness of the feelings of others and a sense of personal honesty.' He was well-liked at his job. His sexuality, Ullman thought, remained fluid and unresolved. 'My own feeling is that his own need to fit in and be accepted is so great that it far surpasses his need for sex in any form.'

Like Falsey before him, Ullman concluded, 'I do not believe that Mr. Boutilier is a psychopath.'

According to Dr. Ullman, Clive claimed he'd ceased having sex altogether, disgusted by the pickle it had gotten him into. He stayed in most evenings. Sometimes he went bowling. He attended mass. He'd moved back in with his mother and stepfather, leaving the roommate behind.

Clive then attended an INS hearing where his counsel Blanch Freedman was grilled by a special inquiry officer. It wasn't looking great that the officer kept guiding the conversation back to the initial letter hastily penned by the appointed psychiatrists rather than the two subsequent diagnoses. Toward the end, the officer addressed Clive directly. He explained that if he were to be deported, Clive had the right to declare where he'd like to go.

Q: IN SUCH CASE TO WHICH COUNTRY WOULD YOU PREFER TO BE SENT?
A: CANADA.

Q: IS THERE ANY REASON WHY YOU FEAR TO RETURN TO CANADA?
A: NO, SIR.

But if Clive had been a US citizen immigrating in reverse, he would have been excludable according to Canada's own Immigration Act of 1952. The Canadian list of prohibited classes included idiots, imbeciles or morons; someone who is or has been insane; epileptics; anyone with tuberculosis or other infectious diseases; the dumb, blind or 'otherwise physically defective' (unless provable they can take care of themselves); drug addicts, chronic alcoholics, those likely to engage in espionage or sabotage, as well as 'prostitutes, homosexuals or persons living on the avails of prostitution and homosexualism, pimps or other persons coming to Canada for these or any other immoral purposes.'

Within two weeks in early August 1965, the INS issued its decision, stating that Clive had been excludable at time of entry due to his psychopathic personality, and was now deportable. Clive was ordered to leave for Canada. 'Whatever the phrase "psychopathic personality" might mean to psychiatrists,' the special inquiry officer decided, 'to the Congress it was intended to include homosexuals and sex perverts.' The INS, he extrapolated, was 'not here concerned with the niceties of meaning indulged in by psychiatrists, but rather with words of legal art.'

Blanch Freedman appealed on the grounds that the decision was void for vagueness. But the Board of Immigration Appeals at the US Department of Justice concurred that *psychopathic personality* is 'a term of art and that it includes an alien upon mere proof that he is a homosexual.' *Time* magazine ran a story headlined THE CASE OF THE ELUSIVE EUPHEMISM on the tussle over terminology as Clive's team sent the appeal to federal court.

In the summer of 1966, Clive lost again in a 2–1 ruling by the Second Circuit Court of Appeals. Irving Kaufman, the judge who sent the Rosenbergs to the electric chair, authored the opinion. 'We do not quarrel with Boutilier's contention that the term "psychopathic personality" is not a model of clarity,' he conceded. But that, Kaufman argued, did not void his expulsion.

In a bombastic, almost camp, dissenting opinion, Judge Leonard P. Moore intoned, 'To label a group so large "excludable aliens" would be tantamount to saying that Sappho, Leonardo da Vinci, Michelangelo, Andre Gide, and perhaps even Shakespeare, were they to come to life again, would be deemed unfit to visit our shores.' Moore added titillatingly: 'Indeed, so broad a definition might well compromise more than a few members of legislative bodies.' (Kaufman described the colorful text as 'the house of horrors erected by our dissenting brother.')

Moore accentuated Clive's many positive traits: Works hard. Member of a big normal family. Almost always has sex in private. Responsible. Correctible. Honest to a fault. Quoting a previous court opinion, he contrasted respectable Clive with those who resist conformity and 'habitually misbehave so flagrantly that they are continually in trouble with authorities.'

Marc Stein has pointed out that Moore's characterization of Clive had a double effect, in that it 'challenged popular stereotypes but suggested that homosexuals without these attributes might not merit equal treatment.'

Boutilier v. Immigration and Naturalization Service was ultimately argued before the Supreme Court in March 1967. By then, Boutilier's attorney Blanch Freedman had become afflicted with scleroderma, an autoimmune disease, but she remained lucid and unwavering in oral argument. She returned to a point from the brief she coauthored with Robert Brown: that homosexuality is an activity, not a recognizable trait like being 'a red-head.' One can't be deported based on the false assumption of an innate characteristic. What's more, if Clive had known the rule, he wouldn't have broken it. He wasn't compulsive. If psychosis involves a lack of shame or guilt, the question was not Clive's transgressions, but whether he was capable of feeling guilty about them.

In the end, she did not persuade enough justices. The decision was announced on the 22nd of May 1967. By that time, Blanch Freedman had died and Clive was lying in a hospital bed.

The *Boutilier* opinion defers to a grim precedent of excluding humans based on essential traits: 'It has long been held that the Congress has plenary power to make rules for the admission of aliens and to exclude those who possess those characteristics which Congress has forbidden. *See The Chinese Exclusion Case.*' This refers to the unanimous 1889 Supreme Court decision in *Chae Chan Ping v. United States,* which upheld the right of the federal government to pass immigration prohibitions—such as the 1882 Chinese Exclusion Act—even when such legislation overrides international treaties. Marc Stein has noted that this was being cited *after* Congress repealed the Chinese Exclusion Act (in 1943) and ceased using the national origins immigration system (in 1965). 'Here,' the opinion continues, 'Congress commanded that homosexuals not be allowed to enter. The petitioner was found to have that characteristic, and was ordered deported.'

Arguing on behalf of the INS, the young lawyer Nathan Lewin reiterated the position that Congress need not specify homosexuals in its list of prohibited noncitizens because the Public Health Service had determined it to be a type of psychopathic personality.

Justice William J. Brennan Jr., one of only three members of the court to dissent, put forward an analogy: What if, instead of *psychopathic personality*, Congress had written 'aliens afflicted with dandruff,' believing it to go without saying that this included homosexuals?

Abe Fortas, the youngest justice and another to rule in Clive's favor, put it this way: the equivalence of homosexuality and psychosis was 'as clear as mud to me.' Fortas advanced the apparently radical proposition that some, but not all, people who engage in homosexual activities can be categorized as psychopathic. (Or, as he put it, according to a note by Justice William O. Douglas: 'ordinarily a homo is a psycho but many are not.')

Douglas, the final dissenting justice, denounced deportation as too high a penalty—equivalent to banishment or exile—to turn on a term as woolly as *psychopathic personality*, which he found 'so broad and vague as to be hardly more than an epithet.' Douglas lamented that in the court's interpretation, 'we make the word of the bureaucrat supreme.' He wrote, 'Caprice of judgment is almost certain under this broad definition. Anyone can be caught who is unpopular, who is off-beat, who is nonconformist.'

The majority opinion was authored by Justice Tom C. Clark, a man who happened to have a flamboyant nephew, Bobby, whom he treated as a son. Unable to forge a connection with his own father, Bobby was a troubled soul, a heavy drinker and opera aficionado who traded Texas for Paris, where he took up residence near his diva, the legendary soprano Maria Callas.

Although Clark was a source of support to Bobby, his *Boutilier* opinion demonstrates no sympathy for the well-being of a homosexual man unrelated to him. (Joyce Murdoch and Deb Price called his opinion 'as impersonal as if the court were ruling on whether a law barring importation of "carrots" could be used to block all foreign turnips.') Justice Clark died without knowing how his decision would limit his own nephew's options. Based on the *Boutilier* precedent, Bobby's French lover—the man who kept him together, showing him a life away from the days on Fire Island lost to champagne—was ineligible for immigration to the United States. So Bobby spent his final years with him in France. Bobby died near Paris in September 1996.

The SCOTUS decision meant that Clive would be sent back to Canada; it also affirmed the authority of Congress to ban homosexuals in general. Since the decision didn't mention Clive's arrest for sex with a minor, it set a precedent for not only those accused of an unlawful act, but all gays and lesbians. Less than a month after the *Boutilier* decision was announced in June 1967, SCOTUS declined to hear the case of a man ordered deportable for cruising public restrooms—or "vagrancy, lewd"—despite being a legal resident from the age of fifteen and the sole caretaker for his ill wife. By December, an immigrant from Norway wrote to *Playboy* magazine anonymously to describe how his apartment was raided and then he was examined by military psychiatrists and deported, apparently for subscribing to two gay magazines.

The mainstream media took little notice of the ruling. Any articles that were published have been heroically archived by Marc Stein, who has remarked that they are often notable for 'downplaying its significance.' The ban would remain in place another twenty-three years. That means you'd have been officially excludable and removable until just six years before we met.

THE HANDFUL OF CLOSE followers of the *Boutilier* case have been led to wonder about the exact nature of Clive's relationship to his roommate, Eugene O'Rourke. Considering the intense strain and scrutiny that Clive found himself under, could Eugene have been what kept him from just upping sticks and returning to his country of origin up north? Years later, some observers would refer to Eugene not as Clive's roommate but as his boyfriend or even life partner. Which sounds like a reason to stay and fight.

The only surviving photo of Clive and Eugene that I'm aware of is torn at three corners. It was probably taken in the early sixties. They appear to be in a novelty portrait studio in Coney Island, posing on a set dressed to look like a saloon. Behind the bar with them is Clive's younger brother Eldred, a dreamboat who went by his middle name, Andrew, along with his wife, Joyce.

A sign on the bar reads:

THE LOST

WEEK END

IN

CONEY ISLAND

Andrew poses as if pouring out a cheeky tipple for Joyce, who seems game. Eugene is doing the same for Clive, who looks sheepish. They glow with youth and possibly booze. They dress lightly, suggesting the day was warm.

Imagine them passing by the fortune teller automaton in Deno's Wonder Wheel and deciding to have their futures read.

Within a few years, Clive will fight for his right to remain in the United States all the way to the Supreme Court. His 1967 loss will mean that his name is forever tied to the equation of homosexuality with psychosis. This gently appealing man will become the personification of an "undesirable" immigrant. He will be deported. But first, just twelve days before SCOTUS issues its opinion, Clive will be struck by a car. His doctor will record his memory loss, confusion, and hostility. Pressed for updates from immigration authorities regarding the young man's deportation, this doctor will explain that Clive is suffering from 'post-traumatic psychosis.' This will mark the first time that Clive is diagnosed as afflicted with psychosis by a medical professional who examined him in person. The case will have become an awful sort of prophecy. Eventually, after several months in the hospital, a shell of the person he once was and unable to care for himself, he will leave behind the United States and Eugene. In 1969, at thirty-four, his little brother Andrew will die of heart failure.

Surely all this would have been impossible to conceive of by four young people on Coney Island amid a lost weekend that should have never been found.

6
OTHER PEOPLE'S INVITATIONS

Our packages got bigger. Letters like autobiographies. Flotsam amassed as if we were magpies building a nest for our mate. One of your overstuffed envelopes spilled glitter when I opened it, annoying me. Mixtapes of ache and atmosphere: "Haunted When the Minutes Drag." "Hobart Paving." "The Wild Ones." I selected songs from the *Hair* soundtrack. You snuck in the Spice Girls. The cassettes were slipped into elaborate covers—foldout, tinfoil, bestickered.

Wouldn't you just like to be in bed together all day, doing nothing? you wrote. *Wouldn't you like that?*

You told me that our bodies fit together perfectly when we spooned in that sublet bed. It crossed my mind: neither of us had held that many other bodies. But you were convinced.

I could be a terrible listener. Like when you put the song "Wichita Lineman" on a mixtape, and checked in with me later: *Isn't it beautiful?* I dismissed it for the schmaltzy orchestration.

But you swam around inside that lyric about needing more than wanting and wanting infinitely.

At the end of rom-coms, the protagonist has an epiphany: *I do not need you, but I want you.* Otherwise it would be too carnivorous or parasitical, not autonomous; one must first be self-sufficient, American-style, to deserve the relationship. One can't need the other person, but should want them, making it an unselfish, high-functioning love. Only then is a happy ending permissible. But I had to accept that this thing between us had begun to feel essential.

Naya pointed out that you looked like the doodles I once drew—the boy of my dreams. How ridiculously cute. I'm sure others found our devotion annoying. But it struck me that people may be deeply uncomfortable with two lovers' attendant vulnerability. Love brings loss to mind.

Plus, falling for you must have seemed like a distraction from building myself up, establishing a career. You compromised my independence and took my attention away. I became an underachiever.

Infatuated with someone who wasn't around, I probably came across as half there myself. I turned down the offer to share another Mission District rental and moved back down to my parents' place instead. I slept in my sister's old bedroom with its Laura Ashley wallpaper, inherited from some spectral daughter who lived in the house before we did, while saving up to visit you in London.

I took an internship with a fashion magazine in San Francisco, driving back into the city a few mornings a week, and was liked by the others there despite, or because of, my newfound air of preoccupation.

First I dropped off complimentary display copies at high-end boutiques. Sashaying through one shop with a ballpoint pen aloft, I drew a line across the suede shoulder of a thousand-dollar jacket. Soon after, I was moved from marketing to churning out short articles. For whatever reason, the publishers decided I was an asset and set about cultivating my loyalty.

I also took a part-time job in a mid-price clothing store at the Stanford University shopping mall. I folded sweaters while my co-worker belted along to the Fugees cover of "Killing Me Softly."

Show me his picture, Kyung Soon said.

I produced the photo booth square that I always carried with me.

He looks exactly like you! she gasped.

We did not resemble each other. What did she detect? A gaze, maybe; our *aspiration*. In the photo, you had a mod haircut and acne on your chin. You wore one of your ugly shirts, a necklace that spelled out STAR in small beads and a name tag on your thrifted jacket lapel that read REJECT in Dymo tape lettering. You'd clearly styled yourself to make someone like me smitten.

You are like twins!

I don't think Kyung Soon detected a similarity in how we looked so much as in how we looked at the world.

ARRIVING AT UNIVERSITY, TWO years older than everyone else, you were grateful that you had all girls for flatmates. Three out of four became friends instantly. The other—the weird one—kept to herself, dropped out and was replaced by another spare tire. The rest laughed easily. They enjoyed your stories about San Francisco and about me.

When you'd first returned to England, you went camping with old school friends, but they didn't quite *see* you, sticking to their memory rather than discerning the new person before them. They didn't ask you to repeat the tales you mumbled, so how could they know the magnitude of San Francisco? It was just another city; I was just another boy. Maybe they sensed you'd been filled and didn't want to be emptied. Thoughts of two gay boys easily turn to ass fucking. You'd figured they would be able to detect the enormity of this shift in your life. But they were *the same,* the only way they could imagine you to be.

Whereas your new flatmates, young and thirsty, had met you this way—alone, but coupled. It was your identity.

There was only one phone, with a very long cable that reached each of the bedrooms. Unless a flatmate was entrenched in a protracted conversation, you could call me from your bed, the cable trailing under the door and down the hall.

You sucked down cigarettes. Sometimes we masturbated, trying to describe touch and scent.

You filled me in about your new friends in the art department. You'd been tasked to bring in a summer sketchbook, a kind of show-and-tell, and it was full of images of me.

You are very much at the forefront of "Who am I?" you said.

There was even a drawing of the stressful dinner party.

Really? I groaned. *Drawn in the style of Kevin Bacon?*

Francis, you corrected.

I planned to visit London for a month from mid-February, arriving in time for your birthday and to hunker down together through the bleakest of winter. The flatmates, you insisted, wouldn't mind. There was so much coming and going already: their boyfriends, each of whom seemed to be a drum-and-bass DJ, plus students from other flats piling in to smoke spliffs on beanbags.

Something each person can be in a long-distance relationship: a destination.

LESS THAN A YEAR since we met in London, I was coming back sophisticated. I worked for a *magazine.* I planned to attend *Fashion Week.* The show invitations had begun to arrive ahead of me, and you maybe took some pride in the sleek envelopes from Owen Gaster, Hussein Chalayan, Vivienne Westwood, landing incongruously at your grubby student accommodation. My reputation preceded me.

Under a flat gray sky and the watchful beasts of the Natural History Museum eaves, I strutted toward the tents alongside stressed-out editors and minor celebrities, all of them wearing so much *fashion.* Was I "in"? Somewhat. Invited to this show but not that one, in actuality further from the industry establishment and closer to the petite East Asian guy I kept clocking everywhere. *So desperate!* I thought, embarrassed on his behalf, internalizing the stereotype of gay Asian men as yappy and persistent. He clutched a camera at his chest, striving for atmosphere shots. No longer able to control himself after the finale of Copperwheat Blundell, he leaped onto the catwalk and snuck backstage.

I took you along to shows that'd given me a plus-one, including Miu Miu, the Prada diffusion line, a momentous addition to London Fashion Week. *You can do fashion illustrations,* I suggested.

The very skinny models paraded, wearing scant fabric in pale hues. A few looks in, I peeped at your notebook. You'd merely drawn a diagonal line with a tiny triangle head. I nudged you, so you did another, much the same: slash, triangle. You couldn't see past your skepticism.

We weren't invited to Miuccia Prada's gala that night, held at a mansion somewhere along the bank of the Thames. We showed up anyway. At the gates we waved our show passes, but the staff had been trained: Not the Same Thing. Alongside us was the Asian groupie with his camera.

He's overzealous, I informed you. *Been seeing him all over.*

He was trying to talk his way in, too; I bristled that we were in the same position.

Well, I said. *Don't think they'll cave.*

You became stubborn. As apathetic as you were toward fashion itself, you wanted in on the hubbub around it. You'd come this close, so why not. You wanted to dip into the decadence that awaited inside, like Baudelaire's 'lover of universal life' who 'enters into the crowd as though it were an immense reservoir of electrical energy.' Baudelaire rethinks it: 'Or we might liken him to a mirror as vast as the crowd itself; or to a kaleidoscope gifted with consciousness, responding to each one of its movements and reproducing the multiplicity of life and the flickering grace of all the elements of life.'

In a blink, there was the hanger-on—grinning broadly and gliding through the filigreed gates on the arm of Stephen Fry, who was entering his Oscar Wilde era. We were impressed; the wannabe was no longer one of us. He'd become a *be,* or at least a plus-one.

It really was time to give up. We went instead to the Soho basement with tobacco-stained walls and plates piled with too much spaghetti, topped with spooned Parmesan. We wanted to be, as author Paul Flynn once put it to me, in the places that let the riffraff in. Being turned away suited us, we decided, even if we would have preferred to *choose* not to join in.

'When one is left out, something else becomes available,' writes psychoanalytic essayist Adam Phillips. 'Exclusion may involve the awakening of other opportunities that inclusion would make unthinkable. If I'm not invited to the party, I may have to consider what else I want: the risk is that being invited to the party does my wanting for me, that I might delegate my desire to other people's invitations. Already knowing, or thinking we know, what we want is the way we manage our fear of freedom. Wanting not to be left out may tell us very little about what we want, while telling us a lot about how we evade our wanting.'

Some version of this revelation came to us in fits and starts. Because marriage was easy to compute, we assumed we wanted in. But, cast out by marriage and immigration law, we began to perceive the freedom in the wildness.

Out of the closet and into what, theorist Judith Butler once asked: 'What new unbounded spatiality? the room, the den, the attic, the basement, the house, the bar, the university, some new enclosure whose door, like Kafka's door, produces the expectation of a fresh air and a light of illumination that never arrives?'

Butler must have been referencing Kafka's parable "Before the Law." In it, a man from the country arrives at a gate, cracked open but guarded by a formidable bouncer in a fur coat. The man seeks the Law and awaits permission to be let through. He is not allowed. Will he ever be? It's a maybe. Not now. He could force his way, the guard says, but would encounter a procession of more obstructionists, each more powerful than the last: "The third doorkeeper is already so terrible that even I cannot bear to look at him." So the man waits and waits. He offers bribes, which the doorkeeper accepts without relenting. Before he dies, the man asks why in all those years nobody else has come begging for admittance. The guard explains that the gate has always been for him alone, then closes it. The man spent his life waiting for a permission that was never forthcoming. He dared not set a foot inside, even though the subsequent heavies could be mere myth. He deferred to the gatekeeper's authority, and diminished himself in a futile attempt to appease.

Though we might know such stories, still the gates continue

to appear. The sight of them seems correct, seemingly inevitable. We sought authorization from a Wizard of Oz, even though we realized he was a pathetic fake. It was easy to imagine that a Miu Miu party would quench some thirst. It was tempting to believe that a neat solution like same-sex marriage would render us resolved and unburdened. Yet a breeze had begun to flow through our thinking. It seemed to carry a message that we could allow ourselves to want new forms of wanting. We could gambol outside the gates. We wanted to be happy. We were mostly, wildly happy.

FASHION WEEK ENDED LIKE a fever lifting. We watched TV. We decided we adored a cooking show hosted by a bossy Singaporean chef who shouted the names of dishes like Busta Rhymes spitting braggadocio. She placed demands on her husband and sous, Ben, a good-natured guy from Ghana who tossed the sizzling ingredients with a grin.

Maybe other viewers, if anyone else watched that show, took their dynamic to be mildly fucked-up. I was heartened by the sight of an interracial couple—not by the notion of "representation," let alone a perfect one, but just seeing them work it out, forging a rapport even if it was, alas, not totally separate from social hierarchies.

I grew up in a household of unexpected connections and frustrating disconnectedness. Dad wasn't a native English speaker. Mom didn't always concur with his family's priorities. In our house, any decision or plan involved some degree of translation—paralinguistic, idiomatic, sometimes angry. Cultural exchange, one might even say appropriation, was a matter of the day-to-day. We misused and mispronounced Mandarin and English words. We presumably agreed on the meanings between us.

My dad, Peter, immigrated to the United States for grad school in 1967. He chose to study in Florida over Stanford because his mindset was "spring break." Indeed, he met a cute blonde there, though she was more bookworm than beach bunny. My mom, Jean, had gone along to a party with her friend Ling, who wanted to meet Chinese guys. I don't think Ling scored that evening, but Mom got talking to the one with a mop of black hair. He smoked cigarettes and wore a white Harrington.

They began to know each other. They both liked Simon & Garfunkel. Peter was also a fan of the Rolling Stones, but Jean was put off by themes like *Satanic Majesties.* They began to see the town as a pair. Its red brick and laurel oaks. The building where Peter had gone to view an apartment, only to be told it was no longer available. The manager made a show of removing the FOR RENT sign from the lawn, then stuck it back in as he crossed the street. The bridge on which Mom was followed at night by yet another creep. They revealed these experiences, then began to share new, better moments together, though some of the area's buildings and trees were sites of their disagreements.

The marriage of Peter's parents, Kwang and Shu-In, had been basically arranged. They were still living in mainland China then, and their union involved a mei-ren (媒人), who served as something like a matchmaker and liaison between families. She offered assurances that the two were of social equivalence. Kwang's father was a university-educated elementary school principal; Shu-In's family owned shoe stores. The mei-ren confirmed that both were raised Episcopalian. The city where they lived, Wenzhou, is sometimes called "the Jerusalem of China" because of its hundreds of Christian churches.

Kwang would cycle past Shu-In's house, smartly dressed, to check her out. He was pleased, and she liked the cut of his jib.

The two were married, then properly introduced at the reception.

They were from a generation in which a wedded pair was tasked with finding something workable from within the practical institution of marriage. They hadn't been led to believe they'd one day meet their future spouse serendipitously. But in later years, their most beloved music—Shu-In's favorite song, "Tian Mi Mi" by Teresa Teng; Kwang's devotion to the Carpenters—involved highly romantic lyrics of chance, swooning, finding true love in a dream.

There remained a cultural expectation that Peter—or Pei-teh, as he was known back home—would marry agreeably, and everyone had this one girl in mind. She was pretty and poised. Pei-teh was a catch. He was one of the highest academic achievers in Taipei, the capital city of Taiwan, where the family had settled. But after meeting Jean, that perfect girl was becoming forgotten. Such an old-fashioned idea as an arranged marriage was eight thousand miles and a half-day time difference away.

On some preconscious level, Jean was relieved that her new beau wasn't white. He wasn't the patriarchal type she knew from military bases in the American South. He wasn't John Wayne—who, Joan Didion wrote with corroded nostalgia, had 'a sexual authority so strong that even a child could perceive it.' Men like that could keep riding.

Jean's family fit the image of an all-American nuclear ideal. But a family home is no guarantee of safety. Open some front doors, and inside—an abyss.

In *The Poetics of Space,* Gaston Bachelard wrote of how 'the house shelters daydreaming, the house protects the dreamer, the house allows one to dream in peace.' This sounds wonderful until a reader questions—which house, exactly? Not everyone has access to a house, let alone one that shelters, protects, and allows each inhabitant to peacefully dream.

So Mom told me less about her family home than about the tree branch to which she escaped. She sat there reading, refusing to come down when a besotted boy came calling. She invented Nancy Drew–type mysteries with her best friend, glamorously named Nancy. They softly wrote themselves into another neighborhood, another universe.

It's often said that because gays and lesbians usually do not grow up with gay and lesbian parents, we learn to make new forms apart from the traditional family unit. But that's not only true of gays and lesbians. Others have their own reasons to reconfigure. My parents also made new forms—fallible, but often actively deliberate—because the ones they'd known were outdated or broken with sharp edges.

When they became engaged, the objections were mostly voiced by Peter's family, who had by then followed him to the States. One of his sisters fell to the floor in tears when she learned that the perfect girl in Taipei was not to be her sister-in-law. After which Jean drove home in her VW Bug, sobbing while Janis Joplin growled on the radio. Peter then divulged that his mother Shu-In had fainted over a mahjong game played with disapproving friends. This got him feeling unfilial, which left Jean fed up.

In the end, with everyone looking groovy, Peter and Jean married in 1972. They chose a Presbyterian reverend who'd married Chinese friends. He'd grown up blue-collar and eventually attended Columbia University. His youthful exposure to a minister who stood up to racism and blind patriotism in their Virginia Tidewater town instilled in him a belief that true faith required him to be a citizen of the world. So it seemed to be from a place of concern and care that, in premarriage counseling, he recommended that Peter and Jean contemplate the challenges ahead as a biracial and binational couple. They assured him they would, but never talked it through with any seriousness.

At the ceremony, the reverend recited "On Marriage" from *The Prophet* by Kahlil Gibran, but accidentally read on and included "On Children." Jean, mortified, took Ling aside at the reception to bemoan how people might conclude it was a shotgun wedding. Coincidentally, when I was maybe nine or ten, I memorized a chunk of "On Children," and it continues to regularly turn over in my mind.

Your children are not your children.
They are the sons and daughters of Life's longing for
itself.
They come through you but not from you,
And though they are with you yet they belong not
to you.

You may give them your love but not your thoughts,
For they have their own thoughts.
You may house their bodies but not their souls,
For their souls dwell in the house of tomorrow, which
you cannot visit, not even in your dreams.

It seems right it was read at Mom and Dad's wedding. They were still just kids themselves.

MOM AND DAD'S CEREMONY took place just five years after the Supreme Court struck down state laws that prohibited interracial marriage, with its 1967 opinion in the case *Loving v. Virginia*.

In 1958 Richard Loving, who was white, married Mildred Jeter, who self-identified as 'Indian-Rappahannock' and was considered to be of Cherokee, Portuguese and African American ancestry. In their home state of Virginia, laws banning any interracial marriage had tightened with the Racial Integrity Act of 1924, which classified "white person" as an individual with 'no trace whatever of any blood other than Caucasian.' (Historian Arica L. Coleman has noted that members of the upper class in the state, 'claiming descent from Pocahontas and John Rolfe, successfully lobbied the legislature to revise the definition to include what became known as the "Pocahontas Exception," meaning that those with no more than 1/16th American Indian ancestry would be legally considered white.')

Richard and Mildred wed in Washington, DC. Back in Virginia, the Lovings were arrested by officers who barged into their house at two in the morning to apprehend them in "illicit cohabitation." Their marriage certificate hung above the bed. It listed their ages (his 24; hers 18) and races (his White; hers Indian). In prohibitive states like Virginia, challenges were faced by couples even when they'd legally exchanged vows in another state. The Lovings were charged and pled guilty. Their one-year prison sentence was suspended on the condition that they leave the state for twenty-five years. While their case proceeded, they tried unhappily to make a life in DC.

The unanimous decision in *Loving v. Virginia* invalidated all remaining bans and provided an apt metonym for the triumph of love over segregation. At the time, most white Americans disapproved of interracial marriage. Nearly half—over seventy percent of white southerners—supported laws banning such marriages.

Even before *Loving,* my parents would have been able to legally wed in Florida, but there was no national safeguard. Legislation had proven mercurial; some of the extant antimiscegenation laws had been repealed in the Reconstruction period, only to be later reinstated. Most laws that lasted up until *Loving* prevented marriage with Black partners, but those of Asian descent were also specified in Mississippi and Missouri. Like Virginia, Georgia only allowed a white person to marry another white person, which was defined by the state as those 'who have no ascertainable trace of either Negro, African, West Indian, Asiatic Indian, Mongolian, Japanese, or Chinese blood in their veins.' Between 1948—the year the United Nations General Assembly unanimously adopted the Universal Declaration of Human Rights, including the right to marry without discrimination based on race, nationality, or religion—and the *Loving* opinion, broad antimiscegenation laws had been repealed in several states, including California, where the classification 'negroes, Mongolians, members of the Malay race, or mulattoes' had been interpreted to include Chinese.

After the monumental Supreme Court decision bearing their name, the Lovings resided with their three children in a house that Richard built on an acre of land, given to them by his dad, on Passing Road; local lore has it that the name referenced people of color who passed as white. Richard and Mildred were now married regardless of state borders.

In 1975 a drunk driver struck the Lovings' car, and Richard died behind the wheel. Mildred, who lost her right eye in the accident, remained in their house and never remarried. She kept a low profile for the rest of her life, releasing a rare statement in

June 2007, just after the fortieth anniversary of *Loving v. Virginia* and on the cusp of the Massachusetts legislature voting down a proposed amendment to ban gay marriage in the state. The final two sentences read: 'I support the freedom to marry for all. That's what Loving, and loving, are all about.'

We've been rightly cautioned against drawing too neat a link between interracial and same-sex marriage, but it's worth noting that marriage has never been something available to everybody except gays. The history of the institution includes explicitly exclusionary and punitive legislation. In the United States and for many years in the British colonies, enslaved people could not legally marry. By the time of *Loving*, some state laws still prohibited whites from marrying Indigenous people. According to the Expatriation Act of 1907, any American woman who married a noncitizen was deemed to have taken on his nationality, thereby stripping her of American citizenship. This made her vulnerable in the ways an undocumented immigrant is: she could be barred from employment, detained, deported.

A woman marrying a Chinese national faced additional restrictions, as she could only leave and reenter under the terms of the 1882 Chinese Exclusion Act, which prohibited immigration by most Chinese laborers and excluded Chinese immigrants from citizenship.

The expatriation law was generally struck down with the Cable Act in 1922, but remained relevant for nearly another decade to women who married a man who was either ineligible for citizenship *or* an immigrant from Asia. This largely affected Asian American women married to Chinese nationals. It would also have pertained to Mom had she married Dad forty years earlier.

Chinese men have entered into interracial marriages in the

States since the nineteenth century. In the aftermath of the Emancipation Proclamation in 1863, some Chinese laborers (or "coolies") relocated to southern plantations, and some married the women they met there. The tenth census of Louisiana, taken in 1880, showed that fifty-seven percent of Chinese men in interracial marriages were wed to Black women. In the wake of the Chinese Exclusion Act, there are records of white female Sunday school teachers in San Francisco and New York who married their Chinese male pupils.

'Sharp distinctions persisted between the prerogatives of American male citizens who married "out" and American female citizens who did so,' notes Nancy F. Cott, an American historian who went on to help author amicus curiae briefs in multiple same-sex marriage cases. Cott offers the example of 'Mary K., an American-born woman descended from seventeenth-century colonists,' who married Taraknath Das, a Hindu native of India, in 1924. Soon after they exchanged vows, his naturalization was declared retroactively 'illegal and void' based on the ruling in the 1923 Supreme Court case *United States v. Bhagat Singh Thind*, which held that a high-caste Hindu man from Punjab was 'not a "white person"' and ineligible for naturalization.

As the wife of a man ineligible for American citizenship, Mary K. was no longer classified as an American citizen herself. They both became stateless. Cott noted that 'while American authorities claimed that Hindus who were deprived of their American citizenship reverted to their former status as British subjects, British law stipulated that any subject who had voluntarily been naturalized in another country lost British nationality.'

In 1926 Mary K. authored an article in *The Nation* entitled "A Woman Without a Country." She wrote, 'Has the American

Government fallen to such a state of degradation that to it the civil rights of its citizens have less value than property rights?'

A fatalistic contributor to *Woman Citizen* opined that the only thing someone in Mary K.'s position had left was 'hope of widowhood.' In fact, she would have been eligible to regain citizenship—if she divorced.

But a nonwhite woman in her position, as historian Candice Lewis Bredbenner has pointed out, would be forever stripped of citizenship. Bredbenner gives the example of Fung Sing, an American-born woman who married a Chinese national in 1920. Fung Sing was 'unaware that she'd irretrievably lost her citizenship' until she left the country and, when she got back, was told she was not allowed to reenter.

YOU TOOK ME TO the bronze Peter Pan statue in Kensington Gardens. Peter Pan has a bowl cut and bare feet, around which saucy fairies are poised to swirl upward, to tickle his knees or peer up his skirt. I didn't ask why you took me there. We saw the boy in each other, and boyishness was wordlessly unifying.

The final line of *Peter Pan*: '...and thus it will go on, so long as children are gay and innocent and heartless.' Dating back to at least 1382, *heartless* could indicate a lack of understanding—not so much callous as immature. The way that J. M. Barrie used the term, lexicographer Grant Barrett has explained, 'is about the undeveloped nature of a child's heart, where they haven't experienced the setbacks of true loss yet, so they don't understand what they're doing to other people when they do something like run away.' The adult Wendy tells her daughter, Jane: 'It is only the gay and innocent and heartless who can fly.' Barrie's meaning, Barrett reckons, is that 'children don't experience the same heartbreak and brokenheartedness of adults.'

Perhaps we were at risk of developing Peter Pan syndrome. What choice did we have but to be gay and innocent and heartless, if it buffered us from heartbreak? Yet, as critic Carol Mavor has postulated, 'Being boy eternal is its own kind of labor... Peter Pan knows how hard it is to live pressured by smallness.'

I was also becoming aware of how standing outside in so many places in London felt like the start of homosexual action. We walked east through Hyde Park, a place with its cruising traditions. In his book *My Father and Myself*, first published in 1968, J. R. Ackerley wrote of the young guardsmen who hung around this area 'with nothing to do and nothing to spend, whistling therefore in vain to the passing "prossies," whom they contemptuously called "bags" (something into which something is put), and alert to the possibility that some kind gentleman might appear' to buy them a few beers and pass over a tip—a pound for a foot guard, whereas a horse guard cost considerably more. The soldiers 'were perfectly agreeable to, indeed often eager for, a "bit of fun."'

The Vagrancy Act of 1898, ostensibly criminalizing prostitutes alongside those sleeping on the street or in makeshift camps, was consistently used to apprehend men engaging in sex acts with other men. In such ways, homosexuality has been legally entangled with vagrancy—clamping down on those who get it on without a roof. You told me about friends who took the risk of cruising in the bushes of parks and cemeteries.

It sounds so cold, I said, sniffling.

I suddenly needed us to be back at yours. I wanted to watch TV with you. Was the Asian cooking show on? Afterward we could draw. We did so side by side on your bedroom floor, which had become one big bed. You'd borrowed someone's spare mattress and pushed it against yours, standing the decommissioned frame against the wall. We sprawled out and changed positions, each doodling a different neverland.

When we emerged from the Underground back in Bethnal Green, the sky swirled ominously, its gray deepening.

We stopped at Tesco. You chose ingredients for dinner. I browsed newfound British specialties. Marmite. Hobnobs. Orange squash, a soft drink meant to be diluted with water—very wartime rationing.

Outside, the clatter of shopping trolleys combined with thunderclaps in the sky.

We crossed the high street and scurried through a small square green, one of those modest open spaces the Victorians maintained to ensure that the East End poor had a place to air out their filth and disease.

The heavens opened. I panicked, then felt elated. You were grinning. We dashed past the brick wall with YOU'RE SO COOL spray-painted inside a heart. We had taken each other's photos in front of it, a couple of poseurs. The rain fell so hard—what you called *chucking it down*—I feared the words would wash away.

Back at the apartment, the girls looked up calmly from their beanbags as we yelped, the water streaming off our clothes, creating another deluge indoors. We took off our squelchy shoes, then stripped down in the bathroom and huddled in the poky shower as it trickled out scalding water.

Later that night, while I did the dishes—what you called *washing up*—a pop song glimmered from the radio on the windowsill. I looked out on the courtyard, now still and dark. No students were out, but I could see lights in rooms. Smoking weed and watching TV and thinking through their dramas. All these young Brits full of sex and doubt.

By the time you came into the kitchen with that little smile on your face, the song—"Everybody Knows (Except You)" by the Divine Comedy—had ended, but to me its sound had become one with the cool wet night.

I wanted it to play again so you could hear it. I now paid attention to everything as it connected to you.

ON FRIDAY EVENINGS, WE went out. You shimmied into a sheer top and showered yourself in glitter. I rubbed black on my eyes and hooked a diamanté dog collar around my tree-trunk neck.

We were descending the stairs into Bethnal Green Station when childish hollering caused us to look up. A group of South Asian boys hung over the edge. They tried out those epithets that sound almost twee to my American ears: *Batty boy! Pooftah!* One, then another, spat.

We were only sprayed with spittle—no loogie. Still, we felt soiled.

On the tube, I sulked, but you sat with something more like disappointment. And irony: it was likely that those kids' family lines traced back to a country where bans on homosexuality were first introduced by British law—Section 377 of the colonial penal code. This was the case in India, Pakistan, Bangladesh, Sri Lanka and many other colonized territories. In fact, I came from a continent that inherited colonial antisodomy laws. In 1610 the Virginia Colony instituted a code that made 'the horrible, detestable sins of Sodomie,' alongside adultery and rape, punishable by death.

And while they might have been taught proscriptive interpretations of the Hadith, they were British schoolchildren, so it seemed to be just as, if not more, relevant that they went to school under the restrictions of Section 28. Under this law, their teachers were not allowed to 'promote homosexuality' or, among other aspects, 'the acceptability of homosexuality as a pretended family relationship.' Section 28 had been in place since 1988, therefore during your education, too.

With that line about 'pretended family,' queers are once again condemned for pretentiousness. It would actually make a certain sense if it were taken to mean that it's unacceptable to perceive of queer families as *merely pretend*, that rather they should be acknowledged as real and valid. But the intended meaning was of course that a gay household can only ever be fraudulent. Maybe we internalized this view, to some extent saw ourselves as *pretended*. Wrong politically, but it aligned with the way our romance was escapist, how we made it up as we went along.

One reason the name Francis Bacon was lodged into your brain: when your art teacher had introduced you to his work, and mentioned he was gay, she was broaching a taboo. Maybe even this could have been construed as breaking the law. Maybe you intuited her risk and carried that with you.

The year prior to the implementation of Section 28, prime minister Margaret Thatcher won a third term decisively. In a now-legendary speech at the 1987 Conservative Party Conference, Thatcher stated, 'Children who need to be taught to respect traditional moral values are being taught that they have an inalienable right to be gay.' She included them among all of the children 'being cheated of a sound start in life. Yes, cheated.' The speech received a standing ovation.

Public disapproval of homosexuality was extraordinarily high at the time. When the office of a gay newspaper was firebombed, a Conservative member of Parliament openly expressed her approval of the terrorist act: 'Quite right too.' She later doubled down by stating she was 'quite prepared to affirm that there should be an intolerance of evil,' meaning the homosexuality, not the bomb. The following month, she was made a dame on Thatcher's recommendation.

Section 28 would not be abolished until 2003.

DO YOU REMEMBER ALL this? I am sure you do. It's mapped out by our small monuments. The Peter Pan. The crude heart on a brick wall. Remember the girl with bleached hair we'd see around town? People called her Bad Laura. She wore a big fluffy white coat to match her peroxide hair. She was hardly malevolent, but came across as slippery and fiendish. She would turn up alone and then swim into a group, a placid expression on her face as she caused unignorable ripples.

While you were in the printing studio—a rare instance when you were actually doing student work, leaving me on my own—I ran into Bad Laura somewhere near the strip joint on Cambridge Heath Road, long before it became a gay club.

She invited me back to her place for a tea that she never made. We sat on her floor. She thrust the soles of her Buffalo platforms toward me, begrimed with the residue of the city.

I have to return to the States soon, I lamented.

Bad Laura responded by proposing marriage. In an offhand way, by claiming she'd almost done it before. Nearly married an American boy—*also named Jeremy!*—for the sake of his relationship with her dear gay friend. And though it didn't wind up happening, she remained as willing as she was then. *Huh,* I said.

I wound up at Bad Laura's place, I told you that evening.

Oh, really? How was that?

I think she proposed to me.

That's nice of her.

I think she's just drawn to the idea of the drama.

A "marriage of convenience" must almost always be a misnomer. It was infuriating to think that I could adore you to no level that would satisfy the law but get hitched and start the paperwork with Bad Laura pretty much right away. If we were to actually begin looking for the right girlfriend to approach, we hadn't even decided which side of the pond we were scouting. My closest gal pals, Xuan and Naya, were too busy getting their adult lives started in very different ways. You were surrounded by university acquaintances who were bound to fall out of touch. The girls you'd known longer were deep in their own dilemmas. Nobody seemed to be in the position to stop furiously writing their own story and become a character in ours.

Pretty much everyone we knew immediately came up with the same hypothetical solution: *if only you could get married.* Such wistfulness was at uncomfortable odds with radical politics. Lauren Berlant has asked, 'Why, when there are so many people, only one plot counts, as "life" (first comes love, then . . .)? Those who don't or can't find their way in that story—the queers, the singles, the something else—can become so easily unimaginable, even often to themselves. Yet it is hard not to see lying about everywhere the detritus and the amputations that come from attempts to fit into the fold: meanwhile, a lot of world-building energy atrophies.'

In our case, we could only ever imagine—though our world-building tended to be insular and phantasmagorical. *Flowers from our planet,* you wrote to me on a card as narrow as a bookmark. *They never die.* Marriage came to only mean the paperwork. Already inclined toward irreverence, we saw practical real-world solutions as some hazy combination of role-play and bureaucracy. Soon I would leave—this time, with no plan for when we'd see each other again. In one sense, we dissociated, becoming, like two kids, *heartless* again. But I was so lovesick it sometimes physically hurt.

7

LEAVE TO REMAIN

We didn't know anyone else in our position.

There *were* others, before and around us, but most, like us, kept their heads below the parapet. Behind closed doors dreaming of, if not Hawaii . . . Denmark? Amsterdam? Some couples were, like us, mostly apart. Some partners did what you would before long: move to the other's country without the paperwork, entering into an unequal arrangement—hidden while their citizen partner remained rooted.

At the end of April 1997, just after I returned to the States, boyfriends Mark Watson and Ander Da Silva received surprising news. Ander, who is Brazilian, would be permitted to extend his stay in the UK (what the British Home Office refers to as *leave to remain*) on the basis of his relationship with Mark, a Brit. They were pretty much the unlikeliest couple to get that.

In 1989, fresh from university, Mark had taken a job as an immigration officer at Gatwick Airport. The position offered generous time off early on. So just a year in, Mark organized an expedition down the Amazon with a group of friends. At a disco in São Paulo, Mark spotted Ander across the room. Ander was swoonable—a model with big dewy brown eyes. Mark's eyes were behind glasses, and Ander had a thing for that intellectual look. They struggled through fragmented English and Portuguese—the language barrier forcing them to slow down and actually listen—until morning. Mark continued on his travels, sending Ander a postcard from each of his subsequent stops.

Then Ander came to England, first living with Mark at his parents' place. The only recourse a transnational same-sex couple had to obtain residency for the foreign partner was to meet a criterion known as compelling compassionate circumstances. A committed relationship did not qualify as compelling enough.

So Mark carried Ander's passport to work at Gatwick one day and, while nobody was looking, stamped it granting permission to stay, and put it back in his pocket.

Over time, they could almost forget the subterfuge. They moved into their own flat in Croydon, South London, and furnished it with mugs, bowls, linens, sofa. They felt real.

Early one morning in September 1993, the pair were awoken by a banging on the front door. Ander answered, then rushed back upstairs in a panic. It was the police, asking to see his passport.

The officers declared the stamp a forgery on the spot and took them both to the police station, where they were separated. In interrogation, Ander lied to protect Mark, who told the truth to protect Ander.

Mark was given assurances that he would almost certainly lose his job but would almost certainly not serve prison time if he confessed. Mark's fear was shot through with anger: Had one of his work colleagues tipped the authorities off?

While Mark was on release, he got in touch with lawyer Wesley Gryk, himself a transplant from the States, who swiftly agreed to act as his criminal lawyer. With Wes present, the couple reported back at the station, where a particularly ornery officer not only charged the pair but denied them release on police bail, declaring them flight risks to be kept on remand. The two fell apart in each other's arms before being detained in separate cells for the night. To put up court bail money, Mark's dad went to a late-night bank and withdrew funds from a recent insurance payout.

Ander agreed to voluntarily depart the country. At the airport, the pair didn't know what to do with themselves as they waited for Ander to board, unsure if and when they'd see each other again. Back at the flat, Mark could barely move for two days. 'You wander around the house and you look at things,' he later recounted to BBC documentarians. 'And you think, well, we bought that together, or we did this together, or we argued over this. The whole place reminds you of the other person, and it becomes very empty. I think, if you're used to living with another person, and that person is gone, and gone completely maybe, it is very, very difficult.'

Wes Gryk suggested Mark attend a meeting of the nascent Stonewall Immigration Group, held at the Barley Mow Pub on Horseferry Road, in December 1993. Wes had been present from the first gathering, held that May, which involved a few binational couples sharing pitfalls and setbacks. 'This was a time,' Wes later recalled, 'long before there were any victories to recount.'

When Mark showed up at the meeting, he brought unique insight: not only his cautionary tale of arrest, but inside knowledge from working at the immigration service, making him privy to ingrained homophobia there. He could attest that making a plea for each case on the merits of a couple's romance was unsustainable. Systemic change was needed, which would require effective lobbying strategies and a sea change in public opinion. While "gay immigration" sounded like a lost cause, Mark reckoned, two humans proclaiming 'we love each other, and all we want is the right to be able to live together—you have a very compelling argument there.' The campaigners needed stories to circulate.

As expected, Mark was fired. What he hadn't anticipated was facing criminal charges. Mark would later describe the day of his court appearance in a gentle tone, almost as if reading from a children's book. Sitting in the dock, he saw on one side his family and friends—'who were almost sort of shining with goodness for me.' To his other side 'was this policeman, who was quite a ghastly, horrible man.' Mark thought, *'I wouldn't swap my place with him for anything in the world. I'm happy where I am.'*

The judge described Mark as a good person. He'd been a stellar student, literally a Boy Scout. Yet one can't betray an appointment to the civil service; an example had to be made of him. Mark was sentenced to six months in prison. His first day of incarceration was his birthday. Mark was advised not to tell anyone he was gay and given the option of being segregated to decrease the risk of homophobic violence, which he declined.

Upon his release, Mark began volunteering with the Stonewall group. The headlines around his case were bringing more couples to the meetings, now held monthly. The group produced a guide, designed like the game Snakes and Ladders, to navigating the tangled appeals process.

The Home Office appeals system was notoriously long. A same-sex couple would submit an application, and though a negative decision was pretty much inevitable, it could take years to process. During this period, the foreign partner wouldn't be able to work or to travel outside the UK, but it bought time. It also, Wes Gryk adds, 'incidentally created an army of volunteers eventually numbering in the hundreds without the right to work in the United Kingdom but with the time, energy and the will' to put in pro bono hours working toward inclusive immigration reform.

In early 1994 the Immigration Appeal Tribunal found it improper that the Home Secretary had dismissed two applications for a same-sex foreign partner. With this, the highest immigration court in the kingdom had finally opened up a consideration of whether homo relationships should have equal status to those of the hets.

ONE REASON WHY "GAY immigration" sounds like an unsympathetic cause is that gays are already perceived to be on the move—a bunch of itchy-footed tourists and neighborhood colonizers. As put by British-based legal scholar Carl F. Stychin, himself a transplant from Canada, the *perception* of mobility can precede us. 'The perceived frequency of lesbian and gay travel has been deployed in the construction of gays as an "undeserving" (because privileged) minority,' he wrote, 'who do not "deserve" what are described as "special rights," because of their *upward mobility*.'

As charted by both researchers and pop songwriters, queers tend to flock to cities and carve out their own urban space. The ensuing gayborhoods can be highly elitist and alienating, with tacit and actual door policies based on gender, race and class. These are the zones of those white gay men who, as described by James Baldwin, have 'the sense of feeling cheated of the advantages which accrue to white people in a white society. There's an element, it has always seemed to me, of bewilderment and complaint.' Plus, the enclaves take on what Stychin has called 'a homogeneity and familiarity across place and time'—a global gay sensibility from West Hollywood to Le Marais that can be seen to erase a given site's former local character. Take the names alone of British gay bars like New York New York in Manchester, the Lisbon in Liverpool, and the Quebec in London. The monikers evince a particular form of cosmopolitanism—the evocation of elsewhere. Even the Stonewall Immigration Group, though focused on British policy, took its name from the legendary Manhattan bar.

Gays and lesbians, wrote Stychin, have been socially constructed as 'outsiders to national culture and as non-citizens.' Voters already prone to favor strict border control and adhere to the idea of a national identity are perhaps unlikely to warm to gay globalists. Gay men have been broadly perceived as a security risk for decades. The irony is personified by World War II codebreaker Alan Turing, sentenced to chemical castration in his lifetime, now the face on Britain's fifty-pound note. By the nineties, gay men were also construed as bearing AIDS.

Stychin has described the public conception that 'both migration and homosexuality have an unfixity and an excessiveness that needs to be contained to prevent invasion: this is a dangerous difference that threatens order, consensus, nation state, and way of life. Like migrants more generally, the (particularly male) homosexual has been a threat because of an inability to know *his* borders.'

SOON ENOUGH ANDER RETURNED, handsome as ever, reunited with Mark, who'd bleached his hair and grown a George Michael goatee. Mark had become so integral to the Stonewall group that they sourced the funds to offer him a paid position. Working to be with Ander had literally become his full-time job.

This time, Ander entered through the Republic of Ireland. If he'd come through the UK directly, he'd have been deemed an illegal entrant, having pretended to enter as a visitor but with the actual intention to stay, and his ensuing application would have been disqualified. The workaround was to land in Ireland as a visitor, then pass without being questioned—hence without making a false declaration—into the UK based on the free travel arrangement between the two countries.

In February 1996, UK immigration law was indeed made more equal. Bizarrely, the Home Office announced it would cease its existing concession for unmarried straight cohabiting couples rather than extend this to gay and lesbian couples. The law had an uneven history: until as recently as 1985, only foreign *females* were allowed to immigrate to the UK with a British male common-law partner—what Wes Gryk has suggested is 'no doubt an historical carryover of a provision created to allow staunch (male) British Empire–builders to bring home their mistresses and concubines to look after them in their dotage.' This was eventually changed to allow for the immigration of foreign male partners. The logic behind ending this pathway for unmarried couples altogether in 1996 seemed to be that the queers could not claim it was unfair.

Between April 1995 and May 1997, however, Stonewall documented some twenty successful applications by a foreign same-sex partner. That meant that although the Home Office had yet to announce a policy for transnational same-sex couples, they were creating a precedent. Wes Gryk noted one possible, and cynical, rationale: allowing in the foreign partner of someone suffering serious HIV-related symptoms might relieve the state of providing resources for the care of that person until their death.

The one case that seemed forever doomed was that of Mark and Ander, given their notoriety. Indeed, they were initially refused, with Ander's presence in the UK described as "undesirable." Then in April 1997, Ander was granted a further year's leave to remain, making theirs the nineteenth successful case.

Was it possible that an old buddy of Mark's at the Home Office felt that the pair was owed one? Just as it's plausible that they had been turned in by some homophobic colleague, so could they have been given the go-ahead by an anonymous ally a few years later.

IN EARLY MAY 1997, the "New" Labour Party headed by Tony Blair—less socialist, more reliant on the power of the market to deliver social justice—won a landslide victory, ending the eighteen years of Conservative government beginning with Margaret Thatcher's election in 1979.

On Friday the 10th of October, it was announced that the UK would implement a new set of guidelines adjacent to immigration rules the following Monday. In the new Unmarried Partners Concession, same-sex partners also qualified, marking the very first time that British law recognized gay and lesbian relationships.

Among predictable exclusions, you couldn't be unhoused or poor. The minimum cohabitation period of four years was blatantly unequal to the previous two-year standard for unmarried straights. Still, it was something worth celebrating. The Stonewall group opened its offices for a party on the night of the announcement.

We did not receive the memo.

You did in fact turn up at a Stonewall meeting sometime around then, but the main thing you had to report back to me was the undeniable charisma of the famous actor you'd spotted in attendance.

We were vaguely aware that changes were afoot, but they always seemed tenuous, and invariably to include some caveat—like the four years of cohabitation—that counted us out. We had not even known each other for much more than a year.

Neither of us felt emboldened enough to reach out to a member of the Stonewall group directly to figure out our options, let alone to ask the right questions. Someone there might have whispered to us the ways in which we could have gotten around the requirements. Like Ander, I could have entered the UK via the open border with Ireland. Then—though I'd be ineligible for gainful employment, and you were still finishing your art degree—we could apply, knowing we would be rejected but hoping to exploit a long appeals process to accrue the required four years of living together. All for a maybe.

YOU BEGAN WORKING MORE hours at a postmodern ceramics shop in Camden so that you could return to San Francisco in the summer. The place was run by a ne'er-do-well who wore a Vivienne Westwood tartan kilt and was said to actually be the descendent of some Scottish viscount or marquess. He slept in the shop, which had no bathroom, so frequently resorted to pissing in one of the many vessels at hand. When a nice tourist couple asked about a particular vase, he took it from the shelf and, despite your attempts to thwart him, turned it upside down to check the price, dousing himself in his own urine. You'd describe such events in a letter, but before you had the chance to send it, you'd have told me on the phone, so that by the time I received your mail, the anecdotes read like shared memories. *You're all I ever talk about,* you told me. But whenever you mentioned your next trip to San Francisco, the postmodern ceramics shop owner figured you were just daydreaming, so when you gave notice, he was shocked, then apoplectic. He found you down at the local pub and screamed in front of everyone there that he would contact US immigration. Tell them that when you came this time, you intended to stay. Which was almost prescient, though that wouldn't be for another two summers. When you related such events on the phone, I could see how I had become an *idea* in other people's minds. The American boyfriend you couldn't stop talking about: privileged, bewildered, uncouth and cut.

I ARRIVED AT SFO with a bundle of gerbera daisies—the brightest, most unnatural-looking blooms on sale at the flower stand in the Castro, my new neighborhood. The zany flowers went with your proudly artificial look; you'd dyed your hair the red of a London phone box. The time with you went by quickly, and, it turned out, the farewells were getting no easier. Apartness loomed, then came like a sucker punch. Without you, I was parched. The sound of each airplane above was distressing.

Back in London, a fashion photographer who wore yellow-tinted glasses took pictures of you in your new digs—a dilapidated house leased by an affable, ineffective man whom you called The Reverend. The photographer posed you with one of the boy housemates together in bed as if you were lovers, though he was actually spending most of his nights in the girl housemate's room. In the photos, your place looks queer and depraved. Ornate wallpaper. Flat burgundy carpets as humdrum and nearly as dirty as those in an old pub. Flakes of tobacco, pencil shavings and lint that could not be eradicated with any amount of vacuuming. Sesame Street toys. An arrangement of empty Silk Cut boxes—*like a Carl Andre,* you joked. *Fire Walk with Me* and "Smells Like Teen Spirit" posters. An indoor garden of plastic flowers.

You made a picnic table out of an old door, and the housemates ate al fresco on clement evenings on the small patio overlooking the wasteland of weeds and impenetrable brambles. You told me over the phone that you planned to make Mexican for everyone based on ingredients you could scrounge at Tesco. I scoffed.

A needy puss with matted fur showed up, then came back daily. You named her, playing off the title of a book that I sent you, Weetzie Cat. You spent whole afternoons combing her. She'd return dreadlocked again the next day, ready to be pampered by your attentive hands. Routines like that quickly formed, none of them permanent.

Your letters became peripatetic. You wrote as you rambled down Regent's Canal. You'd follow the overgrown, abandoned towpath for hours, and arrive at desolate lots that would one day become occupied by an Olympic stadium, megalith shopping mall, craft brewery or street-food yard with all-day reggaeton. Sometimes on these excursions you'd encounter a loud gang of lads. Or another loner, aimless like you, but older and less overtly artistic. You kept your head down. You entered a wooded cemetery and continued your letter to me: *I'm sitting on a bench where fascists once loitered. I scribbled over their Sharpie swastikas with my glitter pen.*

TWICE WE MET IN between: New York City. I flew out for magazine events, and you could just about afford to join me. The first time, my publishers had credit to use at a skanky boardinghouse popular with club kids. A room with a sink, but no private bathroom, had been reserved under my name.

I arrived wobbly, my ears still stuffed with clouds from the flight. Through a half-moon hatch, a disinterested concierge gave me the room number. There was no key to hand over. *Your friend's already checked in,* he explained.

I rattled up to our floor, where the serpentine, bloodred hallway creaked with the ghosts of old-world hookers and faggots. No sign of the living, just the noise of an AC unit, and the smell of bleach or cocaine. Until, there you were: your noggin popped through a doorway. You'd gone peroxide blond, making your blue eyes brighter, somehow bigger. You wore a dozy expression like Falkor the Luck Dragon from *The NeverEnding Story.* You were sleepy but beaming. You radiated as if already being fucked.

I thought: I bet he finds this place delightful. A little seedy, but darkly glamorous. You were euphoric and sure that I would be too when I laid eyes on you. So I was euphoric.

In that hallway, set apart from the crackling metropolis, a space like an old photograph, sepia, blurry, there you appeared, both the moth and the flame.

THERE WAS A SUMMER during those years apart when you could not afford to come to San Francisco, so we didn't see each other for many months. You were moving out of the shambly house. One boy departed, then the boy and girl who'd become a couple, leaving just you to clean up a year's worth of youthful indiscretion, literally in the dark. *I've been rummaging behind sofa cushions,* you confided, *for coins to feed the electric meter.*

I next flew to London to ring in 1999. I was almost grounded by an ear infection. My own fault—I'd tried to dislodge wax using the kitchen sink hose on full blast into my canal. I went to the free health clinic for young gay men, where I complained of excruciating pain. The nurse asked if I performed rim jobs. Very San Francisco. So I made it a gay issue. *I need antibiotics so I can fly to see my boyfriend,* I begged.

You were by then staying on the eighth or ninth floor of a council block not far from Victoria Park. I never got over the jet lag during my short time there, so I'd sit up in your bed—another mattress on the floor—watching the sky shift blues through the window: tar, cobalt, bruise, lilac, cerulean, periwinkle, powder.

One evening I kissed you against the wall in the entry, and you came at me with such desperate hardness that I corrected you. *Kiss me softer,* I said. *Slower.* As bossy as when you first arrived in San Francisco and I criticized your shirts. We'd been standing in a hallway then, too. I detected your sudden sensation of having no escape as I toyed with your trust. But the kissing was nicer. *Good,* I said, encouraging in a fatherly way, and your body told me you were both humiliated and aroused.

IN APRIL 1999, MICHAEL Warner's article "Normal and Normaller: Beyond Gay Marriage" was published in *GLQ*, the scholarly journal of lesbian and gay studies. It had been years since Jack Baker had put forward the reasoned argument that being excluded from marriage made him a second-class citizen, yet until recently, Warner wrote, the cause had not been taken up as a political priority. 'Why not?' Warner asked. 'Was it a matter of lesbian resistance derived from the feminist critique of marriage? Were gay men just too busy snorting poppers at the baths?' The 'norms of straight culture,' he wrote, have been resisted as 'the standards by which queer life should be measured.' Instead, queers had 'cultivated unprecedented kinds of commonality, intimacy, and public life.'

It seemed clear that Warner had experienced fun times, enabled by access he and certain other gay men had to spaces of radical experimentation. But, as unsexy as it sounds, more risk-averse homosexuals had long responded to a lack of federal protections by coupling and maintaining their privacy. In the shadow of the government's queerhunt known as the Lavender Scare, some gays and lesbians developed an essentially conservative domesticity. Legal scholar Dale Carpenter has cited *When I Come Back, I'm Going to Be Gay*, the unpublished autobiography of a circumspect gay man from Houston: 'The 1950s made all of us realize that the only security you have in life is what you build yourself. Education and financial planning coupled with a lasting relationship was paramount.'

Warner persuasively wrote that 'such areas of law as probate, custody, and immigration need far more sweeping reforms than same-sex marriage.' After the landmark *Obergefell* decision, Warner would describe the marriage movement as propelled by a lack of 'thinking creatively about other ways that those rights and obligations might be distributed.'

So how to square these ideals with our own thinking? I fretted we were too sentimental, too swayed by received notions and scared into submission. Did we want marriage? Not particularly. We wanted to be together and passively equated the two concepts. Marriage was always the route, not the destination.

But in Warner's view, marriage is not just a harmless option: 'To speak of marriage as merely one choice among many is at best naive; it might be more accurately called active mystification.' We'd been conditioned to accept the privileging of long-term normative relationships by 'the state's administrative penetration into contemporary life.' He wrote, 'The state merely certifies a love that is beyond law, but by doing so it justifies its existence as keeper of the law.'

I suppose we *were* mystified. It didn't seem like we had the *time* to wait for the dismantling of the systemic suppression of sexual variation, let alone for national borders to be abolished. Queer theory always seemed so *far ahead*. You could have been barred from entering the United States just for being gay a mere six years before we met. An HIV-positive person could still be denied entry.

At times, queer theory has made me feel *less than*, as if I'm too shortsighted to make out the horizon it paints. When I turn toward it, having been diminished by the state, the theory eludes me with its future tense. Reading a text like Warner's is not exactly an experience of being left out; in fact, it seems line by line to indict me. I feel not so much *seen* as evaluated. I am implicated by the very ideas that I agree with, because I can't find a way to live them out. In theory, I'm a disappointment.

IN JUNE 1999 THE UK changed its Unmarried Partners Concession again, lowering the minimum cohabitation period to two years. This remained unequal to immigration based on marriage, which required no prior time living together (in sin). By then we had been an item for three years but didn't have the receipts. Not the right ones, like a utility bill. We'd have fared better with that kind of official proof of living together (even illegally) than a stack of love letters. In the US there remained no inroads at all. There was an annual green card lottery. You had more of a chance through that. You could draw me a picture. I could write you a sentence. These acts meant the world to us, and nothing to the world.

At your graduate exhibition, you presented smoggy sunsets, desert peacocks and tumbleweeds, assembled in video and a tiny book with elliptical text. It was partly told from the perspective of a faded Hollywood diva, like in Andy Warhol's *Heat* or the Velvet Underground song "New Age." You merged your memories (and premonitions) of California with the views of concrete through your East London window.

The work was hazy, extravagant, full of longing. You received no awards and no offers of representation from a London gallery. In other words, done with art school and unsummoned by the art world, when you came to San Francisco in the summer, you could think of no reason to go back. Maybe you unconsciously cultivated that. We both knew what was next in our bodies, like swallows know to cross continents.

8
SAFEWAY

So, that September, reaching your maximum allotted days as a tourist, you decided that sometimes an end needs rewriting.

Nothing to return to, and everything to stay for, was how you put it. We went over the what-abouts until the little things (your stuff in boxes at your sister Ruby's back in London) wore themselves down, while the big stuff (not being able to return to be with her or any of your family) loomed even bigger until we no longer saw it, like a familiar mountain chain in the distance.

I can't stand the idea of being apart from you again, you whispered with a newfound resolve the night before you were booked to fly back from SFO.

Your suitcase was mostly packed, but never zipped. When the time came for the plane to take off, we became giddy knowing your name was being announced throughout the airport—*This is the final call . . .*—then picturing your empty seat. Whoever was next to it would be grateful for the extra room.

We went outside. Into a day that we'd stolen—or stolen back.

Departure day: I used to know it as harrowing—the cusp of loneliness. Now I experienced it instead as disobedient. Still a departure, a huge one, but without parting ways. The city around us was at once spectacular and boring. I felt high on my role abetting a criminal. You shone as if brand-new, but also already at ease. You were doing what one is supposed to do in San Francisco: not leave.

Even though you acted as if you were just passively bobbing along, I saw you as heroic. You became famous in my eyes that day, one of several different reasons I took to calling you the Famous Blue Raincoat—or just Famous—in my writing. *Not that I'm famous (yet),* you had written in your first letter to me. It's a tender irony that probably the most famous move you'd made was to become a secret.

When you're nervous, it shows. And that tremble was there, but at the same time, a new calmness stepped through. You appeared Californian now. Tanned already. I never felt as much a citizen as I did when we became outlaws.

We passed the Castro flower stand. *Your florist now!* I said. We were headed nowhere, maybe Café Flor. *Your café!* We were going to have to teach you once and for all how to pronounce *water* in a way comprehensible to American waiters. But you refused to learn how to calculate the tip. You figured I'd always be there to figure out fifteen percent. We passed the usual mean gays. Now they were your problem, too.

We scrambled up the rocks near the children's museum atop the craggiest hill in the Castro. We stood there as if it was Everest, surveying the Safeway sign on Market Street; rainbow flags; people like ants; cars in traffic, forced to slow down in proximity to one another, navigating the crowded, prickly, glistening city.

I WAS—NOW *we were*—living on 17th Street where it met Market and Castro, with three sympathetic girls who each rocked a Wednesday Addams look and jointly subscribed to *Martha Stewart Living*. One of them had heard of a Scottish Highlands–themed hotel that was pretty much always hiring overstays, and indeed you were given work there right away.

I'd draw a bath for you after your shifts in the repulsive kitchen, where the chintzy plates piled high like cairns. Why didn't they put a boy who looked and spoke like you in front of the guests? It seemed that pretty much all the staff were paid under the table. You scrubbed pots alongside older folk from El Salvador. Other young Europeans, who had, for instance, arrived for a rave and never departed, made the beds and vacuumed. The pretension of making everything look like rural Scotland wound up sapping the life out of the place. By the rancid smell of the water in the vases, one could tell the owners were haughty and remiss.

People, you told me as you soaked, *keep mentioning someone who used to work there. Dylan.*

Nice name.

My parents almost named me that.

Would have been so cool, I said.

It would have been too much.

Your hair had grown out, revealing its waves, framing your face in near-ringlets, now free of the red dye and bleach. Gold glowed from within its chestnut brown. You dunked under the water and reemerged. Your cushy little lips, your snout.

Anyway. Dylan?

They keep mentioning that he went Somewhere Better. I should look into that.

Definitely. We gotta get you the hell out of there.

We kept up the plans and speculations, you in the water, me perched on the toilet seat lid, until the whorls of your skinny fingers became baggy raisins.

Time to rinse off, I said. *I'll get in the shower with you.*

We scrubbed each other. How did I clean my back before you came along? I wasn't the type to buy myself a brush. I could barely say what my back looked like.

I look like E.T. the Extra-Terrestrial, you announced, your hands clasped behind your neck, suds sliding over your narrow shoulders and smooth, slightly distended belly, then knobbly knees, curled toes, unbelievably high-arched feet.

I laughed a little too loudly, and you put your arms around me, pulling me in, wanting to be assured that I was smitten notwithstanding the tum between us.

We got out together, dripping wet.

THE MYTHS AROUND DYLAN, the former dishwasher who'd successfully escaped, did not stop coming.

He followed the lesbians, an Australian cook with stretched earlobes explained. That sounded promising.

Specifically, Dylan had moved on to a vegetarian café called the Bloo Legume in Cole Valley. *Much better than here,* someone always wistfully sighed about this Shangri-La.

You showed up at the Bloo Legume looking like the genteel English folk singer Nick Drake, wearing a crocheted top and brown corduroy bell bottoms. The manager, a sturdy dyke with short dreads, offered you a job on the spot. And there, on your first shift, was Dylan beside you. It turned out he was Welsh and had grown up in Argentina.

I can't imagine! you said, plopping black dal. *Patagonian Welsh!*

I recommend, if you haven't read it already, the Bruce Chatwin book, Dylan said. *You can't make out where the truth ends . . .*

You wanted to be his friend. He spoke of *In Patagonia* and *The Street of Crocodiles*; of Paul Klee and Robert Walser, and the apparent smallness of each; of Neutral Milk Hotel, the Portishead live album, and how *Nirvana Unplugged* was wholly different from the rest.

He preferred the short stories of his namesake, Dylan Thomas, to the famous poems. In your eyes, his life as an expat, even an undocumented one, seemed like a road trip rather than a dead end. He was baffled and melancholy, but very *present.* He was weirdly, hesitantly, somehow perfectly articulate. Also, he asked questions and actually listened.

I can't go back to Argentina, he said cryptically.

You had tried so far not to give much thought to *back there.* How would you let your parents know? As with so much else, you wouldn't, exactly. They'd figure it out. They'd wonder but wouldn't press. You'd send letters, illuminating a life in San Francisco, conjuring a sense of adventure to compensate for the precariousness.

They liked thinking of you on an adventure. When you were fifteen or so, your dad dropped you off at a beach with a tent, a Trangia stove, and an Ordnance Survey map. You walked for miles along the cliffs, camped in one or two different places, survived on Super Noodles, crisps and tea. In some town somewhere, you bought a copy of *Viz,* the bawdy adult comic, a tiny act of transgression. There wasn't much else on which to spend the small amount of cash you had with you. Good thing, because a storm was coming on your last night, and you needed what was left to pay for a room in a B&B. The couple that ran the place were a little shocked. What were you—a runaway? Maybe you were running *toward* your dad, his approval. But you really did like being out there on your own.

Like you would one day yourself, your parents had uprooted. They'd moved to South Africa when Brits were incentivized to do so, and that's where you were born. It was a place with an abhorrent political system—but *away,* and under the sun. People think of you as a very English boy, but your early days were barefoot and beachy. Your first body of water was the Indian Ocean. You walked among protea, spekbooms, and blue chalksticks. You laid eyes on elephants, hippos, giraffes, kudus, springboks, baboons, lions, cheetahs, zebras. Your family returned to cloudy England just before the antigay legislation Section 28 came into effect.

Years later, just around the time that you began your overstay in San Francisco, postapartheid South Africa was reforming its immigration laws to welcome foreign partners in a same-sex relationship with a citizen or permanent resident. Whether that presented an opportunity for us because it was your place of birth, we were oblivious. South Africa was far away, and we didn't think to pay attention to its legislative developments.

Sometimes a sight in San Francisco would trigger a memory of the place—a groundcover of blue chalksticks, a certain kind of warm weather. At the rate you were going, you said with something approaching pride, you'd live on a different continent each decade.

It seemed that your dad was pleased he had passed his restive DNA on to you. The impression of a pioneer spirit kept your parents from interfering with your reckless move. You let them picture your California as mountains and rivers, which indeed it sometimes was, though you wrote the letters detailing all that from grimy dive bars and flamboyantly decorated cafés.

*JERR-*EMY*?,* ONE OF MY housemates began through a terse smile.

I knew I was in trouble. A used glass left in the sink was enough to get me a written note. They did adore you. Another of the girls had a goldfish that was twenty-one years old, and it was more high-maintenance than you. But after some months, the presence of another male body, no matter how quiet and slim, was beginning to take its toll. You make your noise in other ways. As if subconsciously balancing out your gentility, you have a surprisingly heavy gait and a tendency to slam doors.

Yep? I grimaced.

The bath mat, she said. *Can I show you?*

It was hanging over the tub, as was the policy, but saturated—I could practically make out the prints of our four soaking wet feet.

Maybe you two could dry off a bit more before getting out?

I was defensive but could see what she meant. We were constantly taking baths together. We were always dripping and leaking all over the place.

Sure, right, I said, then blurted: *Don't worry. We're going to look for our own place.*

THE TIME HAD COME anyway to move out of the Castro. Too pricey, too precious. Back in the Mission, a few blocks but a world away, with its acid-fried troubadours, third-wave feminists and grandpappy poets, was surely where we belonged.

The problem was high earners now wanted in, too. The neighborhood was a site of displacement upon displacement. Some eight thousand Latinx residents would move out over the next decade and a half.

On a Saturday morning, we rocked up to an open house on Harrison Street, somewhere south of 24th. It was a one-bedroom apartment amid a row of grubby Victorians shoved together like clothes on an overstuffed rack.

The queue of prospective tenants trickled down the stoop, then flooded the block. It was made up of childless couples in North Face fleeces. Many were clutching résumés. I didn't know there was such a thing as a résumé for renting. A woman in a cheerleader ponytail sussed out the competition and whispered hot takes to her boyfriend, a presidential-looking Asian jock. She held a steaming paper cup in one hand and in the other a folder stuffed with evidence of her worth.

People like that couple prompted us to adopt the phrase between us: What would a real person do?

We shuffled through the railroad flat as if touring the historical re-creation of a dust-bowl flophouse. There were windows on one side only—prison windows, high above sightlines and barred. A shaft or two of dirty sunlight flickered on the floor.

Still too expensive.

We exited past the two smug real estate agents who collected paperwork from better-qualified candidates.

WHAT WOULD A REAL person do?

We're looking, we reassured the girls.

But moreover we were being looked *at* by the managing agents. We couldn't disclose your presence on an application. We'd have to score a lease under my name alone. You were only a Guest. What were the tenancy laws, exactly? How many nights is a Guest allowed to stay over before being considered an unlawful occupant? Not many. We supposed we couldn't rent a place where the landlord was likely to be around, as it wouldn't take long for them to figure out we are two separate people. We could only declare one income, so we'd puff up my measly stipend, plus get my dad to cosign. And we now understood we couldn't afford the Inner Mission. We began to look farther out.

An adventure! we convinced ourselves, in truth devastated we didn't get to live in the throng of nutjobs but down some forlorn street with only the occasional loon drifting through.

On a drizzly midweek afternoon we took a 49 bus southbound, crossing Cesar Chavez Street, a loveless gulf that seemed to me to mark the city's boundary. It had been widened several decades ago, when it was still called Army Street, to serve as a thoroughfare to a never-built freeway, then renamed in homage to the labor activist.

A few men wearing 49ers merch and dusty chinos hung around where the pickup trucks pulled in and dropped off day labor. Undocumented, maybe. Cesar Chavez himself was known to refer to paperless strikebreakers as 'illegals,' even 'wets' or 'wetbacks,' and said to encourage comrades to report their presence to la migra. A border patrol organized by his union, the United Farm Workers, was known as the 'wet line.' In his 1974 letter to the *San Francisco Examiner,* Chavez attempted to clarify his recognition of 'the illegals as our brothers and sisters.' The position of the UFW was that they should be given amnesty and legal documents; based on this, it appeared that what he stood against was a system that created cheap, voiceless labor rather than citizens.

If you too had become an "illegal alien," it was as if from a different planet. White and well-spoken, you were never going to wait for day work on that sidewalk. You had a job at an organic café. When a local weekly reviewed the place, they described the waitstaff as angelic. It was not hard to see how sometimes the moves we made that cast us outside norms actually highlighted our privileges.

Yet still we had been alienated by government systems, not just personal whim. When you became undocumented, in a way I did, too.

Years later, in his dissent from the majority in *Obergefell*, which legalized same-sex marriage across the United States, Justice Clarence Thomas wrote that even without marriage, same-sex couples had not been without liberty: 'They have been able to travel freely around the country, making their homes where they please. Far from being incarcerated or physically restrained, petitioners have been left alone to order their lives as they see fit.'

Of course Thomas omitted the lack of access faced by a transnational couple like us, along with countless limitations endured by other queers.

But I marvel at the freedom-conjuring. It's almost as if Thomas was unintentionally suggesting that same-sex marriage marked the end of a great period of anarchic felicity, a time of seeking and soaring. It's almost as if Thomas was saying, perhaps with a tinge of envy: *You had it all, without the boring stuff.*

I wiped condensation from the bus window, taking in a smeary view of the outer-city doldrums. Outside the law but together. On the lam and on the way to an apartment viewing.

The city began to flatten and sprawl. We no longer recognized what was around us. When we passed the Mission Street Safeway, it seemed as though dusk fell. It was as if the outskirts were deeper in winter.

The sign of the Safeway on Market Street just east of the Castro was a beacon. The aisles of that location were full of glamorous goths and gays. I projected that the clientele of this remote Safeway wouldn't be much to look at.

The bus drove on. Past Zante Indian Pizza. We vowed to try it. Past dingy storefronts that claimed to facilitate tattoos or taxes but were surely never open for business. Nearly every place looked like a front. The road plateaued, and we alighted in front of an empty laundromat. We walked along the ridge of a sloping field. At the bottom, an austere public housing project squeezed into the shoulder of a ravine of freeways. The smog was cut through with the scent of invasive fennel.

We'd often gaze at the fog romantically. Now that we were up in it, we could barely see. We almost missed our turn down a steep street that ended abruptly, a cul-de-sac with no final house, just the precipice above the freeway canyon. This formed a wind tunnel; we were practically blown back. Our windbreakers rippled. Light shone from only one or two windows of the uniformly glum houses. They looked like they were lining up to jump off the cliff.

Our destination was the house next to last on the right. A tarped military jeep was parked across the street.

We descended into the basement apartment, which didn't hold much promise until we saw that, because the house had been built into the slope, it was level with a backyard at the rear. Inside, it was roomy, with something of a welcoming flow.

Ever since you missed that plane back to England, we constantly had to *keep our story straight.* On the bus ride over, I'd hashed out what to say to the agent. That you were just along to give a second opinion.

Now looking around, I delivered comments in a stage whisper.

Can you imagine me cooking here? I gestured in the sizable kitchen.

Sure, you obliged.

It's a lot of closet space for Just One Person! I remarked on the catacombs-like walk-in.

Our relationship, built on apartness—longing—had entered its phase of subterfuge—pretending. We had practice. Growing up, like other gays, we were tacitly and directly instructed to evade, if not outright lie. We learned to dodge, deflect and deny in order not to stand out. But this only fostered an inner alien quality. Now I'd found an alien partner in crime. We saw through alien eyes—distance vision. Stuff like renting an apartment could become a curious experiment.

We couldn't wait to play house.

There was only one other pair present. A girl and boy whom I quickly profiled not as lovers but friends, maybe queer. Recent graduates of Oberlin or Evergreen. They'd have to repurpose the living room as a second bedroom.

Hello, hi, we said.

They do not instill confidence, I evaluated gleefully.

The agent handed them applications, which they began to fill out, tripped up by comparing answers. I whizzed through the form. Magazine job. Tick. Inflated salary. (The publishers wouldn't pay me more, but promised to claim that they did.) Dad as a cosigner. Tick, tick.

Meanwhile, the agent delivered selling points to you in a half-assed manner. You pointed at me and shrugged, believably indifferent.

How did you get to be the superior liar? Something changed after you missed your flight. Your naturally low-key deportment had morphed into elegant nonchalance. Uprooted, you settled into yourself.

I finished the form, feeling cutthroat. I presented it in a magaziney way to the agent, who seemed sufficiently impressed. The other two were still filling in their separate forms. I smirked goodbye.

What ya think? I asked once outside.

Not sure... you began diplomatically.

We've just GOT to get it, though, I said. *Right?*

THE NEW CORNER STORE guy was named Sam, as was the last. He was unharried compared with Sam in the Castro. Less drunken gays to contend with. On our first Friday night, we procured the next-to-cheapest bottle of red and a pack of Parliaments. We settled into a session of Rainbow Tumbling Tower II, a stack-and-pull block game like Jenga but with colored pieces.

My first thought, at the hard bang, was that our tower had tumbled, but that wasn't it. Our column still stood, and this was far more commotion than a few wooden blocks could make. Had something fallen in the kitchen? Had the refrigerator exploded?

Earthquake, I informed you. I'd been waiting for the day I could "show" you an earthquake.

But that didn't seem right either. I jumped up. You remained on the floor, looking about six years old in front of the colored blocks. My stomach lurched. It was obviously the INS, come to take you away.

I ventured into the kitchen. Nothing out of place.

Stay there! I called back.

I rushed to the bottom of the entrance steps and looked up with a grimace. An unfamiliar light shone down the stairwell. Yep, an INS raid. How to best respond: Hysterical? Composed?

The light was broad and bright, as if I were standing on subway tracks facing an oncoming train.

Headlights.

A car had crashed through the front door. Is that something that happens? The street was as steep as they come, but still the chances were slim that a driver would lose control and careen into our house. It must have been a neighbor parallel parking, gassing it without shifting into reverse. I climbed the stairs slowly, as if approaching gingerly would prevent the car from going up in flames or rolling farther inside. Imagine if I was run over by a car inside my own house! How would you explain it to friends? How would you explain yourself to the police?

Through the gaping maw that had only recently been the front door, I glimpsed the street, felt the cool night air over the crunched car hood. But no driver.

A woman emerged from the house one or two up.

I was driving! she panted. *It was ME!* Except she was barefoot and in pj's.

It clicked that the actual driver was someone else, maybe her husband, father or sibling. Whoever it was, they'd never pass a breathalyzer. They had stumbled inside, and she'd taken their place.

No need for police! she cried, without making eye contact.

Yeah! I chimed. *Probably no need!*

Though it was only the two of us, we were speaking in a directionless way, as if raising objections at a group meeting. Each of us with something—someone—to hide.

But she was unlikely to suspect I was harboring secrets. She was too busy being blatantly fucked. I was the innocent victim. She was hardly coloring in a backstory that involved me hiding a fugitive downstairs.

I rushed down to give you an update. *Keep out of sight!* I urged.

You were cozied up under an old blanket on the floor—no couch yet—leafing through a book of Stephen Shore road-trip photos.

Up above, the dim street turned red and blue from the strobe of a squad car.

The woman had backed the sedan up, peeling off more of the house, crinkling its vinyl cladding. She appeared again, this time in jeans.

She presented herself to the police as hopeless at parallel parking.

I presented myself as suffering from shock. I handed over the number of the management company.

I'm a renter! I declared. *I rent.*

I took on *renter* as an identity, in the way the neighbor went with *bad female driver.* We stripped ourselves down to a single attribute. *Renter* meant I couldn't get involved even if I wanted to.

Eventually the police were satisfied this was a matter for insurance companies, a matter for the morning.

This was not a rite of passage we could have seen coming. I had not carried you over the threshold, or vice versa. Instead, some drunk drove it down.

IT WASN'T ACTUALLY THAT hard to get to sleep, considering we'd been left without a front door. The sound of the freeway came through ferociously, a reminder that the driver had been lucky not to go over the cliff. With time, we would teach ourselves to reimagine the thrum of cars as ocean waves.

The bedroom ceiling glowed with stars and planets and comets. We figured there must have been a child there before us. Maybe a single parent. Maybe a whole family. Maybe immigrants. Whoever they were, they'd affixed dozens of stickers, transforming the room into a planetarium. Whatever their situation, they felt compelled to live it out beneath a fake open sky.

'The private individual, who in the office has to deal with reality, needs the domestic interior to sustain him in his illusions,' Walter Benjamin wrote. He described 'the phantasmagorias of the interior—which, for the private man, represents the universe. In the interior, he brings together the far away and the long ago. His room is a box in the theater of the world.'

Maybe you and I both once pictured ourselves as open, communal, inhabiting a field, not a cave. Now we found ourselves in fortification, self-protective, contrary to our political ideals. Hannah Arendt: 'The only efficient way to guarantee the darkness of what needs to be hidden against the light of publicity is private property, a privately owned place to hide in.' But we were not owners. We were renting.

The next day was the first time I met Lorenzo, the owner. He finished removing the deformed door from its hinges.

Sorry, he said. *Another day for a replacement. Maybe two.*

No problem! I shouted. I took it as an opportunity, confident that Lorenzo would be cool in exchange for my not making a fuss about being left doorless. I could give the impression I was the type to be on time with the rent and keep my gripes to myself.

I detected in Lorenzo himself the air of someone with something to hide.

You, already so quiet, were learning to disappear. When noticed, you'd nod and smile, a little prince. Gradually, when Lorenzo worked on this or that around the property, you let yourself be seen. You telegraphed *no problem.* So no questions were asked.

BY THEN, WE WERE no longer using rubbers. Sex was unprotected in that it was condomless, but it took on an intense and meaningful form of protection in another way, in our development of trust. We shared knowledge of risk. We had been cautious. I could fill you. You desired that. We came to know trust as both robust and fragile. Unprotected by either of our governments, we sheltered each other. We found a way of feeling safe together—interior.

Whether or not you were born a male, or a citizen, the right for us to have oral and anal sex at home was not protected across the United States.

More generally, the right to privacy is not explicitly stated anywhere in the US Constitution. Rather, it has been found, gradually and tentatively, by some Supreme Court justices through penumbra, a metaphorical reference to the outer edge of a shadow. One could say: the gray areas.

The relevant Supreme Court cases often regard the interior of not only a household but a body. In *Griswold v. Connecticut* (1965), which protected a married couple's choice to use contraception, justices found an implied right to privacy in various amendments in the Bill of Rights. The Third Amendment says a homeowner is not obliged to provide living quarters to a soldier during peacetime; this scenario, which now sounds unlikely and antiquated, has been interpreted to imply that a private home should be free from state interference. The Fourth Amendment enshrines 'the right of the people to be secure in their persons, houses, papers, and effects, against unreasonable searches and seizures.' The opinions in *Griswold*, and subsequently *Roe v. Wade* (1973), invoke the due process clause of the Fourteenth Amendment, which proclaims, using the same language as the Fifth

Amendment, that no person shall be 'deprived of life, liberty, or property, without due process of law.'

Since the 1930s, the term *substantive due process* has been used to describe such instances of "reading into" the Bill of Rights in order to establish a protection not explicitly spelled out. This remains a bugbear for certain members of the court. With the June 2022 decision in *Dobbs v. Jackson Women's Health Organization*, Clarence Thomas called substantive due process an 'oxymoron' and a 'legal fiction.' *Dobbs* overturned both *Roe* and *Planned Parenthood v. Casey* (1992). Thomas had been biding his time for years. In his concurring opinion on *Dobbs*, Thomas wrote chillingly and directly that 'in future cases, we should reconsider all of this Court's substantive due process precedents.' He specified *Griswold* as well as *Lawrence v. Texas* (2003), which finally struck down remaining state laws against private consensual sodomy, and *Obergefell*, the 2015 same-sex marriage decision. Thomas reiterated his previous declarations that substantive due process is 'demonstrably erroneous' and that the court had a duty to 'correct the error.'

The penumbra analogy resonates with me beyond its legal usage. Those of us threatened to be exposed under spotlight may be impelled to keep to the shadows. The way I see it, we have agency not just in emerging into light, but in our right to inhabit the darkness. Yet the precarity of these penumbra precedents—and the compulsion of powerful justices to "correct" them—makes me mindful that shadows are a very different place to choose to be than to be forced back into.

EARLY ONE MORNING IN July 1982 in Atlanta, Georgia, Michael Hardwick, a dishy bartender in his late twenties, tossed a beer bottle into a trash can outside the disco where he'd been installing insulation through the night. An exceptionally vigilant patrolman ticketed Michael for drinking in public, warning him that if he didn't show up at his court date in eight days, he'd take it as a personal affront.

Michael did miss his spot, almost immediately after which the cop, twenty-three-year-old Keith Torrick, paid a visit to his apartment. The friend who answered the door relayed the situation to Michael, who duly went down to the county clerk, paid the fifty bucks and thought that was that.

Accounts vary about what happened next, but it goes something like this: On a sultry morning in August, Torrick, under the impression that Michael hadn't sorted it out, returned with an arrest warrant. Again, he was greeted by a houseguest—some hungover buddy crashing there. He said he didn't know whether Michael was in or not. So Torrick began looking around, finally pushing open the bedroom door. There, Michael and another man—a married teacher from out of town—bobbed between each other's thighs by candlelight. Torrick looked on.

'He must have stared for 35 seconds,' Michael later recounted to the *Washington Post.*

The *Post* reporter, Art Harris, was far from the only one to describe the tall, handsome bartender as looking 'like some GQ model.' Michael had been a gymnast, a druggie, a landscape architect, a failed health food store owner and a Sanskrit student. At one point, he considered becoming a Buddhist monk. Blond waves framed his big, friendly features. He looked playful and ripe.

Yet apparently all this was lost on Torrick, who laughed

off the accusation of a prolonged gawk. Sure, he stood watching Michael in his bedroom for maybe five seconds—but only 'because I was shocked. It sort of grossed me out.'

Michael was indignant about the intrusion. 'Ranting and raving about how I had no right to be in his house,' as Torrick later put it. 'I would never have made the case if he hadn't had an attitude problem.'

Torrick confiscated a small stash of pot, stood sentinel as the two men got dressed, put them in a single pair of cuffs and marched them to the station. Michael claimed that the officer then ensured the nature of the charge against them ('cocksucking') was made clear to their new cellmates.

Torrick later insisted he wasn't a hater. Among complaints lodged against him, not one was 'from a gay.' He even moonlighted as security at a gay club called the Bulldog Lounge. At fourteen, Harris reported in the *Post,* a man who'd given Torrick and a friend a lift wound up propositioning them: five bucks for a trip to a gas station bathroom. 'He never told his father,' wrote Harris; he would have disapproved of the hitchhiking. Harris drew a melancholic parallel: Keith Torrick was raised 'to believe boys "don't cry or hug."' Michael Hardwick 'doesn't remember his father ever hugging him.' Michael added that he believed the lack of physical contact was the reason he was gay.

After pleading guilty to reduced charges, the visiting schoolteacher hightailed it. Michael pled guilty to marijuana possession, incurring another fine of fifty bucks. But the sodomy charge presented a unique opportunity. What if, unlike most men who kept their head down for the sake of discretion, Michael fought it? The local ACLU got in touch to explain this might be the chance to strike down the state's sodomy law. Michael's case was pretty much perfect. He'd been arrested in the privacy of his home with a consenting adult. Out to his family and employed by a gay bar, he had a lot less to lose than others in his position. Another arrest under such a constellation of circumstances might not come along for years.

Then the charge was dropped by the Atlanta district attorney, who had the foresight to imagine how invasion of privacy would play out before a jury.

This meant that, in order to proceed, the ACLU lawyers had to sue in federal court. They did so on Valentine's Day 1983, declaring the law unconstitutional because it violated Michael's right to privacy. Michael was the plaintiff, alongside a straight couple under the names John and Mary Doe who took the view that the case had a 'chilling effect' on other people's sex lives. Georgia state law prohibited oral and anal penetration no matter the sex or marital status of those involved. Among several interviews conducted by Joyce Murdoch and Deb Price for their book *Courting Justice,* one clerk described the straight coplaintiffs as 'a married couple interested in variety.' But a judge removed John and Mary Doe from the suit, then dismissed Michael's case altogether.

In 1985, Michael and the ACLU were victorious in appeals. The 2–1 circuit court decision found that Michael's fundamental constitutional rights had been infringed, and remanded the case back to district court, challenging the state to produce a compelling state interest for disallowing the guy a candlelit session of sixty-nine. Murdoch and Joyce describe Judge Frank J. Johnson Jr. telling his clerks: 'Personally, I think it's disgusting. But until we find a cure, society ought to tolerate conduct of this kind between consenting adults in the privacy of their home.'

Instead of demonstrating a compelling state interest, Attorney General Michael J. Bowers pushed the case to the Supreme

Court. Bowers was advancing a censure of homosexuality, despite the fact that sodomy was outlawed even if performed by a man and woman in the Peach State. Sodomy had been illegal in Georgia since 1816, originally carrying a life sentence. (As his legal team put their brief together, Bowers himself was in the middle of a decade-and-a-half-long extramarital affair with a woman who later announced to the press: 'As far as sodomy is concerned, Mike Bowers is a hypocrite.')

In October 1985, SCOTUS agreed to hear *Bowers v. Hardwick*.

Representing Michael Hardwick, legendary Harvard legal professor Laurence Tribe would base his argument on the right to privacy implicit in the Fourteenth Amendment. While the state attorney general 'focused a spotlight on the penis in Michael Hardwick's mouth,' Murdoch and Price noted, 'Professor Tribe attempted to shift the spotlight to the cop in Hardwick's bedroom.'

Murdoch and Price unearthed a Dictaphone memo made by Justice Lewis Powell while reviewing the case briefs. Among his thoughts: 'I must say that when Professor Tribe refers to the "sanctity of the home," I find his argument repellent. Also it is insensitive advocacy. *Home* is one of the most beautiful words in the English language. It usually connotes family, husband and wife, and children.'

Oral argument took place on the last day of March 1986. 'The principle that we champion is a principle of limited government,' Tribe attempted to clarify. 'It's not a principle of a special catalogue of rights.' He recited a Robert Frost line, getting it just slightly wrong: 'Home is the place, where when you go there they have to take you in.'

Michael Hobbs, arguing the case for the state, reasoned that, 'Concededly, there are certain kinds of highly personal relationships which are entitled to heightened sanctuary from state intrusion.' That, he enumerated, meant marriage, children, kin. 'This Court has described those relationships,' Hobbs argued, but not gay intimacies, as 'personal bonds which have played a critical role in the culture and traditions of the nation by cultivating and transmitting shared ideals and beliefs.'

SCOTUS oral arguments play out in the space of a television drama episode. Each side is given just half an hour to present their case. Afterward, Michael Hardwick was convinced that his lawyer Laurence Tribe had presented the superior case, and dozens in their legal camp went to lunch in hopeful spirits. Michael himself slipped away with Evan Wolfson, a junior attorney with the Lambda Legal and Education Fund, into the streets of DC. The cherry blossoms were in bloom. 'We had this unbelievably romantic day. It was a lovely spring day. It was gorgeous,' Wolfson shared with Murdoch and Price. 'We actually kissed in front of the White House.'

Two days later, in the conference vote (when justices determine a likely disposition in advance of the final decision), the majority held that Georgia law had infringed Michael Hardwick's rights, with Justice Powell tentatively casting the deciding vote against the state. That night, Powell's clerk Cabell Chinnis went out to drinks and dinner in high spirits. Out of professional propriety, he kept the reason for his celebratory mood to himself. Handsome young Cabell was the latest in what Murdoch and Price have described as 'Powell's unbroken string of gay clerks,' an inexplicable phenomenon in stark contrast to the self-contained septuagenarian's insistence he'd never known a homosexual. Powell's legion gay and lesbian clerks had witnessed the grandfatherly justice routinely shoo away gay-focused cases over the years.

Cabell Chinnis had never outed himself to Powell and didn't seize this moment to do so. Surely on some level the justice must have surmised. Confounded by the case briefs, for instance, Powell had specifically approached Cabell, even though he wasn't the clerk assigned to the case, to inquire why homosexual men didn't copulate with women. Because they can't get an erection, Cabell bluntly explained. Figuring the vote was in hand, he saw no reason to disabuse the judge of his naive (or willful) conviction that he'd never met a gay man, let alone one so like himself, a gentleman from Virginia with an Ivy League degree.

Then Powell changed his mind. Perhaps it haunted him that when he'd asked in oral argument if this was only a matter of sodomy, Laurence Tribe had responded, 'I think it is somewhat broader to be candid, Justice Powell. I think it includes all physical, sexual intimacies of a kind that are not demonstrably physically harmful that are consensual and non-commercial in the privacy of the home.' Which would likely sound a little loose to a traditionalist.

Whatever his reasoning, Powell now wouldn't be able to save face and switch back. So in this tightest of 5–4 votes—'4½–4½!,' Powell himself noted self-deprecatingly—the final decision in *Bowers v. Hardwick* upheld Georgia's right to criminalize sodomy. In the majority opinion, Justice Byron White reasoned that there is no constitutionally protected right to engage in homosex, all but ignoring the fact that Georgia law prohibited anal and oral sex no matter who the partners were.

A concurring opinion written by Chief Justice Warren Burger referenced the penalty of capital punishment for male-male sex under Roman law as well as the eighteenth-century English politician William Blackstone's proclamation that the transgression was 'of "deeper malignity" than rape.'

Justice Harry Blackmun's dissent was rare in evoking an actual person affected by such rulings. 'Homosexual orientation may well form part of the very fiber of an individual's personality,' he wrote. In the face of criminalization, gays and lesbians could be left with 'no real choice but a life without any physical intimacy.'

When word got out that Justice Powell had wavered, critics of the ruling were given their villain. Among queer observers, speculation ran rife around the predicament faced by a hypothetical gay clerk. Literary critic Eve Kosofsky Sedgwick described the gossip as a 'train of painful imaginings.' As she wrote in *Epistemology of the Closet,* 'The question kept coming up, in different tones, of what it could have felt like to be a closeted gay assistant, or clerk, or justice' who might have had some ability to alter the course of 'this ruling, these ignominious majority opinions, the assaultive sentences in which they were framed.'

If Cabell Chinnis hadn't presumed Powell's vote was locked in, he would have been ready, he later said to Murdoch and Price, 'to take the most aggressive measures that I could have taken, including, to put it colloquially, pleading on bended knee on the floor. I was prepared to say, "You're hurting me personally, you're hurting people I care about. You need to understand there's a human face to all this."'

In 1990 Powell himself addressed his *Hardwick* decision before a group of students at New York University Law School: 'I think I probably made a mistake in that one.'

Michael Hardwick died near Gainesville, Florida, of AIDS-related complications in June 1991. His obituary did not mention his role in the landmark case nor his subsequent activism.

In 1998 the state of Georgia struck down its antisodomy laws of its own volition, declaring, 'We cannot think of any other activity that reasonable persons would rank as more private and more deserving of protection from governmental interference than unforced, private, adult sexual activity.'

BY THE YEAR 2000, when we rented our first weird, damp apartment, eighteen states still had sodomy laws on the books.

What's more, we had no idea of what rights you had, if any, living undocumented in the United States.

'In decisions spanning more than a century,' according to an ACLU position paper published that year, the Supreme Court has held that constitutional guarantees apply to every person within the nation's borders, 'including "aliens whose presence in this country is unlawful."' A foreigner has no guaranteed right to enter the country. But once inside, an undocumented person shares certain rights with citizens.

The relevant language has been extracted from Supreme Court cases that arose in the wake of the Chinese Exclusion Act of 1882, which banned the immigration of Chinese laborers for a decade, as well as the Immigration Act of 1882 and subsequent legislation declaring several categories of people excludable and deportable—such as paupers, lunatics, anarchists and those afflicted with loathsome diseases.

In *Wong Wing v. United States* (1896), SCOTUS ruled that an unlawful resident has the right to a jury trial before criminal punishment. Wong Wing was one of four people arrested for violating the Geary Act, which required all Chinese residents to carry a permit at all times. Before deportation, the men were sentenced to sixty days of imprisonment with hard labor. Wong Wing filed a petition for a writ of habeas corpus, the legal challenge to internment without trial, and was denied.

The Supreme Court's majority opinion did affirm the Chinese Exclusion Act, stating that no limits can be put on Congress to 'protect' the country from 'aliens whose race or habits render them undesirable as citizens, or to expel such if they have already found their way into our land.' Yet it also held that to declare unlawful residence an 'infamous crime, punishable by deprivation of liberty and property, would be to pass out of the sphere of constitutional legislation.'

Wong Wing was the first Supreme Court decision to explicate the constitutional rights of noncitizens, establishing that the Fifth and Sixth Amendments in the Bill of Rights protect even the illegal and undesirable from sentencing without trial. However, it also delineated that deportation is not punishment for a crime—'It is not a "banishment"'—so neither is being held in custody pending removal. In the words of the court opinion, such detention 'is not imprisonment in a legal sense.'

Wong Wing referenced a prior decision, *Yick Wo v. Hopkins* (1886), which held that when the San Francisco Board of Supervisors denied business licenses to every single Chinese person who ran a laundry business out of a wooden building, it amounted to the biased enforcement of a discretionary law. Many Chinese laundry owners were not American citizens, but *Yick Wo* established that 'the rights of the petitioners, as affected by the proceedings of which they complain, are not less because they are aliens and subjects of the Emperor of China.' Significantly, *Yick Wo* explicated that the due process guarantee of the Fourteenth Amendment 'is not confined to the protection of citizens.'

The subsequent decision in *Yamataya v. Fisher* (1903)—or the "Japanese Immigrant Case"—held that a foreign national has the right to appeal their deportation through the court system. Kaoru Yamataya had arrived at the port of Seattle two years prior. She was fifteen years old and pregnant, without a set destination.

As told by Washington State public historian Eleanor Boba, within days Kaoru was found in a Japantown boardinghouse by Thomas M. Fisher, whose title was Immigrant and Chinese Inspector. Kaoru's male companion, Masataro Yamataya, was sent to prison on suspicion of bringing Kaoru in for the purpose of prostitution. Also arrested and ordered deported, Kaoru was placed in the interim at a home for unwed mothers. She gave birth to a baby boy and named him Thomas, as if in homage to her persecutor. He died of pneumonia at two months old.

The case prompted more than a little speculation, and much remains unknown. Eleanor Boba has gathered a range of reports that only raise more questions: Was Kaoru an aristocrat, banished for her indiscretion? Was she just hoping to learn English and take up sewing? Did she briefly escape to Salt Lake City between confinements? Was Masataro her adoptive father? Her uncle? One journalist from the *Seattle Star* described Kaoru fetishistically: 'an aristocrat from the top of her little black head to the tips of her tiny toes, and is more than passing fair.'

In 1902 Masataro was tried and found not guilty of trafficking. The next year, Kaoru's case went before the Supreme Court. Her lawyers argued that Thomas Fisher had overstepped his authority, acting as 'prosecutor, judge and jury.' They pointed out that Japan was recently given most favored nation status; in other words, it wasn't China.

The justices voted 7–2 against Kaoru and ordered her deported. Yet *Yamataya v. Fisher* established her right to due process of law. This set a precedent that would go on to be cited in hundreds of court cases—including those regarding Trump's 2017 executive order banning immigrants from some Muslim-majority countries. Kaoru, though, deemed to have already received her due process—she'd gone all the way to the Supreme Court, after all—was out of options for staving off deportation.

Then Kaoru disappeared. Some say she was spirited away. According to Boba's findings, she evaded authorities for over three years before being discovered in Portland, jailed in Seattle and sent on the *Shinaro Maru* to Yokohama. Kaoru is an extraordinary example of the significance of foreign fugitives, elusive in their lifetime even as they make American history.

Did these precedents mean that if the door was struck down again, and it was by an authority ordering your deportation, you had some thin legal claim to stay and fight? That if we had the wherewithal and the access to the right legal aid, we could have, like Kaoru, taken our case to the Supreme Court? Maybe you too could have gone all the way only to suffer a humiliating loss. But really we were too lost in our own world to think through such legalities. Plus, we didn't cast ourselves as public figures.

The gay marriage movement needs a pair of poster boys, opined a blond intern at the magazine whom I called Le Petit Prince. *And that is clearly not you two.*

His implication being we were too weird, too wimpy. That sounded about right.

I am telling the wrong story, in terms of the triumph of gay marriage. We did not appear like two winners, a pair of rectilinear grooms in tuxedos. I'm sure we came across more as a cautionary tale.

VALENTINE'S DAY 2000 WAS your first in the States, and only our second spent together. Who knows what we did to celebrate; something with red wine and red sauce. That day, Jerry Nadler (D-NY) introduced the Permanent Partners Immigration Act in the House of Representatives: a bill for the tens of thousands of binational gay and lesbian couples like us, through which we would become eligible for spouse-like immigration benefits.

The bill would die in the House Subcommittee on Immigration and Claims, but Nadler would go on to introduce versions with various names and cosponsors nearly every year for over a decade.

You turned twenty-four on the sixteenth of February.

You still looked like a baby, so you'd show your passport to the bouncer or bartender when we went out. You'd wiggle nervously, as if they were the gatekeeper of the whole USA. A bouncer, hoodie up, could appear to you like the giant guard in the Kafka tale. But they'd impassively shut your passport, and you were all set. Deeper inside the pages was the stamp that marked your entrance the previous summer, with no stamps since. You were further away from lawfulness with each day. But that's nothing a bouncer or bartender was looking out for. They were unconcerned with the crossing of national borders. You were old enough to be in such places: have a drink, play pinball, watch a band play. Sometimes you'd slump over in a booth and fall asleep. I'd watch you in your dive-bar slumber, your puffy petal lips parted and wet. In such moments, you looked like you were still on vacation. Pooped from sightseeing, blissed out, jet-lagged. A traveler without a return ticket on resplendent, inhospitable terrain.

THEN IN EARLY MARCH, over sixty-one percent of voters in California approved Proposition 22.

Already, from 1977, the California Civil Code explicitly defined marriage as a civil contract between a man and a woman. But a separate provision, validating marriages from outside the state, remained ambiguous. As a precaution, Prop 22 closed any possible loophole that would recognize a gay marriage from elsewhere.

The previous year, for instance, in December 1999, the Vermont Supreme Court, in what the *New York Times* called a 'bombshell ruling,' required its state legislature to either legalize gay marriage or create a form of union between same-sex partners that equals the benefits that come with wedlock. This would result in Vermont enacting the nation's first same-sex civil unions, to be followed by same-sex marriage within a decade. So the majority of voters in California were declaring that no lesbian brides in Birkenstocks from the Ben & Jerry's state would be legitimized out here.

The Family Code would now declare that 'only marriage between a man and a woman is valid or recognized in California.' Prop 22—also known as Limit on Marriage, the Knight initiative (after its author, state senator Pete Knight, the father of a gay man) and the California Defense of Marriage Act—won by a far bigger margin than predicted. I felt betrayed. Our own state turned out to be just another place where we were unwanted guests.

WE BROUGHT IN HOUSEPLANTS. A creeping succulent was suspended from a ceiling hook. Known as a string-of-pearls, but I kept thinking: anal beads. The tentacular foliage around our place was a hangover from seventies San Francisco, in turn a throwback to Victorian days. Rebecca Solnit has described it as an 'aesthetics of horror vacui'—or fear of empty spaces. Which may explain, as Solnit enumerates, all that 'clutter, ornament, jewelry, print, pattern, texture, flourish, tassels, fringes, tendrils, frizz, dangly bits, lace, laces, buttons, and other distractions for the eye.'

We scavenged a wooden armchair from the curb, with a gash in its orange vinyl seat—its ass crack.

We actually spent money on a cumbersome octagonal coffee table, awkwardly refinished with a distressed effect, as well as a frumpy velveteen couch and a charming handmade quilt.

The manager at the Bloo Legume gave you her old yellow Formica kitchen table. A San Francisco staple.

We rescued a giant Wrigley's Doublemint display box from the garbage left out by the corner store and installed it above the stove.

We taped a David Shrigley photograph near a light switch; it depicted a coconut painted with the words TRY TO BE HAPPY.

An image of a boy catching air torn from *Transworld Skateboarding*, paired with a Situationist International quote about public space, hung above the toilet in a plastic frame.

A Jenny Holzer wooden postcard with the aphorism PRIVATE PROPERTY CREATED CRIME leaned against a hardback copy of *Reyner Banham Loves Los Angeles* on a chipboard shelf.

A very large woodland landscape painting from the Salvation Army was drunkenly spruced up with holographic stickers.

On the turntable: Joan Armatrading's "Whatever's for Us, for Us." *Dusty in Memphis* by Dusty Springfield. Buffalo Springfield's "Expecting to Fly." Neil Young, of course—*After the Gold Rush*.

We found a way of feeling safe together—interior.

9
A DELICATE DANCE

It seems that every historical account I encounter—of those who came before us, subject to old law and sometimes catalysts for new—takes place in a rented apartment.

Miguel Braschi lived with Leslie Blanchard for a decade on East 54th Street in Manhattan. Leslie died of AIDS-related complications in 1986. In a familiar pattern of the era—Sarah Schulman once wrote that she 'could literally sit on my stoop and watch it unfurl' in the East Village—the landlord was poised to oust Miguel from their rent-controlled apartment because his name was not on the lease. Miguel claimed he should be able to stay under the state's Rent and Evictions Regulations, which prohibited the eviction of a surviving spouse or family members.

Miguel, who'd been a devoted caregiver to Leslie as well as his lover, was granted a temporary injunction. In March 1987, this was reversed by the Appellate Division because 'homosexuals cannot yet legally marry or enter into legally recognized relationships,' and were therefore ineligible to invoke a law intended to protect people in 'traditional, legally recognized familial relationships.'

Miguel's appeal seemed unlikely to prevail. A short article in the American Bar Association journal predicted a ruling in favor of the management company. It was entitled "We Are Family?" with the strapline "Not If Non-Traditional." The novel case, the article explained, had 'particular resonance in the age of AIDS.' Surviving partners were realizing that if they weren't the leaseholder of a rent-controlled apartment, their right to remain there was precarious—'and Manhattan landlords can raise rents spectacularly.'

In July 1989, there was a surprise final reversal at the New York Court of Appeals. The opinion in *Braschi v. Stahl Associates Co.* stated that 'a more realistic, and certainly equally valid, view of a family includes two adult lifetime partners whose relationship is long-term and characterized by an emotional and financial commitment and interdependence.' This marked the first-ever legal recognition of same-sex relationships by an American appellate court.

It's worth noting that when, a month later, Andrew Sullivan published that seminal article of his, "Here Comes the Groom: A (Conservative) Case for Gay Marriage," his argument was specifically shaped by his view that *Braschi* set a reckless precedent. Sullivan cautioned that domestic partnerships weren't merely second-best, they created a loophole for benefit scroungers. He feared that after the ruling, which was also inclusive of straight unmarried couples, any manner of so-called domestic partners—a senior citizen and her live-in nurse, say, or two frat buddies—

could become eligible to claim rent control, joint health insurance, and so on. The way Sullivan saw it, marriage was an act of privatization.

Not long after the case concluded, Miguel died of AIDS-related illness. So near to the end of his own life, he battled for other people's right to stay put in a rental.

JUST BEFORE THE *BRASCHI* decision was announced in the summer of 1989, artist Felix Gonzalez-Torres installed a billboard above Village Cigars on 7th Avenue near the Stonewall Inn. Where normally one would encounter an advertisement, Felix erected a long black rectangle, suggesting a blackout or void. But what might be taken to be a redaction could also be considered a portal.

Written along the bottom in elegant white lettering were simple phrases that alluded to queer historical incidents. These included the 1895 conviction of Oscar Wilde on counts of gross indecency in Britain and the recent Supreme Court case upholding laws against oral and anal sex. The last reference was to the gay bar uprising that had taken place nearby on Christopher Street twenty summers before.

Each of these events involved fierce tensions between private lives and public opinion, along with the nuances of how people move between these overlapping spheres. Eve Kosofsky Sedgwick wrote around this time of 'a culture where same-sex desire is still structured by its distinctive public/private status, at once marginal and central, as *the* open secret.'

The 1989 New York Gay Pride was held the last Sunday of June. Stoned drag queens shrieked at sequined superheroes: *Happy Gay Day!* Gay cops marched. The Gay Men's Chorus sang "New York, New York." RuPaul was there somewhere, in white lingerie, cackling. The streets rightfully rumbled with anger and, despite the illness and loss, fizzed with sex and serendipity. Seventies-style daisies were in; this was just before the release of the Deee-Lite single "Groove Is in the Heart." Everybody lost whoever they came with amid the biceps, rainbow flags, marching bands and bubble butts. Without cell phones to help them find their way back to their friends, boys in ACT-UP T-shirts and Dr. Martens drifted like dandelion clocks.

Felix Gonzalez-Torres was there that day, along with his lover Ross Laycock. Their close friend, artist Carl George, recounts how, having moved back to his native Canada to access better health care, Ross was increasingly anxious about crossing the border. Though immigration rules remained cumbersome and archaic, traveling through had usually been no big deal. But then, as Carl puts it, AIDS *put all of these laws on steroids.*

To distract from his facial lesions, Ross grew a beard and wore a baseball cap and concealer makeup when passing through US immigration. Border patrol officers were trained to look for telltale signs of the disease. Ross's handsome face was completely purpled in sores. But, wearing pink button-front trousers, a striped matelot and a Yankees cap, he marched with his friends and was able to behold Felix's billboard, which was at once silent and screaming. Felix, Carl recalls, would split from the group to confront counterdemonstrators, grabbing and ripping up their signs, which said stuff like GAYS DESERVE AIDS.

Ross was raised in Canada's remote Northwest Territories, where he drove a snowmobile to school. His father died when he was young. His childhood best friend had been taunting wolves from his snowmobile when it ran out of gas, and the boy was devoured by the beasts. Ross initially studied biochemistry, but was distracted by fashion. He befriended Carl on the job as the two new visual merchandisers at Holt Renfrew, the classy department store in Montreal. By then, Ross was strapping and confident. Carl was bookish, less assured. But they became as close as brothers. Ross made sure of that. *He was tall, athletic and handsome, and wore clothes well,* writes Carl. *He had a certain personal style, but mostly emulated the looks from* L'Uomo Vogue*—creating a uniquely Canadian sprezzatura.*

Ross decided to study menswear design and moved to New York in 1980 to attend the Fashion Institute of Technology. He rented a place across the street from Barney's. Among those who spotted gorgeous Ross around town was Calvin Klein, who asked him to model. But Ross didn't want his focus stolen away from the making of clothes. Eventually, though, Ross would drop out of FIT—*realizing,* Carl tells, *he was not a menswear designer, but a menswear shopper.* Once on a trip to Italy, Ross pulled a thread from a marriage tapestry at the Palazzo Medici and sent it to Carl, who could've killed him for his egregious act of bravado and beauty-thirst.

At Ross's urging, Carl soon followed him out. They roomed together. First, they briefly sublet a Greenwich Village studio from the doctor whom Larry Kramer fictionalized as Irving Slough in his 1978 novel *Faggots.* Their next place was among the wrecks of the East Village, where David Wojnarowicz stenciled images of flame-licked houses and falling men onto local walls. The area was populated by Puerto Rican and Dominican families, Catholics from Poland and Ukraine, Jews from Central Europe and Russia, heroin addicts, artists and those Carl calls *otherworldies.* This mélange suited him much better than the clones and leather queens of the West Village.

Carl and Ross were shown the huge two-bedroom by a local real estate speculator, a hot guy with a big dick whom Ross, of course, had met someplace or other. Carl was far from besotted. The guy promised he was about to rid the place of drug dealers. They mostly believed him, and signed the four-hundred-and-fifty-dollars-per-month lease. The following week, they awoke to a person yelling outside their new abode: *This is my apartment. He pushed me out of my apartment.* He was an older Black man, and when the roommates encountered him later in Tompkins

Square Park, he shared more of his experience. The man was able to score another place in the area, but Carl's eyes were opened to the cavalier displacement around him, leading him to years of tenancy activism. Though living in the States illegally, he and Ross had become a part of the city.

Carl reckons that Ross met Felix at Boybar in late 1982 or early 1983. Ross was a waiter—regularly headhunted for his good looks and alacrity—at restaurants like Café des Artistes on the Upper West Side and La Coupole, a branch of the Parisian restaurant on lower Park Avenue, where he made five hundred dollars a night in tips. Felix was also waiting tables, at a small Italian restaurant in Murray Hill, while studying photography. Felix was born in Cuba. As a child he was separated from his parents and sent to live in Spain, then Puerto Rico, where he began the academic studies that would take him on scholarship to New York.

Ross and Felix fell in love—*instantly and madly,* Carl recalls. *Inseparable from that point on.* Ross began to spend most of his time at Felix's—a modest ground-floor studio apartment on the corner of Grove and Bedford, the intersection later used for the establishing shot on *Friends*.

It was probably sometime in early 1984 that Ross realized he had AIDS, or what was then referred to as GRID (Gay-Related Immune Deficiency). He returned to Canada for the free health care and because continuing to live illegally in the US was, Carl says, *untenable, even dangerous.*

Although now they were often apart, their love grew. Ross wrote to Carl, using his characteristic lower case *i* among capital letters, 'LiFE WiTH FELiX iS CHEERY AND I CAN SEE THE DEFEAT OF THE ENEMY iN SiGHT.' This bond seems to my mind integral to Felix's developing body of work, which immerses the viewer in rituals of mating and mourning by way of seemingly banal materials. *The New Yorker* would describe Felix posthumously as 'one of the greatest and most groundbreaking artists of the late twentieth century.'

For a while, Ross would still sometimes travel back to New York. Or he and Felix would meet up in Europe. In Los Angeles, when Felix was teaching there, the two stayed at the Ravenswood Apartments on Rossmore Avenue. 'The street name literally declares: More Ross,' art historian Miwon Kwon has noted. It's a storied place: legend has it that when the Ravenswood developers attempted to deny entry to Mae West's boyfriend and chauffeur, a Black former middleweight boxing champ, she bought the whole place and took the penthouse. I'm sure Ross and Felix would have loved this tale. Ross once wrote on a postcard to Carl: 'JUST REMEMBER—BE BiTCHY AND YOU WiLL BE POWERFUL.'

Felix would go up to Toronto for the summer and set off camping with Ross in the Canadian wilderness. There, the pair were enchanted by beavers. At first, reading through their dispatches to Carl, I took *beaver* to be code for hot guys. 'DOLL,' Ross wrote, 'BEAVERS EVERYWHERE AND BUTCH TOO! LiFE BECOMES SEDENTARY AND LOVE GETS CRAZY.' Carl clarifies that, while Felix thought of sturdy Ross as able to *build anything, like a beaver,* out there in the wild, they were literally sitting on rocks gazing at the industrious mammals.

Felix once delivered a typed note to Carl, a kind of instruction for after he was gone: 'remember to tell them about me and him.' Coming across this document—then held with other correspondence between the three friends at the Visual AIDS archive in New York—I was overcome, almost disturbed by, euphoria—a sensation as if at once falling and being enveloped.

I feverishly grasped at this literally paper-thin connection to the deceased artist and his own alien lover.

In this request, Felix longed for their love to be known. What follows are a string of extraordinary phrases evoking cities, musk, letter writing, the bills that documented time spent on the phone, and how their love survived 'the distance, the fear, the nos, the donts . . .' Felix ends with words to pass on to those who really seek the truth; they should look out for a pair of beavers building themselves a home, 'a very romantic dam, somewhere.'

I write to Carl, daring, at risk of sounding proprietary, to state that I couldn't help thinking that when Felix wrote 'tell them,' he meant *us*. Carl responds graciously: *"them" is us, all who followed, an instruction guide, a "how to" manual—to deep, life-changing, intensely personal love.*

Carl sends me a photo of bare-chested Ross taken by Felix on one of their camping trips. Thick, fuzzy and beaming, Ross fills a Muskoka chair, his black Labrador Harry panting by his side. Carl includes another snapshot, of Ross at that New York City march in June 1989, revealing the stark contrast in his declining health.

By that time, Ross had enrolled at the University of Toronto to finally finish his biochemistry degree. When activists took over the stage at the Fifth International Conference on AIDS in Montreal, they read out a series of demands informed in part by Ross's scientific insights.

Meanwhile Carl continued living without legal status in the States. He became a member of ACT-UP and other coalitions. As part of the PWA (People with AIDS) Health Group, he helped import drugs from other industrialized countries that showed some promise of treating opportunistic infections but were not yet approved for use in the States. *Of course nothing worked,* Carl says, *but desperate people who were dying within months were willing to try anything that showed some promise.* They imported enzymes from Germany, frozen egg lipids from Israel and dextran sulfate from Japan. Thousands of doses of dextran sulfate were packaged by an activist doctor in porcelain teaware and shipped in boxes labeled "gift shop merchandise." Carl, risking deportation, heavy fines and imprisonment, signed for these deliveries at JFK. From this contraband, doses for Ross were mailed to Canada inside a teddy bear, along with "birthday greetings" from Carl. Thousands of pills were sewn into various plushies. Felix and Ross wrote a grateful, melancholy letter to Carl describing the period as 'TiMES OF CONStaNt BiRthDaY GiFTS.'

The activism was inspiring and horrific, Carl tells, *a dichotomy that still gives me hope and nightmares.*

According to Ross's letters to Carl, in Los Angeles in the spring of 1989, Felix was stressed by the semi-illiteracy of his students and refused to accompany Ross following one of those maps to celebrity homes. But Ross also wrote to Carl of the glorious weather and indescribable light, of the "SURFS UP!" morning skies and how the 'SUNSETS ARE SO PINA COLADA.' Around a year later, he typed, 'Life with La Gonzalez improves with each day.'

I ask Carl if they would have gotten married if that had been an option. Carl can only speculate. Ross may have been the one to reject marriage on principle. *Felix was the romantic,* Carl writes. *He would cry when he'd see an old Cuban couple in Miami holding hands.* Then again, there was the time when, on the cusp of a visit from Felix ('the boy'), Ross divulged that he'd been covertly learning Spanish, which seems a deeply romantic gesture, an act of holding another person at their root.

Ross died in 1991. Before that, Carl was bathing and taking

care of him, and helped fulfill his final wish—that his ashes be put into a hundred small bags so that Felix could take him wherever he traveled and spread them over the places they loved.

AIDS was taking Carl's friends and, as he has put it, scared the sex out of him. Friends compared notes on the many memorial services they attended. Deeply traumatized, grappling with survivor's guilt, Carl describes himself in this period as *mostly a lone wolf.*

But animal behaviorists tell us that a lone wolf is also known as a *disperser.* By separating from its natal pack, it can avoid inbreeding and establish new territories. They can be considered social creatures in that they are integral to the health and survival of the species. Maybe in a way that's how I see Carl's solitariness—as a contemplative search for new forms of intimacy and allyship.

Carl finally became an American citizen in 1993, reciting the Pledge of Allegiance led by newly appointed Justice Ruth Bader Ginsberg. He had initially been denied and ordered deported, eventually only sorting out his status through a friend's mother, a wealthy old East Coast Republican WASP with the right political connections.

Felix died in January 1996. A few months later, you and I met; not long after, I encountered Felix's art. I initially became familiar with two works. In *"Untitled" (Perfect Lovers)*, a pair of identical clocks is displayed side by side, rims touching. They are set at precisely the same time, but as they tick away, will eventually fall out of sync. In *"Untitled" (Portrait of Ross in L.A.)*, visitors are invited to take a morsel from a pile of wrapped candies; the exhibiting institution is meant to replenish them to maintain the ideal weight of one hundred and seventy-five pounds, the size of Ross in healthy days.

These works are sometimes spoken about alongside and in contrast to those that the right-wingers loved to censor in the period—the nudes of Robert Mapplethorpe, the legible activism of Wojnarowicz. What can one object to about two clocks? So an unspeakable love is smuggled into the museum. Felix once commented that he wanted to be like a virus, infiltrating and replicating within an institution. The candies are ingested, some observers have suggested, as a kind of Communion that represents Ross's diminishment.

Felix's art is intended to be continually open to new readings. I happen to read an elliptical love story, expansive and incomplete. Ross has become a beloved figure in art history—a muse's muse. I think this is because of the reciprocity: Ross was something other than a fetishized boy or brute. He brought another mind, another point of view. He looked alongside. In the art, Ross may only be present in the abstract, but he was very real.

By the time you and I moved into that basement apartment, where a multitude of mold spores nefariously floated, the candy piles and clocks had become active in my imagination. Everything around us could be a totem. I saw ordinary objects anew; or rather saw myself, and us together, as capable of transformation.

But I did not know then about the national borders that stood between Felix and Ross. Looking back and going on a hunch, I reached out to their confidant, Carl, who unfolded their experiences with a uniquely naked erudition. I told him how, for you and me, borders had yielded a kind of identity—more so even than *gay,* maybe: the being apart and becoming stateless. He writes back of *the feeling of statelessness during that time, especially for gay people living in NYC, busy as activists but always cautious not to be arrested and deported. Most especially for those who found love with Americans and for whom, the thought of separation was devastating—like yourself. It was a delicate dance for Ross and Felix, but their times together were filled with joy and only deepened their love for each other.*

For his 1993 work *"Untitled" (Passport #II)*, Felix printed spare black-and-white photographs depicting birds in flight on cardstock. These were then folded and stapled, to be opened like a passport booklet. Into the one that he gave to Carl, Felix inserted a translucent sheet with words by Langston Hughes: 'There's a certain amount of traveling in a dream deferred.'

What right do we have to claim a cultural inheritance, and what's just looting stuff that's been buried? I ask Carl if I can write what he has shared with me and he agrees, generously responding: *It's all true, and it's our history.*

He then sends me an essay that he wrote about another friend and artist, Gordon Stokes Kurtti, who died in 1987 at the age of twenty-six. In it, Carl describes the process of remembering back to that period as 'my mind meandering through endless dark hallways, doors slightly ajar and stairs to nowhere.'

I was taken aback to read his vision, so similar to my own. I'd been writing about living alone in Los Angeles and imagining unknown men inhabiting a black-walled hallway. The moment your cherubic face appeared in the unnerving corridor of the hotel in New York. The London vestibule in which I made you kiss me differently. Why have I been thinking through hallways? Is it bathophobia—a fear of the abyss? I wouldn't exactly claim to have that fear, but I would say I am overwhelmed by the uncertainty of distance.

Gay identity is widely considered as a homecoming, but I know it more to be a setting adrift. In dire circumstances faced by others, exile has been not only disorienting but horrifically violent. But for some of us sometimes, exile could be a kind of magic. Back then, before marriage, in the wilderness.

10

OTHER PEOPLE'S ISLANDS

There *was* a *there* there; it was just around the corner.

A few blocks north of our blustery street, the area became a neighborhood. Rows of houses wrapped around a dusty hill, said to be home to a lone coyote. Steep stairways provided pedestrian shortcuts. In one spot, whimsically: a pair of twin metal slides, with a bump near the top to provide users a boost. The neighborhood had its own main street—a route like a ridge, lined with organic grocer, pet supply store, bookshop, bakery and so on. The wooden Victorian facades resembled an old Western set, in which there's no actual building behind. We soon gave in to the mellow. Bluegrass banjo and fiddle rose from the coffeehouse patio. The aroma of Sierra Nevada wafted from two taverns, one pseudo-Irish, one quasi-lesbian, which eyed each other suspiciously from across the street.

There were also two video stores, which seemed surely one too many, though we'd soon learn the local population was devoted to spending the night in. Strolling at dusk and peering into the windows, we could immediately tell ours would not be Celebrity Video, with its slatwall fixtures and slumping posters for no-longer–New Releases. It had to be Video Hut, which had a train set in the window and sloppy, crammed shelves.

You'd wake at five in the morning and pedal to the Legume on a too-tall bike. Another hand-me-down, this one from a yuppie customer. I worried its thin tires would get stuck in a streetcar track. When that did indeed happen, you only scraped your knee, a great relief because we were convinced you couldn't go to a hospital without being deported.

You'd work the breakfast-to-lunch shift and then, afternoon by afternoon, explore the seven square miles of the city, finding ways to stretch its boundaries. Before home, you'd stop at Video Hut and check out two movies at a time. Many of these entailed American landscapes as seen by awestruck Europeans: *Paris, Texas*; *Bagdad Cafe*; *Model Shop*; *Zabriskie Point*. The directors placed the little lives of lowly drifters within a vast expanse so that the films were at once intimate and huge, and I believe they made you less homesick because their particular dislocation was not about looking back but about taking in the Kodachrome view.

Video Hut was manned by a long-haired guy in a shawl-collar cardigan like The Dude from *The Big Lebowski*. He approved of your choices, and perhaps moreover that you didn't annoyingly pontificate about your returns. So he offered you a job each time you came in until you gave up resisting.

By that point, The Dude was a day or two away from selling the business. His only other employee was a middle-aged guy who'd amassed a small fortune in tech and just hung around hoping to meet women. He had no reason to stay. The store's new buyer had been promised the business came with staff, so that meant you. All this you were surprised to learn on your single training day with The Dude, who then swiftly split for Bali.

The long-standing man-cave atmosphere of Video Hut dissipated as soon as the new owner marched in. Frank was half the height of The Dude, and dressed as a kind of mafioso Liberace, or cholo Elton John, in baggy shorts and fedora, a ring on every finger and spectacles the size of sunglasses, with a diamanté top bar. You wondered how you'd be heard over the keys jangling off Frank's pocket chain, his humming "That's Amore," the nylon man bag swishing against the silky baroque shirts, his manicured fingernails tapping the register. How would you cope in Frank's blingy din?

Frank had only just moved to the city. Though he was of mixed heritage, he strongly identified as Italian, and formerly ran a deli in the exurbs, where he lived with his wife and two daughters. He was closely involved with their lives and the church. He then moved into a condo somewhere closer to the city to wrestle with his gay demons. When he spoke of that brief, lonely period, I pictured the glow from a chat room and the ice cubes melting in his Manhattan. After decades of Catholic guilt about the very thought, he walked into a gay bar on Polk Street and met Crispin right away. Within months, Frank was shopping for a house in San Francisco for the two of them to move into, along with Crispin's prizewinning Brussels griffons. The pooches, Frank was quick to boast, were the same breed as the one in *As Good as It Gets.* Crispin, who'd trained dogs for competition until too debilitated by AIDS, was rumored to have been the inspiration for the flamboyant character in *Best in Show,* the mockumentary by Christopher Guest.

Frank, who purchased Video Hut from a small-business broker, knew nothing about movies. To be fair, he had his preferences, which you learned quickly: *The Godfather.* Musicals like *Easter Parade.* Anything with a good dinner table dispute, however short of the bar set by *Moonstruck.* He'd howl on cue at the predictable zingers in *Big Momma's House* and swoon over the dance sequences in *That's Entertainment!* as the videos rattled away on the TV monitor perched on a crossbeam. The customers—most of them; some turned tail never to return—found Frank refreshing after a decade of The Dude carrying on about *The Conversation* and *Deliverance.*

Crispin wasn't able to work Video Hut shifts as they'd intended, and in fact his waning health would require more of Frank's attention than planned. So Frank hired his neighbor Lydia, as well as offering you more shifts, enabling you to give notice at the Legume.

I was still employed by the magazine, now operating out of a proper office downtown. I took to visiting you on my way home in the evening, and inspected Euro gay arthouse covers—*Come Undone, Water Drops on Burning Rocks, Get Real*—that might provide decent softcore. Then, overcaffeinated and indignant about another unrealistic deadline, I quit in a huff. Having become jobless, I hung around Video Hut until Frank put me to work, much to Lydia's chagrin.

Lydia, salt of the earth and just past thirty, brought her big, hobbling dog to work and left her gun at home. She wore her hair lank like preteen Jodie Foster, then cut intimidating bangs. Her go-to recommendations were *Paper Moon, Christiane F.* and *The Little Girl Who Lived Down the Lane.* I dreaded my shifts with her because she'd rebuke me as I tried in vain to find a given New Release, arranged on the wall by order of arrival, not alphabetically. *There! Can't you SEE?* Lydia would snap as I searched for *Under Suspicion* or *Reindeer Games,* each of which looked like the rest—worried faces in sepia tones, the title bold black and red.

You noticed the backstock didn't include *What's Love Got to Do with It*. So Frank brought that in, then dozens of titles at your recommendation. He took nearly every customer request, too. *I don't care if they're the only ones to ever rent it,* he'd confide. These additions to the library, however random, were cultivating loyalty, one would-be cinephile at a time.

You busied yourself tearing the place apart and putting it back together section by section. I'm sure this looked to Lydia like you were quietly attempting a coup but just making a mess.

I've come to know, Frank proclaimed, *that what looks like a disaster in the meantime is going to turn out beautifully. You have to trust him. He takes his time, but he gets there in the end.*

You hand-lettered new signage. You created a wall divided by auteur, from Almodóvar to Wong Kar-wai. You subcategorized: *Spaghetti Western, Creature Feature, '80s Teen.* You replaced the term *Foreign* with *International*.

The train set came out of the window. You couldn't resist adopting it. We carried the set into our bedroom, where it sat forlorn, the green turf soon indistinguishable from the encroaching mold. Frank then suggested you display something in the shop window of your own.

You'd been taking photos: A bulldozer on which someone had arranged felled branches. Partially obfuscated views through various windows. Chain-link fences. The wind through my sister's hair. Buildings like noses. Stop signs stenciled to make political statements. Humans wearing visors and neon T-shirts, hands on hips, watching the Fleet Week Air Show. A motel that advertised itself with the slogan SLEEP BY THE SEA. The images never seemed like violations. They were not judgmental. People weren't punch lines. You glimpsed unknown, unfinished experiences. We say of photography that it captures a moment, but it seemed to me that you set it free.

You named the exhibition *Other People's Islands*. These were open scenes as viewed by someone trapped. You could no longer cross national borders for fear of not being allowed to return. Taking these pictures, you somehow transcended the state of being stuck. As much as we wanted the situation to change, for the time being it gave you perspective. I wondered if the camera was something for you to hide behind, then began to understand your Pentax K1000 to be not a shield but a passport.

ONE EVENING, AFTER BEER and a shot or two of tequila at the lesbian saloon, we descended the steep, windy slope back to our place and a streetlamp went out.

Oh, see, you said, fingering the air. *I do that.*

What?

Put out streetlamps when I walk past. Have you not noticed? I'm sure I've mentioned this before.

What possible explanation? We proceeded to speculate wildly. Were you extra-electromagnetic? It was very alien-like of you. Only much later would I read that Hilary Evans, an author of paranormal phenomena, coined it 'Street Light Interference,' identifying those who possess this ability as SLIders. Some SLIders, apparently, put out lamps with startling regularity, no matter the type of bulb. Some have proved capable of powering off a whole batch at once, or in sequence as they glide spookily down the street.

Carl Jung used the term *synchronicity* to describe a *'meaningful cross-connection'* that appears to have no verifiable cause. Like when something—say a type of animal, word or melody—comes to mind, then enters the room incarnate, or becomes a recurring motif throughout the day. Like how certain individuals are inexplicably struck by lightning again and again—or put out lamps.

Why you? Were you turning off what Emily Dickinson called 'a certain Slant of light... that oppresses'? Turning toward the darkness that Walt Whitman described as 'gentler than my lover'? Ridding the sky of artificial light so that we two moths could orient ourselves according to the genuine moon? In *A Lover's Discourse,* Roland Barthes cites psychoanalyst Theodor Reik: 'The darkest place, according to a Chinese proverb, is always underneath the lamp.' It's like you were telekinetically shooting out the lights so that we could bask in an illuminating dark. There are far more sensible explanations. 'Cycling,' a spokesperson for a streetlight engineering company commented to the *Washington Post*. What kind of sorcery is that? 'It means the bulb needs to be replaced.' Pure coincidence. Confirmation bias. Apophenia—the delusional, solipsistic, potentially schizophrenic search for meaningful connections. Whereas in fact, mathematics professor David Hand asserts, 'Extremely improbable events are commonplace.'

So there we were, finding ourselves forced into philosophy. I'm not sure we'd ever really interrogated the question of whether our meeting was *written in the stars*. We were figuring out how to be present together, attentive, intersubjective, half aware that we could never be on precisely the same wavelength, but could make something of the tuning.

I have magical powers, you joked. *I'm special*.

Maybe, I had to admit, I perceived the phenomenon in an opposite way—not about your agency (your ability to extinguish bulbs) so much as your tininess within an enormous world (the unpredictable fluctuations above reiterating your insignificance).

I sometimes thought of you as *small*. Your slender form, your quiet voice. The effort that little asthmatic body took to speak up. You landed minor roles in school plays. Whereas I'd almost always gotten the lead. You seethed with resentment when I created Halloween costumes for us—you as Country Mouse, me as City Mouse. I shrugged it off—the bumpkin role just suited you better, *no?*

But it was gradually dawning that what happened when we came together wasn't about me wielding some power, like your director or casting agent. Instead, you could disabuse me of the fallacious notion that I was *somebody*. There was something more sublime available to us. In another notion taken from Emily Dickinson:

I'm nobody! Who are you?
Are you nobody, too?
Then there's a pair of us—don't tell!
They'd banish us, you know.

In an alternate version, the ending was written: 'they'd advertise, you know.' To be *advertised*, I guess, would amount to banishment from nobodiness. More and more, other sorts of banishment—from society, from respectability—were appealing to us. To remain in nobodiness, we could be expansive. At one with the night.

The lamps continue to baffle me. To this day, you put them out regularly. The only meaning I can grasp is in how we respond. It gives us pause. I become aware of the change in light around you. In our attentiveness, we come closer to attunement.

There it goes, you'll say. It can be tempting to think you're hoaxing. (Usually I hadn't noticed the extinguishment until you pointed it out.) But I'll look up and spot unilluminated glass, and perceive how the darkness has deepened.

Your true superpower must not be putting lights out but observing the change.

Also, it was a relief to find a person with whom to *not understand*. Not overcoming a mystery, or reshaping it, projecting language onto the unknown, but plunging into its fathoms. Never totally unafraid—who can be?—but less scared of the dark.

WE PLAYED HOUSE.

We played the Moldy Peaches.

Our stuff was getting moldy. Mushrooms, the biggest clocking in at something like four inches, sprouted between the tiles in the shower. The shoulders of unworn sweaters were taken over by fungi.

We played "Les and Ray" by Le Tigre, a song I understood to be about how the sound of a piano from a gay couple's parlor brought hope to the young girl living next door.

Also on repeat, Cat Power's "Colors and the Kids."

You suggested we could handle adopting a cat.

Like when? I asked.

Like Saturday.

Clementine was a smart, lean tortoiseshell rescue with a clipped ear tip. If she could sing, it'd be in the angelic, raggedy voice of Emmylou Harris. Over the first day and night, we kept playing with new names, until: *What name did she come with again? Clementine—perfect.*

A cat's cat, our friend Niki said.

LET ME PULL IT back out and push it inside again slowly, so you know better the shape, the ridge. Time to slow down again, like listening to a long composition. Sit on it. Turn around. Not out of shyness, though that hovers around you like a halo. But reverse so that you can stare at my hairy trunks. Glide up and down, focused on my two handsome feet, in socks or bare. Take in my thighs, the *dadness*, and crave being bred. I'd have gotten you pregnant so many times we'd be bankrupt. All our phantom children like good ideas that arrive only to disappear in a blink. I pull out and move around to your face, plant the furry cleft over your eyes, nose, lips, cheeks. I want to smother you with the aroma. I want to defile your pretty face, already sizzling with stink from all the nuzzling beforehand—what made you want to get fucked in the first place—your snout like a dog at the park. I want you to love when your elegant face reeks like the base of the man who's inside you.

UNDERNEATH THE GLOW-IN-THE-DARK SKY, we exchanged more stories about other houses.

The imagined ones. As a kid, you designed a villa enclosed by a glass semidome that maintained a tropical climate. A waterfall tumbled down a central five-story edifice built to resemble an escarpment. Windows and doors opened from its cliff face, overlooking a jungly courtyard. Each morning, you rode a waterslide from the top bedroom into a lagoon, where you bathed.

The half-imagined places we'd actually once lived. You told me about your childhood in South Africa.

How could your family live there during apartheid? I demanded to know.

Your mum and dad each had an ex-spouse to forget. Each was emerging from unexpected life turns, and were probably swept up in the idea of forging a new path together on a new continent.

The cleaner was named Ethel. You liked to keep her company, meaning get in her way. She brought along her baby son Diko. You gathered that when Ethel and Diko returned home, it was to a segregated township.

You constructed bivouacs for your little sister, Ruby, using words alone or materials like sticks and blankets: hot-air balloons, ships, rafts, cabins, and dens. At Hobie Beach, you made sand sculptures of vehicles onto which you could both climb aboard.

In your backyard stood a playhouse, what the Brits call a Wendy House after *Peter Pan*, with interlocking planks that could be rearranged so that it transformed into a different edifice—a shop, for instance. Imitations of adult life, but irresponsible. *Heartless*, as J. M. Barrie might say.

You were there until age ten, old enough to read the WHITES ONLY signs and to find them disturbing.

I told you how my father's family moved to contested land.

Then called Pei-teh, my dad first immigrated at the age of one. It was 1946. One of his earliest memories is encountering the geishas who lived upstairs from their first apartment in Kaohsiung, Taiwan. The group of young bar hostesses adorned themselves in hand-me-downs from half a century of Japanese rule.

Taiwan was once considered terra incognita, then the site of centuries of violent disputes involving not only nearby China but several other nations. Its Indigenous inhabitants are Austronesian. It's said that by the twelfth century CE, Chinese fishermen could be found living on the Penghu Islands in the Taiwan Strait, and that smallholdings had been established on Taiwan itself by farmers from China and Japan.

Taiwan was dubbed Ilha Formosa—the beautiful island—in the sixteenth century by Portuguese seafarers. The next century, Spain took over the area that is now the port city of Keelung, and eventually the whole island was dominated by the Dutch East India Company. These imperial powers encouraged immigrant labor from China. Southern Ming general Koxinga, the son of a Fujianese pirate, expelled the Dutch in 1661. After Koxinga's death the next year, his son Zheng Jing succeeded and promoted more Chinese immigration. The island was formally annexed by the Qing empire, which ruled—save certain aboriginal regions—for two centuries. It was ceded to Japan in 1895 as a result of the Treaty of Shimonoseki, which ended the First Sino-Japanese War. Uprisings of native populations were quelled. In 1945, at the end of the Second Sino-Japanese War, governance was taken up by the Republic of China—specifically the Kuomintang, or KMT, the nationalist government led by Chiang Kai-shek, with Chen Yi installed as chief executive of Taiwan Province.

My grandfather Kwang, who held a position as a customs inspector, was transferred to Taiwan in this period, bringing along his wife, Shu-In, and Pei-teh.

As the changes brought by the Chinese regime took effect, Taiwanese people became increasingly resentful of the handover. Factories formerly under Japanese rule were seized, along with domestic properties. A range of industries became Chinese monopolies; the price of rice inflated some four hundred times within a couple of years.

Things boiled over on the 27th of February 1947, when the Tobacco Monopoly Bureau confiscated contraband cigarettes from forty-year-old widow Lin Jiang-mai at the Tianma Tea House in Taipei. She was struck in the head with the butt of an officer's gun. The patrons were angered, and officers opened fire. One of the wounded bystanders died the next day. Members of the resistance nabbed control of a radio station to broadcast reports that soldiers were shooting at demonstrators.

In the chaos, Chinese nationals like Pei-teh's parents, assumed to be allied with China's KMT regime, felt at risk of attack. In their area of Kaohsiung, a Taiwanese fishing boat captain was trusted as the de facto neighborhood leader. As Taiwanese uprisers appeared in the streets, he took in Pei-teh's family along with a couple of single men, also from mainland China.

The family story goes that as the rioting moved closer, my grandfather Kwang and the other men retreated into the captain's attic to hide. Kwang would later recount how one man had a cough, and the rest covered his mouth to suppress it. The man's cough has resonated in family lore for decades. The infuriating tickle in his throat. Self-sabotage? His body desperate to make itself known, like a giggle in a sermon, amid the thrill of the men's collective fear?

Little Pei-teh stayed downstairs with his mother. Because Shu-In was raised speaking Southern Min, a form of Chinese also spoken in Taiwan, she could pass for a longtime resident. For the time being, Shu-In would be the one to run the errands to gather provisions for the family, not speaking enough to raise doubts.

The crackdown by the KMT was brutal, with reinforcements dispatched from the mainland. A 'wholesale slaughter,' according to a *New York Times* bulletin published near the end of March. The *Times* reported some ten thousand Taiwanese, or "Formosans," had been killed by Chinese troops; massacred by machine guns, according to witnesses, indiscriminately and 'without provocation.' An American described instances of beheading, mutilation, and rape. A Briton explained that the Taiwanese who had taken control in Takao—the Japanese name for Kaohsiung, where Pei-teh and his family lived—were unarmed. It was Chinese troops, he said, that took to the streets, raping, looting and shooting hundreds dead. Two women recounted how Taiwanese rebels had used the radio earlier in the month to 'caution against violence.' The reporter attested that the witness accounts were supported by foreign embassies. Eventually, an estimated eighteen to twenty-eight thousand were killed. The lives lost, as remembered in the *New York Times* many decades later, included 'much of the island's elite: painters, lawyers, professors and doctors.'

Meanwhile, the Chinese Civil War was raging on the mainland. Once defeated by the Chinese Communist Party, Chiang Kai-shek retreated to Taiwan, where he led the remnants of his Kuomintang party. Martial law was declared on the island at the end of 1948, then ratified in May 1949. Known as the White Terror, this state would prevail for thirty-eight years, making it the longest period of martial law in history at the time it was dissolved in 1987.

While they still lived in Kaohsiung, the fishing captain would pay visits to the Lin family, who treated him respectfully. His seafarer's skin was tanned and weathered, and Pei-teh was always happy to see him.

OUR FUTON NESTLED IN an alcove on the side of the house built into the hill. I frequently thought about the worms squirming in the damp earth on the other side of the wall, mere inches from my head. It was like being buried alive, in contrast with our pathetic attempts to spruce up the built-in shelf above us with cute objects—odd vinyl monsters, a tissue box cover crocheted by Japantown seniors, the boom box on which we played noise music to help us get to sleep: the groan of Mogwai, an early live Sonic Youth album called *Sonic Death*, the blistering guitar seizures of Lightning Bolt.

The warren!, said Dylan when he encountered our basement life. Slightly the wrong word, as a warren is not just a single burrow but a whole network. Yet in some abstract way our subterranean domicile *was* connected to other people who have lived literally or figuratively underground.

We'd begun to hear footsteps and soft voices directly upstairs. We knew the genderqueer housemates and their cats who came and went on the very top floor. The mystery sounds emitted from some mystical in-between zone. We never laid eyes on those residents. We figured it was a family; the softest voice was a baby's gurgle. Maybe they were unlawful residents like you. They never hung out in the backyard, unlike the kooks from the attic who used the patio as a workshop for their latest cabaret ensembles.

Our kitchen door was often open. We took morning coffee on a concrete slab in the weeds out back, surrounded by insects buzzing around our ears or crawling over the top floor's glitter spills. The yard backed onto the field of wild fennel, so the air was scented with that tingly, jagged aroma. Clementine marched around, glancing in anticipation of feline encroachers, ready to make clear this was her turf.

Coming back into the kitchen one morning, I was startled by a change I couldn't quite place—that vertigo-like state of perplexity before what exactly has shifted makes itself known.

A palm leaf cross had been woven into the hog-wire fence perpendicular to our back door. It was positioned too close to our place not to be intended specifically for—or against—us.

It seemed obvious that the beige wisps had been folded into the Christian symbol to ward off demons. In order to stay fixed, it was impaled on a wire that had come away from the wooden frame. I was put in mind of the fence that young Matthew Shepard was left to die on in Wyoming a couple years before.

Was this the work of someone from the in-between apartment? Had they done it early one morning? In the cover of night? Were they protecting us from yet more worldly sin entering our domicile—or protecting themselves, keeping our perversions locked in? Was one of the children sending a plea for help? Or was it the adults telling us to keep away from their kids?

I'd been convinced that moving in with my one true love would be all about entering into a comforting center, only to be made aware of the boundaries. The wind blew in through the lacunae. A car crashed through the front door. Unseen neighbors cast a binding spell. I felt invaded, erratically and minutely, as if by pinpricks.

I invaded you—squelched into your center. We were full of each other's juice and combined into a tart new fragrance. I could never get far enough inside. I worked my hips to thrust my dick taller, as if standing on tiptoe. After sex—which didn't quite smell like two full-grown men yet, still pubescent, raunchy, sun-kissed, slightly pooey, clammy but clean—we smoked in bed. Our stomachs were flat and fluttering. We were fuzzy here and there, in some parts totally smooth.

We had to wonder whether the neighbors who'd "blessed" us, or those politicians who damned our moral turpitude in the halls of Congress, carried with them some image of us fucking: the buttery thickness and sweet musk, initial pain, long strokes, thrusts, anticipation. The ritual tasting of oneself on the other. The sameness and difference, all viscid. Our spooge in ropey strings like bright white Silly Putty.

Or maybe all this never even crossed their minds at all. I could never know if they were freaked out because of, or ignorant of, our actual bodies, in all their grimy glory. Was fornication, its sounds and tastes, too intense to let in, like a country on the other side of the world some would rather disdain than visit?

I WOKE UP TO the news on the radio alarm clock. Because the reader's voice had lost its usual NPR polish, I knew something of magnitude had happened. She sounded genuinely panicked.

I drew a few conclusions rather swiftly that morning: of course the attacks would need a name, and I predicted it would simply be the date. September 11th. Only understatement would suffice. And of course it was 911, the digits to phone in an emergency. I also figured that George W. Bush had just secured another term. Patriotism would get a boost. Any gap we could have slipped through would be sealed. The catastrophe would be called by its date, and the reaction would cement our current impasse.

Indeed, by the end of 2001, Bush announced the formation of the Office of Homeland Security, later the Department of Homeland Security, integrating agencies including immigration. It was reported to be the largest government reorganization since the start of the Cold War.

We were among some thirty-six thousand binational same-sex couples residing precariously in the United States. 'I have to say, I have some element of worry,' stated Tony Sullivan in an interview. It was Tony's claim to be with his lover Richard Adams that had advanced further than any of its kind through the US court system. 'Anything to do with immigration since September the 11th is all that much harder.'

The two were still living illegally in Los Angeles. As Richard put it: 'We're more in the closet now on one level than when we first met.'

In 2003 the newly founded Immigration Policy Center derided scattershot overreactions: 'Calls to impose a "moratorium" on immigration, halt the issuance of student visas, close the borders with Canada and Mexico, eliminate the Diversity Lottery visa program, draft harsher immigration laws.'

The IPC lawyers depicted a climate of extreme fear: 'Because all nineteen of the September 11th terrorists were foreigners, some observers have been quick to blame our vulnerability to terrorist attacks on lax immigration laws.' The IPC argued that 'there is little that is "lax" about laws that subject a long-term permanent resident to deportation for pulling someone's hair.'

RENTER IS BASICALLY A synonym for *sucker.* In the era of the video store, people desperately jumped through hoops to borrow a bulky plastic tape or, later, flimsy DVD. It was the norm that if you didn't have a credit card as collateral, you had to put down a hundred-dollar cash deposit. The renters were vassals hungry for shreds of story — or bare breasts, car chases, triumphant ballads — dispensed by video store feudal lords. I worried that when Frank pulled up in his champagne-colored Lexus SUV, locals would think we were all on the make, but time and again they remarked how nice it was to see local business succeed.

The 1994 film *Clerks,* which I despised, enshrined the image of video store staff as slackers and goobers. Men who couldn't get laid, so got their rush issuing opinions. *The video store guy.* But video stores also had a kind of magic, storefronts that rented windows to other worlds. The products of the behemoth entertainment industry became subject to regional taste — to the staff's recommendations and their power to decide which posters go on the wall and which are kept rolled to be given away. Every film became local.

That's why people disdained the chains. The uniformity — literally, royal blue polos — of Blockbuster destroyed the image of the video store as autonomous space. The indie video store clerk–customer relationship was often fraught, but intimate. The spats over late fees. The debates over the cinematic merit of *Ghost World.* Everyone had an opinion about the ending of *Mulholland Drive,* and the next customer would shout *No spoilers!,* to which we'd retort: *There's no way we could give it away.*

A lot of people were infuriated by David Lynch's opacity, but nearly everyone was sold on *Donnie Darko,* the way it served up nostalgia in the form of a fever dream. Alejandro Soler, a fetching young Colombian with the curly locks of an emperor's favorite—supposedly living in San Francisco with an uncle, though we could never figure out who that was—would trail you around the store like a puppy, seeking more recommendations. *Another one just like Donnie Darko,* Alejandro would whine, then return disappointed at each of your lesser suggestions.

Wes Anderson was especially divisive. Lydia liked only *Bottle Rocket,* with its depiction of downbeat motel life. When it came to *The Royal Tenenbaums,* the consensus was that the style was an affront to substance. I took the contrarian stance of defending its surface qualities, and we stapled the *Royal Tenenbaums* poster to the utility room door indefinitely.

That was the first of several video store transgressions. We limited New Release posters to two per week, displayed back-to-back in a single suspended plastic sleeve, and permanently installed ones for *Billy Liar* and *Masculin Féminin.*

But we were still *neighborhood.* When I scolded a kid for punching the dangling New Release display, his mom, swaddled in a pashmina, with a fistful of complimentary hard candy, went ballistic, and Frank had to give me a talk.

I'd tried to be avuncular, I clarified, *telling him he should show respect.*

Frank said that was the problem. I'd have done better with *KNOCK IT OFF.* Frank explained that in *neighborhoods,* people let the bratty progeny of PTA moms remain the problem of those PTA moms. I took from this that the only way to survive other people's version of community is to let them believe it is exactly what they want it to be.

Frank taught you, and you in turn instructed me, to sweep the front step of the shop each morning. We became known for doing this dutifully, cleaning the sidewalk all the way to the curb.

Customer feedback drove me to pretension. My favorites shelf featured the films of Éric Rohmer and Tsai Ming-liang and

Céline et Julie vont en bateau. My exasperated insistence that Yasujirō Ozu *DOES* live up to his reputation *ACTUALLY* cost us some points with an embittered local journo who subsequently wrote: *Most of the staff is nice most of the time*. But on a Saturday night, when there were so many customers they had to queue to be served, and friends greeted one another while their kids circled their knees, we put crowd-pleasers on the crossbeam TV—*Overboard, Three Amigos, Goonies*—and customers lingered with camaraderie.

Dogs and children and transmasc musicians were named Scout and Huckleberry and Jo. There were no membership cards at Video Hut. We looked customers up by typing in their names, which drilled many into memory. Cassie Denton, the drummer in a post–Riot Grrrl band. BoBo Halk, gradually spending all she earned as a corporate big shot on the rocks. Sebastian Credenza, a hypnotherapist. There was no way I would let that guy hypnotize me. Belinda Day DiMarco, a private detective, and her husband Bill DiMarco, a public defender. We wished we could watch the TV series of their life.

The place was international. Fellow Brits treated you with a special kindness, aware you were far away from a proper cuppa tea. Beautiful, bald Dahlia, who learned to cook in the Caribbean, then in London, checked in on you tenderly and genuinely listened. Likewise Siobhan, crawling with gap-toothed, paint-splattered blond children like a tree full of squirrels. She never seemed otherwise lucid, but spoke intently to you about your frame of mind and reassured you that, hey ho, life is always some kind of muddle. We renamed Jonathan, a tall Yorkshireman, Giles after the "watcher" of *Buffy the Vampire Slayer*. The thing about a "watcher," alas, is they can't fight your battles for you.

The place was intergenerational. Giles's partner Babette was a mature French woman with a miniature bow in her curly hair, who taught me the secret of ageless Parisian chic: *Know your style.*

The bewitching Natasha Railton was into Americana singer-songwriters like Townes Van Zandt and Steve Earle, and in a relationship with a musician/Trader Joe's bagger twenty years her junior.

I guess I'm a cougar. She shrugged.

What's that? I asked.

She tilted her head and drawled, *Jeremy!*

We made friends with Elaine Reymus, a former New Yorker, and were impressed she'd done titles for Jarmusch films. I asked if she'd ever gone to Studio 54.

Did I, she said. *I was one of the girls.*

We knew which sexagenarians still enjoyed a toot of cocaine as an aperitif, and which ones regularly smuggled joints back from Amsterdam in emptied-out ballpoint pens. Several customers were usually stoned. Some drank heavily. Some of them, including BoBo, the former mogul, died.

Older gay men flirted harmlessly. One recounted how he'd been approached downtown by a twink who wanted to call him daddy. I thought this would flatter him, but he was perturbed.

Every time Joshua Goodick left the shop, you'd comment, *I bet it is.* I took pride that renowned sex-positive writers and filmmakers had accounts. Rebecca and Dexter worked in the sex toy industry. Once, Dexter nipped behind the counter to show me the submarine tattoo on the shaft of his penis.

The adult section was separated by a curtain, and the most shameful thing about it was that the selection was so bottom-of-the-barrel. Frank thought it should be gotten rid of altogether. *It's a family business,* he'd tell customers, somewhat misjudging a clientele that prided itself on liberalism. There were those who did concur, some in a second-wave feminist way.

Initially, the adult section just provided a source of amusement. One night as Frank and Lydia cashed up, they put on one of the more remarkable XXX films, *The Mighty Midget,* an airborne superhero fantasy starring Bridget Powerz, sometimes billed as 'Bridget the Midget.' It was Crispin, who'd shown up at closing with the dogs, who put them up to the viewing. To Frank's mortification, a smartly dressed couple peered into the window just as the protagonist spread her red feathered wings.

Bristling at the thought that he might appear like anything less than a paragon of virtue, Frank became convinced the adult section should be eradicated. At first you resisted the idea. You didn't want to be censorious.

In our basement apartment, you and I had been posing naked for each other, perched on a skateboard or lying back on the futon. Then some of those images circulated on a website to which we hadn't exactly given permission when we, for whatever combination of reasons—narcissism, youth, an exhibitionist streak—submitted the scans.

We enjoyed looking at the other pictures on that website. We enjoyed renting porn in the Castro, which is also where we headed to get our own photo rolls printed. You weren't ruffled when the cashier there passed on an enthusiastic compliment, having overseen the development of several explicit nudes. I was sure he meant you. Your cock was so fetching, like an English gentleman, tall and polite yet entitled. Boys had said nice things about mine in person, but I had the inkling my penis was unphotogenic.

I don't have an issue, Frank said of pornos generally. *We should all have the freedom to do what we want.* He adopted a lecturing tone. *But I say leave it there, in the Castro. Or on Polk Street.* It riled you up slightly. But he finally won you over with: *Look, if we're not going to do it right, let's not do it at all.*

Frank wound up giving it all away. He would announce the clear-out to select, mostly male customers, first attempting a discreet wink but then, overcome with his own magnanimity, bellowing like a circus barker. Those who were game took as many tapes in their subject area as they could carry.

Mangia, mangia! Frank cried out, unsure how exactly to mark the occasion, reverting to his flair as dinner host.

We put aside the classic straight flick *Deep Throat* for ourselves. Collector's item, surely.

One or two of the porn recipients were never to be seen again because that's all they'd ever come in for, but Frank's generosity made loyal customers of the rest. They returned regularly to nab whatever other escapism they required—action, arthouse, New Release.

Frank cut the losses of those who didn't get him, and treated the rest as kin. *It's a family business,* he kept repeating, and you cringed, but his instincts were generally correct, albeit sometimes in an oblique way. Bringing down the stud walls that had boxed in the adult section, for instance, allowed more sunlight to pour across the shop floor.

Video stores were a borderland between public and private. A pause before the night's sequestering. We sent people home with images and ideas. Customers returned the containers with the contents intact, yet with the movies now also inside them. We got back mangled tapes, eventually scratched DVDs, in plastic cases dusted with suspicious white powder (or, with baffling regularity, daubed with purplish jam). The videos were returned through the slot in the counter that you turned into the mouth of a Totoro, the tweeness of which was undermined by the way we squalled *In the slot!* at any customer who left their returns on the countertop.

We were regularly present in people's lives by way of our recommendations. On the couch at home, we crossed their minds. And several came into the shop bearing this or that opportunity. We become more entangled in their lives. Elaine Reymus, for instance, gave us part-time work in the evenings folding paper for her new stationery-and-event-planning business.

Rebecca and Dexter presented us with the chance to take in a second cat. Theirs had given birth to a litter.

There's one just waiting for you in a sock drawer, Rebecca cooed.

Take the little panther, Dexter growled.

Within two weeks, we had Isabel, a blithe little black kitten. Another thing that needed you to stay.

FRANK WAS THE MOST unlikely of gay father figures. For starters, you and I had been together for longer than he'd been out. His adorable daughters were at relative ease with being in their awkward mid-teens. They'd been raised to see the world as a place of stability, but now understood it as a matter of adjusting. Sometimes the elder—other times both—attended the dinners at Frank's house.

We'd ring the doorbell, making Crispin's Brussels griffons hysterical. Settling them back down was a big group event.

Mangia! Frank would bellow over fulsome bowls of pasta, wearing his frilly apron for effect.

We'd quiz Crispin on whether his arena performances really were the inspiration behind the dandy in *Best in Show.*

Ye-ess, intoned Crispin from below streaked, razored hair. *My matador jacket was just like that.*

When Crispin's mother, a Filipina widow, was there, she sat in the corner, muttering away to herself in apparent contentment. Crispin was called a 'survivor,' in that he'd been early to access antiretrovirals and lived a remarkably long time after his HIV diagnosis. This meant that in addition to the usual poking and prodding, he'd been treated as a case study. I got the feeling that years of living with both HIV and Hep C, not to mention changes in his combination therapy regimen, had not only enfeebled his body but damped down shades of his personality. When we arrived, he'd invariably be in his seat already, propped up and primped. He spent all his energy on an established repertoire of anecdotes, almost as if scripted. He was always sweet, but somewhat cosmetic, defaulting to a goody-two-shoes delivery—everything was *wonn-derful! greayte! am-ay-zing!* I figured this belied depths—maybe a dirtier, cattier sense of humor; a wicked streak. This did not strike me as inauthenticity. It just felt apparent that things had been different once upon a time, and maybe were different, in other ways, after we left. From her place next door, Lydia reported with something like bitterness, she endured shouting matches between caretaker and cared-for.

But while the dinner party lasted, you and I sat comfortably with the compromises of the evening. Nobody would expect or want us to stay long. At a certain point, Crispin would need to get to bed. Family members both quite young and very old were present, so best not to be too unguarded. Frank was hosting, so best not to be political. He had been a registered Republican. There was a particular *realness* at that table—something that seems impossible to achieve in situations where the expectation is that those gathered are so like-minded they will always take the same view. Instead, it was small talk yet somehow big. It's just that we spoke of details rather than systems, and in anecdotes, not generalizations.

I thought of Frank's ex-wife back in the suburbs, who probably still felt confused and left behind. Here we were, this motley crew brought together by happenstance, shoveling spaghetti in the chaos that came after the illusion was shattered of how things were supposed to be.

11
LEAVES LIKE TWINKS

The road trips: A long, sticky ride in the car with just you—the six-minute songs, the dust. You directing me to turn onto some ominous track through a field of tall something. Me wanting head—as I drove, or parked on the side of the road. Later, we'd fight. The fuck-off sun, the hollow sound of the wind in heat, the mammoth horizon. The thought of pulling a Thelma and Louise. Plunge off Highway 1!

The sun's astonishing exit. Jumping on a motel room bed. The boys who served us in diners and gave the impression they would come back to our room if asked. Fetching ice in buckets with plastic linings. Scrapes. Bruises. Another fight. Like an avalanche, leaving us both in rubble. The next mornings.

Your index finger on the map on your lap. You and your ideas of going a little bit farther, higher, never returning the same way, getting lost, being impossible to find. You wanting to not just explore but disappear, become cloudlike. Or, at least: wander, then sit by a fire as if licked by its flames and fall asleep in the day's ashes.

The sound of things outside the tent—probably just something harmless. Probably just a critter. Who doesn't love a raccoon? The footsteps.

The rivers. The rocks. Sitting for a sunburn, gabbing about desire and mistakes. Feeling my molecules expand. You, literally a tree hugger. We'd gather pebbles. You'd choose a delightful souvenir, and we'd buy it. Even though "You Ain't Goin' Nowhere."

Whiskey. A bar we figured was probably safe. Headlight after headlight. The final stretch. A delicious melancholy, almost unbearable.

Equipment. Smoke. Dark green needles. Pale new leaves like twinks. The resting faces of passengers and drivers. Bored teens. Their dashboard feet. Alongside us, but separated. Dirty-soled socks. Pop another Combo in my mouth, please. Combos—disgusting, but so good, right? Rude waitresses. The line from *Twin Peaks* we made our own: *You wanna hear about the specials? There aren't any.*

A sky we've never seen. Finding our way back in the dark. We'd hike and, on the return, at your urging, take some ill-advised, less-trodden path, racing against the encroaching darkness with me afraid we'd never reach the car.

The shooting stars, but you'd dozed off, leaving me alone with the miracle. Speculating about who's been in this cabin before. About who's next door now.

Big, bad coffee. Teenage boys popping wheelies. Boys with nothing to do. Trying to have nothing to do ourselves. A pathetic picnic on a traffic island. Nearly running out of gas. Worry over tires. A stone in the lug hole. Watching a miraculous sunset from the waiting room of a mechanic's garage. Steely Dan.

Bathing. Licking asshole. TV. Nothing on, switching channels. The smell of past smokers. Smoking out front. Blue-green, chlorine. The salty sea. The salmon swimming upstream. *There's that person,* said of strangers—fellow tourists or locals who, let's be honest, look like they've never left the place we're moving through.

Take Pacheco Pass—or avoid? How Gilroy smells like garlic. Driving the Grapevine, like that song by Pavement. *And Then Nothing Turned Itself Inside Out,* Yo La Tengo. *Teatro,* Willie Nelson with Emmylou. And of course when she sang with Gram Parsons. Her voice like a coyote who got her PhD in nevermind.

All the men who want to fuck you. That man in the hot springs acting like it was a bathhouse. There are kids present! Me, your great defender, which just meant pulling you closer in the ripples. My navigator, which means the boss. Tiring, and yet never, of driving. Stores with porches. Grab another lighter. Junk food. Denny's. Big, slick commercial country music in the gift shop. American flags. Other things in red, white and blue. National Rifle Association stickers. Ex-military men. Glory holes. Families on vacation—or on the run? Churches—big, new and spookily unspooky. Abortion billboards. Christian *food.* Unfathomable meat. No dogs allowed. So many rules. Trailhead, or just anywhere? The sound of pulling into the gravel on the side of the road. The whizz of cars, putting in mind ships passing. Ditches.

Peacocks in the desert. The elation when we finally encountered them. In front of an opera house. *An opera house in the desert.* Other man-made curiosities. Rusted Dust Bowl relics.

Overtaken by nature. Train tracks to nowhere. Wanting to stay in the scorching endlessness. Tumbleweeds, tumbling down the side of the highway like restless hitchhikers. Car crashes. No cops in sight. So many cops everywhere. River-saturated shoes. Sand between toes. Driving barefoot. Driving relaxed. Driving unrelaxed.

The landscape—a foxed page onto which we'd jot down our many thoughts.

Highway 17. Bugs on the windshield. Wiping away the blood of the humans they sucked. *Don't tread on me.* Fear. Your fearless climbing up unclimbable things. A turn into a valley at dusk. Infinite ravines. Daydreaming about isolated houses nestled there. Cabins that smell of mildew and cedar. Redwoods. Joshua trees. Everything like Dr. Seuss. Everything like *Twin Peaks.* Everything like the past. Hard to envision the future. Meth. Graffiti. Mysterious insects. Visitor centers. *There's that person AGAIN.*

Driving at "the flow of traffic." Roadkill. The scenic route. The death wish route. Up to Fort Bragg. Down to Los Angeles. Again and again. The time we slept in a lighthouse, soaked in a hot tub on the edge of the world. Seeing something we think is one thing (a white wall) when it's something else (a sand dune). All of the movies about people going off-grid and getting murdered in gruesome ways. The smell of fresh air. Almost forgetting about home. Because of that, being at home. In the away. With curious, intelligent, soft you.

Out there, in the desert, even more than the forest, I could finally see. See so far in every direction, perceiving no threat, until it dawned that I was inside the threat itself—the wild distance. I've never felt such a ferocious sense of peace. I am minuscule. Dusty, made of stardust, one with the landscape, as if I could vanish into the earth but still retain all of my giddy, goofy energy, the in-jokes and pop culture references, the nineties R&B, the pastiche. Or: I am bigger in the bigness—so, all the more love for you, who too has become rocks and sagebrush, cactus, and sun and air. We are both stretching like a highway. The haze of heat above the tarmac. The way that two lanes don't make any difference when there are no other drivers there.

12
LOVELAND

Exactly what, the cats must have wondered, are we doing in this big room watching Jeremy kneeling naked before the twitchy artist with the bird on his shoulder?

The cockatoo fanned its tail and scooched across Vladimir's neck while he leaned into a camera on a tripod.

Okay, okay, Vladimir said. *Settle, Leonora. Gosh. I think your cats are making Leonora nervous. Are they antagonizing? Anyway, I think I've got enough.*

I pulled on my undies. In a blink, Vladimir was at his desk, transferring the images of my body from camera to iMac. I retreated to our bedroom, hoping Isabel and Clementine would both follow.

I could hear the printer, then the *tink-tink* of Vladimir's brush against his jar of murky water. Going back to his painting. Adding in the shape of my body. The frantic *tink* again; his sigh.

This was becoming a routine. *Jur-mee! Can I just borrow you for a minute?* Vladimir would then ask me to disrobe again. Once, he added: *Now, can you just act as if you're casting a fishing rod?* This time it was: *If you could just get down on one knee . . .* He directed me to raise my arms forward, as if offering up a large plate.

Clementine was affronted. Isabel was still blithe. They seemed at a loss as to why we hadn't returned home yet. No more backyard. Clementine yowled through the window at the parking lot sadly. We had moved into a loft. The space was exhilarating. You could make big art that involved a big mess. I dubbed it Loveland, after the name of an olive-green wall paint on a color chart. I never used the paint itself, but circled the word *Loveland* on the strip and taped it to the front door. *I suppose you're being ironic,* Edward, Vladimir's other half, wheezed. Vladimir disapproved of the name. Too soppy. He kept saying, *We'll think of something else.* But I knew it would catch on.

Vladimir (never Vlad) was a customer at Video Hut, a little younger than you, and nearly as skinny, with pale red hair pulled tightly into a nub of a ponytail. He laughed in falsetto, as if being tickled. He proudly identified as gay and an artist—honorifics you hedged around awkwardly, like a teen loitering in a convenience store parking lot in the hope that some grown-up would offer to buy beer without being asked. Edward, who worked in advertising, already seemed middle-aged, though he was slightly younger than Vladimir, so the youngest of us all. Edward was corpulent and wry. He spoke with the sibilant delivery of an orally fixated aristocrat.

Two of their friends—she a taciturn designer of clubby fashion, he a scrawny electronica producer—had offered to hand over the lease on their loft. They were, of course, moving back to Berlin. The rent increase was a little steep, and Vladimir and Edward figured the space was big enough for two couples, so they asked us to consider joining them. We thought we were going to look at the place out of politeness and idle curiosity. But then we entered. It was a former adult learning center on the second floor of a plain office building that shared a parking lot with an army surplus emporium. The sunlight-filled main room—the studio—was the size of a tennis court. I imagined blasting *Ladies and gentlemen we are floating in space* through it. At the far end was a soundstage, and behind that a utility area with deep sinks. The other side was divided into a kitchen, living room, small but airy bedroom (for us) with a door on either side so that it was also a kind of corridor, and a large, carpeted master bedroom (for Vladimir and Edward). Our rent would be slightly cheaper to compensate for the difference in size. We agreed to move in.

Vladimir was despondent when he got a look at our stuff.

Such an ugly coffee table! he shrieked. True, but I took umbrage that he had the gall to say it.

Our whimsical objects, relocated into the airy loft, appeared remarkably inelegant. Our musty books, records and clothes smelled like we'd arrived from a tomb. Our new housemates had a sleeker yet kitschier aesthetic. Edward had shipped out a collection of mid-century furniture, all procured for next to nothing around the exurb where he was raised in Arizona. Teak and teal, wicker, atomic starburst patterns. Bric-a-brac that telegraphed *housewife.* It was as if a nuclear family was being held hostage somewhere and Vladimir and Edward had forged a life with their stuff.

The ugly table was quickly repurposed by Vladimir as the platform upon which his life models would pose. I used to eat off that, I thought, as men planted their bare soles and asses on it. Vladimir was all about the classical form. I hadn't realized his art was so figurative. We'd spoken about Felix Gonzalez-Torres, for whom a portrait could be a candy pile or two clocks, so I thought his own art would be more conceptual, but he mostly strived to paint High Renaissance male nudes.

The life drawing always seemed destined to become sex, and sure enough, Vladimir and the model often retreated into the master bedroom. He also held occasional, far less erotically charged group sessions. One early evening I awoke from a nap and figured I'd get stuck into some writing. Stumbling groggily into the studio in the boxers I'd spooged into before falling asleep, I came upon a circle of middle-aged women sipping merlot, laser-focused on a model wearing only a braided anklet striking a pose excruciatingly close to "The Thinker."

When no model was at hand, Vladimir would ask you or me to pose. I was catnapping the first time he knocked on the bedroom door and asked if he could draw me asleep. I was in a thick pullover hoodie and boxer briefs. *Can I?* he asked gently, then pulled the blanket down to my knees. I pretended to continue snoozing, agreeable to a new experience of inhabiting my body. I later figured out he put the sketch up for sale on eBay.

From then on, when he was painting one of his arcadian landscapes populated by cavorting men, he'd call me over to quickly strip off and pose.

Vladimir's cockatoo Leonora Carrington seemed to be on the verge of polysyllabic speech. Capable of thwarting a nefarious scheme. Able to finger a suspect in a lineup. It put me on edge. When nobody was looking, she'd glance my way and raise her crest.

Edward stumbled home in the evenings, swiftly mixed a cocktail and collapsed with hopes of being entertained by some observational wit over bong rips. He was avuncular and pooped. *Tell me about your day,* he'd sigh, as if it was an obligation but genuinely craving anecdotes from our relatively laid-back lives. Little catch-ups were, after all, meant to be a perk of living with other people, and I felt unsporting. You and I could only really provide myriad variations on the arguments we held with customers over late fees, none of them particularly engrossing.

If he'd been for an after-work drink with colleagues, Edward could be lairy. His hand would grace my back, though it seemed possible he'd lost his spatial perception along with his glasses. He'd mutter a line about *unwinding* and whimper my name. It was harmless, even while it recalled the misbehavior of bosses from the era of his furniture collection. It could seem as though you and I had been brought in as two more decorative tchotchkes.

In the runup to Folsom Street Fair, where leatherfolk with exposed low-hangers crawl on leashes and lick boots, Edward announced that we should go as a group. And, he added, try to make a quick buck. He turned to you. *We'll sell you,* he laughed. *Our most valuable commodity.* Why were both of them always trying to *sell* us?

Edward's VHS porn was unashamedly, maybe deliberately, left around the place. He was fond of the Young and Innocent series from Dolphin Entertainment. Vladimir and Edward watched these in their bedroom, but evidence suggested they also enjoyed them openly in the living room when we were away.

A pair of brunet twinks, visiting from somewhere outside Miami, almost immediately disappeared into the master bedroom. Edward would periodically stride out in his silky robe and fetch snacks. Vladimir stayed in bed with the boys. I imagined, as in the classical paintings that inspired Vladimir, the group of them lounging with calves displayed splendiferously, dangling bunches of grapes. Their presence made the place seem like a porn set.

Vladimir's local friends were more articulate. They'd be invited to one of Vladimir's "salons," where they weighed up virtue and vice by way of Rousseau and the Marquis de Sade, twirling puka shell necklaces and stroking an actual or phantom goatee. Or they'd come over one-on-one to whisper deeply with Vladimir. I sometimes got the impression they were plotting his escape from under Edward's tacit control. Edward made pretty much all the money, and though I never witnessed him being anything other than kind, an impression hovered that Vladimir saw himself as trapped.

One of the free-love friends in particular, with the tight curls of a South American soccer player and a notebook full of prose poems, openly gazed at me. I once caught him and Vladimir snickering over images on the iMac that I felt positive were my nudes. Were they pervs? I enjoyed the idea. They reminded me that the city was full of pervs. I wanted to be one, too. Why were you and I so restrained?

In one sense, we'd become outliers. But on another level, we had internalized what kind of couple would be worthy of immigration and conformed to that model. We seemed to think of ourselves as plaintiffs, always on the verge of entering court and ready to portray ourselves as anodyne and well-behaved. We were prepared to put on the record our loyal devotion, which implied monogamy.

Immigration laws, Carl F. Stychin has written, operate to "tame" citizenship seekers and 'put them in "their place": that is, within a recognizable, manageable, and normalizable guise (and, if not normalizable, to exclude them).' The approvable foreign partner is demonstrably moneyed and performatively monogamous. But Stychin added that 'it is worth remembering that with discipline inevitably comes resistance, and successful citizenship claims no doubt will also facilitate new relationship forms and experiments in living as transnational citizens which are not so easily managed. The ability of law to manage and to discipline into a recognizable form is never totalizing, and subjects are not necessarily as docile nor as unimaginative as we may sometimes think.'

In the 1984 book *The Male Couple,* the authors (a male couple) cited a study of one hundred and fifty-six men in gay relationships, lasting from one to thirty-seven years, finding that only seven couples—none who'd been together over five years—were exclusive. As if monogamy is just a phase for gay men to grow out of. Which stands in contrast to public advocates of gay marriage depicting decades of gay rights progress as parallel to a lifespan, suggesting time had come for those still spreading seed, stuck in the adolescent stage, to mature and settle down.

In 1998 conservative gay pundit Andrew Sullivan wrote of how a 'proclivity for quick and easy sex' was 'in fact a desperate and failed search for some kind of intimacy' that evidenced 'both our wounded self-esteem as homosexuals and our general inculturation as men.'

To which queer theorist Michael Warner retorted: 'Even if gay men did suffer from "wounded self-esteem," the most likely result for them would not be promiscuity—which calls for a fair amount of courage and dignity on the part of those who defy the stigma and abjection associated with it—but a compulsive idealization of love and a desperate need to have validation conferred on their intimate lives through state-certified marriage.'

I think we basically wanted to have our cake and eat it, too. Vladimir and Edward liberated this desire by osmosis. Their carnal risks felt more playful than dangerous. They scored regularly. I figured you and I could achieve great things.

We would begin to negotiate new borders, those around our bodies.

WE NEEDED A FIRST third. To practice. We used Craigslist. Chances were high that our selected guy was a poseur when he described himself as a skater, code for what he *wanted* to be, also who he wanted to serve. Skater meant desirable-because-hard-to-get. It meant masculine, but not in a frat boy way, which had begun to seem camp—all those performative *Bro!*s peppering short sentences. Skater meant earthy yet airborne; it meant sweaty—dirty, but not diseased; a scruffy sort of minx. A skater was on his own plane, on four wheels gliding away.

I'd owned a board on and off since I was a kid, and could maneuver with some elegance, curve and not fall, but could never quite catch air. I rode one short distances in Los Angeles but abstained in San Francisco, where skating was serious business. Anyone who saw me arrive at a curb would see I could not ollie. This threatened my gender security. Like popping a wheelie on a bike, the ollie is a way for a young man to showcase his potency, his ability to get it up.

The Craigslist "skater"—a little older, maybe thirty—was pretty clearly even less authentic. He arrived with a board, its wheels clean, the deck neatly threaded through hooks on a specially designed backpack. In other words, he showed up with a thirty-two-inch phallic symbol on his back.

I took him by his clammy hand. He said he had seen me around, then glanced at you like he couldn't believe his luck. He was stocky and cumbersomely tall. Not ugly, but we were out of his league. I knew he was going to get off. I wanted him to. I knew that, unthreatened, I could keep my erection. I felt ready.

He wound up humping us both at once, sliding from thigh to thigh, breathless and shaky. He turned over and orgasmed like an earthquake. His legs spasmed as if they were about to cut loose. I briefly thought it was possible he could die.

So we were capable of *that.* We had a superpower as two. All the warm, sticky inches between us.

That was a surprising choice, said either Vladimir or Edward, standing together closely. They seemed truly astonished. *Tell us everything,* one or the other demanded. I shrugged and began prepping for dinner, feeling cavalier and slutty.

The next guy was very cute—a cocky runt with a short mohawk and tight bod. That evening, while I firmed up the plans via Craigslist, you got it into your head to show Vladimir and Edward and me a BBC adaptation of *The Lion, the Witch and the Wardrobe.* You remembered it being terrific, but watching it again on a bootleg tape, it turned out to be amateurish and painfully slow.

I answered the door, and the mohawk dude joined us on the soundstage. He sat next to you on the floor, and it was soon clear that you two were fondling each other under the blanket while the rest of us sat on the couch making occasional comments about *The Lion, the Witch and the Wardrobe.*

Can we go to your bed? he asked you. I joined.

It was slower this time, and the room filled with his sexy humidity. Afterward, it seemed we'd done something beautiful, like a dance, meditative and sensual, like sex in the seventies. He kicked back, his arm above his head, the pit fuming.

I don't really like three-ways. He yawned.

No? I asked, as if unbothered.

Nah, he said, petting you. *I invariably like one much more than the other. So someone just feels left out.*

He side-eyed me while you snuggled into his chest. He stroked your waves, which seemed more golden since we'd emerged from the basement. I knew you so well. We had history. I was covetous.

You asked him life questions, as gay men do after fucking. I waited for him to gather up the energy to get his clothes back on and leave.

After that was the businessman at the W Hotel. I'd made the arrangements, then gone to the dentist. Which got a little bloody, so when I met you in the hotel lobby, I was obsessing over my mouthful of tiny abrasions, fretful about the risks of swilling precum. Now every little panic about disease would involve protecting not just myself but you.

The man opened the door to his room with a towel around his waist. Hairy-chested, average-looking, intense. He was surprised to hear your English accent.

He's a California boy now, I said.

Oh yes, he is, he said gluttonously.

I felt like a pimp.

Seeing the businessman's arousal silently empowered you. The scenario, it was clear, was really turning you on. You were dealing with capitalism as best you knew how!

There was very little afterglow chat. The whole thing had been orchestrated as a corporate alpha male fantasy, and we left so that would remain relatively intact.

Then there was the construction worker we seduced at the Phone Booth, tugging him away from the girl for whom he was doing a sleazy impression of Justin Timberlake. His pals from the site thought we were hilarious and explained that he was their foreman. *He's so hot,* they agreed, which made me insatiable. Back at ours, his verbal directions for how exactly he liked to be fingered left me with a much clearer anatomical understanding of the prostate. Adding a bisexual to the mix, it turned out, could provide a less ideological, more bodily form of edification.

Drunken fumbles. Drawn-out pursuit. There were boys who insisted on being alone with you—*the weird ones,* I pointed out, like the self-proclaimed cum guzzler with OCD, who wore cycling gloves at all times and told you that your sperm had a questionable flavor. The ones who zeroed in on me were generally boyish and fey, some emitting a fervor that struck me as patricidal.

On another household movie night—this time a Cassavetes—a guy who'd once modeled nude for Vladimir showed up. He was a striking brunet with soccer thighs and the unignorable scent of clean scrotum. He wore Hello Kitty socks. He sat near us on the floor.

I love Hello Kitty, he whispered when we commented on the socks. *She's so cute.*

We began extracting other likes: Sigur Rós. Camping. The color "toothpaste." When he said the word *cute* again, I felt pretty sure he'd also apply it to us if given the chance.

All of his caverns must be deep, I thought: mouth, belly button, asshole. I was eager to snout around in it all, with his sweet, tangy fur on my cheek.

Wait—what's your name again? I asked. It remained my job, as the American, to ask the obnoxious or embarrassing questions. As settled as you were, you still played the role of polite guest.

Edward, he replied. *Ed Cashwell,* he added, distinguishing himself from our housemate. It didn't suit him.

Can we call you Cash? I asked.

Yeah, I do get that from some people.

We made a plan to go camping. It seemed butch, therefore hot, to go camping with a guy we called by a riff on his last name.

After that, when Cash knocked on the door of Loveland—no buzzer, so one had to pound really hard, or shout at the windows—it was to hang out with us.

The three of us felt shitty that we'd pilfered him from Vladimir, but not enough to stop cultivating the friendship. We became addicted to the bond, relaxing and gently euphoric. We listened to Deerhoof, did shots with lime and salt, tried to imagine life in Iceland.

Cash had a kitty, too, but it was vicious. Hence the name Sid. When we went to his place, we'd take turns planting our face into Cash's squishy buns, while the other kept watch so that Sid didn't bloody our forearms and calves.

We drew sexy stories out of Cash, like how when he was a teen in Ventura County, he used to pull over after work at a stadium and jack off because he'd been in proximity to so many male bodies all day.

In deep kisses, our three mouths found a union I didn't know possible, like all talking at once. We ventured into one another's armpits. *Dirty Dollar,* you called him. His big tan feet were always poking into the middle of the car or the bed.

You could smell that Dirty Dollar coming. What's more, you felt seen by him. *It's always the quiet ones,* he took to saying about you. Your horniness cracked him up. When it came to you in a round of 'which *Golden Girls* character?,' he'd bellow, *Blanche!* Meaning the trampy one. Cash chided you in locker room tones; he knew what to say and how to say it. *You're secretly Blanche!*

Everybody, I was figuring out, liked being friends with you, because everybody likes having a secret.

AMONG THE UNUSUAL TALES of same-sex marriage I have read, and I've read many—take those of Emperor Nero alone: in one nuptial, he assumed the role of the bride at a lavish floating feast with a fleet of tugs helmed by catamites; in another, he had the young slave Sporus castrated and called by his dead wife's name—the one that plays in my head with the most sparkling and gruesome detail took place in Rome in the sixteenth century.

Or rather *almost* took place. An exchange of vows never happened. Historian Gary Ferguson's fascinating microhistory of the nonevent, *Same-Sex Marriage in Renaissance Rome,* starts from the travel journals of French essayist Michel de Montaigne. In March 1581, Montaigne recorded his encounter with a Roman who regaled him with the amusing gossip of a group of 'Portugais' (Portuguese) men who, a few years prior, entered into 'une estrange confrerie' (a strange brotherhood) through a church wedding ceremony at the San Giovanni Porta Latina, or the Basilica of Saint John at the Latin Gate. The story went that the men took Communion, read the relevant gospel, 'et puis couchoient et habitoient ensemble' (and then slept and lived together). Ferguson points out that *habiter,* or *to live,* was at the time 'a common euphemism for having sexual relations.'

Other accounts dug up by the historian suggest that this was a part of ongoing transgressions at the Latin Gate, possibly involving a network of more than two dozen men. On the last of such festivities, some eleven participants were arrested. According to more than one record, numerous more were present but fled. It's possible, writes Ferguson, that some were part of a heavily monitored populace known as '*conversos* or so-called New Christians—Iberians of Jewish descent converted to Christianity, often under compulsion.' One report does not mention any marriages at all—just the 'enorme, abominevole et nefando vitio' (enormous, abominable, and unmentionable vice).

In 1578, various records concur, eight of the men were executed for their participation in the aborted marriage ceremony. Montaigne relayed the speculation of Roman *esprits,* or wits: it occurred to the men ('these sharp folk') that they might legitimize their form of sexuality ('this other action') through marriage 'if they authorized it with ceremonies and mysteries of the Church.' Ferguson notes the mocking tone of the wits; the immigrant men, in re-creating traditional wedding vows, were perceived to be 'adhering uncritically to an orthodox view of sin and sex and to marriage as both institution and sacrament.' The irony being that while the men figured marriage would absolve them of the sin of their sexual deviance, it was their profaning of sacred rites that led to the executions.

Some scholars, working from inaccurate translations, have mistaken the gossip of Roman *esprits* (wits) for the official approval of Roman *esperts* (experts). Most notoriously, overeager historian John Boswell considered the ceremony a form of adelphopoiesis, the Eastern Orthodox rite of "brother-making." Though adelphopoiesis has been interpreted in myriad ways—a 'community molecule,' posited Russian theologian Pavel Florensky—Boswell averred that it was essentially akin to same-sex union. But by the early modern period, such rites were actually no longer in practice in the Roman Catholic Church. Boswell's theory of adelphopoiesis was one of several claims in his 1994 book *Same-Sex Unions in Premodern Europe,* which was derided as a repository for wishful thinking. Boswell was accustomed to being criticized by both theological scholars and gay activists for allowing his yearning for a gay-tolerant Christian lineage to predetermine his historical findings. He was convinced the Church demonstrated 'general equanimity' regarding such unions. How to explain, then, the gallows?

In his quest to find a queer continuum across centuries, John Boswell may have actually done better to inspect the saucy details of the men's sexual exploits. After Boswell's death, Gary Ferguson did this work. He found scraps of testimony that add up to a yearslong soap opera of carnal pleasures with a rotating cast. The men coupled up in a dizzying array of combinations. Some were known as *commare* (variously *godmother, gossip* or *mistress*) for taking a passive role, therefore considered womanlike. Others aren't so patently identified by their sexual proclivity, or fall in line with what would today be called versatile. Some hanky-panky is not so much the stuff of a bottom and top, but two sides. The men gave head and jerked off, then talked about it using filthy colloquialisms, like they were gabbing on the Christopher Street pier. They spoke of male bodies with hunger and delight. They referred to one another with a range of slurs and, touchingly, to themselves collectively as '*friends*' or simply '*us*.'

Some of the pairings between males of similar age and class could be construed as akin to modern-day *gay*, in contrast with the historical norm of pederastic relations between men and boys. The Latin Gate group did include age-gap configurations, too; some arrested youth claimed to have been forced. This may have been sadly true. The remote location tracks with the prevalent practice of taking kidnapped youths to a vineyard or other secluded spot on the outskirts of town. Such a declaration could also have been a young man's defense against capital punishment. Indeed, at least one young captive had his life spared. Ferguson found that other adolescents were depicted as actively involved, like two youngsters dressed as hermits who covertly guided new participants to the Latin Gate. There are atypical depictions of the younger partner doing the topping. One nubile fellow was encouraged to 'get married here' to an older priest, taken to mean that the man of the cloth would bottom. Ferguson's research suggests that it's possible the term *marriage* could have also been code for foreplay or ritualistic initiation, even 'recruitment,' into a 'secret society.'

Who knows what power dynamics were actually at play. But Ferguson uncovered how, in their variety of formations, the men perverted not only procreative sexuality but "acceptable" norms of male-male sex that had for centuries reiterated social hierarchies. 'The ancient Romans had no problem with homosexuality,' historian Stephanie Coontz has observed, 'and they did not think that heterosexual marriage was sacred. The reason they found male-male marriage repugnant was that no real man would ever agree to play the subordinate role demanded of a Roman wife.' Homosexuality came with a series of rules: a man might permissibly bed a young male, or *puer*; a free citizen could sleep with a member of the *infames*, such as an enslaved person, sex worker or entertainer—people without legal and social standing. Historian Catharine Edwards wrote that, as could be the case with women adulterers, 'a man who allowed himself to be penetrated by another man was also termed infamis.' To be a *pathicus*, a man who took the passive role, also meant bottoming socially.

By contrast, the men of the Latin Gate circle were no strangers to a flip-flop. Battista, for instance, a brawny and bellicose boatman, is unusual in historical records: a hard man who bottomed.

Out in the world, these men were of low status. Going by the bigger picture that Gary Ferguson has drawn, it's probable that the prosecution of several had to do with, as much as anything else, their position as poor itinerant laborers. At least two were friars—devout men of the mendicant orders who lived in poverty. Only one of those ultimately executed was actually Portuguese. Six were Spanish. Battista was described as Albanian and called himself 'a Slav.' At the time of his execution, the only item he had to bequeath was his cloak, which he left to charity. Ferguson has listed these men's few worldly possessions. Some donated what little they had; others left behind only debts. A few willed small sums of money for a mass to be held on their behalf, in a ritualistic attempt to prevent their damnation.

Their group description as "Portuguese" may have been a conflation of political subjugation with sexual submission. During this period, Rome's population doubled, and the majority of new immigrants were men. They took positions as household servants or worked the land or in construction. Many could not afford to marry. 'Perhaps not wholly surprisingly,' Ferguson notes, it was these men 'who found themselves most frequently in court accused of the crime of sodomy.'

Under interrogation, the accused provided contrasting versions of the day's events. The men frequently attempt to downplay the festivities. They feign ignorance and depict muddled social plans, presenting themselves as unaware that they were profaning sacraments. Just a bit of a get-together—with, yes, some hazy rumor of a possible wedding in the mix. Some of the accused incriminate others, or assert they were coerced. Their testimonies are tinged with fear and envy.

Marco Pinto, the sole accused actually from Portugal, lived on the basilica grounds, so surely must have connected the group to the site. 'Pinto ran San Giovanni as a place for buggery,' testified a man named Alfaro, although that was after he was strung up with ropes. Pinto did seem to be exceptionally horny. Of all the witness statements that Ferguson has accumulated, Pinto provided some of the most explicit. Like: 'I put my cock in his ass and did what I wanted to do.' Or: 'My lord, my pleasure is to bugger and I've done it many times, but now I don't remember how many I've buggered.'

As for the day's would-be grooms: one was a friar, the other a man enough past his youth that his taste for bottoming could be considered a choice and not an obligation. In some ways, the outlaw wedding was comparable to an arranged marriage. It all seems to have been at the behest of the rest of the group, not so much initiated by these two would-be grooms as foisted upon them. The others organized the date and the elaborate feast, featuring chicken, a traditional wedding dish to symbolize potency.

On the Sunday of the wedding, the friar-groom was supposedly too sick to show up, therefore escaping arrest. Ferguson has not been able to discern: Did he get a heads-up? Or actually help arrange the raid himself? Was it all a trap? Though the nuptials were thwarted, the reception went ahead. The cock, after all, had been cooked. Then the party was busted, and the unlucky ones caught.

For all of his research, translating his way through the archives, twice journeying to the Roman church—by then a popular destination for traditional weddings—Ferguson has been left wondering whether it was all just a bit of fun. It's plausible that the men were put to death for a lark, incriminated by their use of the sacred vocabulary of marriage.

The records are too few and full of gaps to be conclusive. What was going on, exactly? Some chaotic mix of parody and piety? Why precisely was it considered such a heinous crime? There's much we'll never know. 'Like the histories of other persecuted or conquered individuals and peoples,' Ferguson wrote, 'that of the men who met at the Latin Gate contains many holes.'

In their final hours, each of the condemned was accompanied

by a "comforter"—a member of the Confraternity of San Giovanni Decollato wearing a pointed hood and pointy shoes. Ferguson documented how these terrifying figures would urge the convict to repent, make arrangements regarding his property and debts, and finally walk alongside him to the site of execution, singing psalms and repeating pious words. They held up a tavoletta—a paddle-like object with images of Christ's crucifixion or a martyr's death—in front of the face of the condemned. This practice was intended to both shield the doomed man from the crowd of spectators and focus his attention on spiritual matters.

The eight condemned men were hanged in the public square at the Castel Sant'Angelo in the city center. Their corpses were then carted to the remote Latin Gate, the site of their transgression. Ferguson clarified that this was an unprecedented spectacle. Normally if a body was to be burned after hanging, it would happen immediately in the vicinity rather than after being 'paraded through the streets of the city, traversing its entire breadth from the northwest to the far southeast.' To heap their corpses on a pyre where they sinned—along with, as has been told, the trial records—must have been a ritual cleansing. More arrestees waited in prison; it was said that 'they will be baked in another batch.' But that lot seems to have been spared in the end.

At moments Ferguson's precise, scholarly account gives way to lament—'the obscure lives of these early modern immigrants to Rome were suddenly transformed by their encounter with power, an encounter that focused on them a brief but intense beam of light.' To me, engrossed in Ferguson's research, two things stick out: This was not only a commitment ceremony between two men but a group activity. And the group was punished not only for aspiring to an unsanctioned union but for multiple forms of border-crossing.

The party—then the subsequent pyre—was located at the very edge of the city. The condemned men had crossed borders in search of work. Perhaps they also sought some form of enlightenment, as well as the bodies of other men. Whatever happened at the Latin Gate, it was messy. The main characters were poor, promiscuous and unreliable. Their deaths are maddening and tragic.

Because the trial records appear to have been burned along with the bodies, Ferguson had to consult a spotty array of dispatches, partial copies and subsequent accounts. From these fragments, he has deciphered something more complex than a pair of sentimental male lovers. These men don't provide the most convenient model for traditionalist gay marriage advocates. More than anything, we can divine some sketch of a subculture—replete with utopian potential and unsavory infighting. In their testimonies, more than one of the men painted a picture of the day in a domestic light. It was a gathering marked by the bustle of food preparations. The various tasks and the anticipation suggest something like community.

Were they being willfully heretical or naively attempting to absolve themselves of sin? Or was it all just a joke? It wasn't necessarily one thing or another. Ferguson's detailed account presents the possibility of a kind of earnest pastiche—an exploration of the possibilities of identity within recognizable social structures. It's what the men had to work with. This seems to be much the way humans stumble through identity still. However conscious they were of the significance of their actions, Ferguson has posited that the men enacted 'a striking form of polyvalent—*queer*—appropriation.'

SO WE WERE OUT of the fog. We ate breakfast at a café with a huge orange sun painted on its yellow floor. We ordered everything *with avocado.* We biked to Rainbow Groceries on Harrison, which actually smelled of food, not just plastic.

With this or that boy, we'd fall into an erratic rhythm, ripe and sticky, fooling around, then afterward talking at length about things we did and did not like. We sipped lukewarm coffee and chain-smoked. We discussed whether it was too early to start drinking until we needed a drink.

There was always one errand that someone needed to run but kept procrastinating. Like exchanging a pair of shoes or purchasing a tool or getting a haircut. Hours, then days, would be designed around this single mission, which we came to view as a herculean task and everyone's joint concern.

Small gestures of trust led to mutual protection. I think the boys felt comfortable around us because we were mindful of each other and the cats. As a unit, you and I always had someone to call us out, but also accept, when we made a mistake. So we could take little risks. We were living our days in the silver linings.

One evening several months into our time at Loveland, a bunch of acquaintances—haiku writers and ukulele players, connoisseurs of Agnès Varda films, readers of *Close to the Knives*—were over for drinks. I took two of the art fags aside.

Can I ask your opinion on something? I asked.

I led them to Vladimir's latest and largest arcadian painting. There you were in a corner, strangely small, cupping your hands to drink from the stream. And just off-center, I was naked and bent on one knee in the water's shallows. My hands were raised, as I'd been instructed to pose. A wreath had been added between my fingers. Standing on a small boulder above was Vladimir himself—nude, contrapposto, holding his dick and pissing. With a magnificent arc, urine streamed through the hollow of the wreath as I held it aloft.

Is this fucked-up? I asked, pointing to that part of the picture.

Uh, yeah.

Totally fucked-up.

I have to say I was gobsmacked, I said, now emboldened. *It seems...*

Very passive-aggressive.

Who does that, right?

Yeah, it's pretty shocking.

OK, I said. *Thanks. I wasn't sure if it was just me.*

Leonora cackled. Vladimir put on one of my Joy Division records. The big room was impressive. A party here had the glamor of an exhibition opening. The cats hid under our bed. You and I had emerged and opened up. I was writing more, and being more widely read. Your art expanded. It was more willing to take up space. You were less knotty and more experimental. We could be capacious. I felt more important in the open plan and under high ceilings. I could swan around. I'd leaned into my wiggle. My shoulders relaxed. There were many projects to be undertaken. But when I saw that painting, I realized I couldn't live in Loveland forever, or even much longer.

13

JAMES DEAN'S PENIS

The first time I heard "Milkshake" by Kelis, I was in a VW camper van, racing against the night through the remotes of Oregon, scared for my life.

Earlier, we'd pulled up to the campsite you had planned for us, at the end of a long track through inexplicably unfriendly trees, only to find it deserted and locked up. Just more forest, behind a gate. A dead end in the woods.

We'd been touring the Pacific Northwest for several days. Cash christened the van Shady Lanes. I did most of the driving. From the back seat, Cash and his new best friend, my sister Jenny, would chant in falsetto: *We want Dairy Queen!* to test my composure, while you navigated, dutiful finger on map. *We'll be somewhere near something soon,* you'd report, playing Mom. *Twenty miles or so.* You'd pat my knee and turn back to "the kids." *You can have your Dairy Queen. Anyway, we can fill up the tank then.*

One night in Northern California, a cluster of large rocks came into view, lapped by waves off the coast. We recognized it from *The Goonies*—the formation that matched the holes in One-Eyed Willy's doubloon. We sat on the shore until we became chilly, then headed back to our campsite. We strolled through the near-silent town and beheld a shirtless teen jogging down the middle of the street. In a river in Oregon, you were swept away by a strong current and disappeared around the bend. Gone. For the first time in who knows how long, I prayed. Then there you were, minus the inflatable, pulling yourself upstream by the vines and roots on the bank. In Washington we posed for photos in front of the lodge, falls, diner, and sheriff station from *Twin Peaks*. We continued north but you couldn't cross into Canada, so we basked like seals in the sun on the bobbing docks of Orcas Island.

The terror I suffered when I first heard "Milkshake" was based on threats we concocted ourselves, but fair enough: you and I, still emerging from childhood bullying, were now outlaws and feeling conspicuous out there in rural America. Gay sex was not yet legal throughout the United States. The change in law would come only days later, with the announcement of the SCOTUS decision in *Lawrence v. Texas*. But it was all so fresh, still alive: our legislated marginalization. The sight of your finger keeping our place on the map undid me—as if you thought you could exert some control over this big bad country.

It was maybe around eight at night. We were on our way back down to California. We stopped at a gas station. It was Cash's turn to pump. He stood alongside a pickup with gun rack and two enormous men who were somehow Caucasian-presenting. They both wore camo, as did the small boy traveling with them.

We cruised deeper into the night. Jenny tried her best to calm down us increasingly anxious gays. She'd taken on this job generally. Such as when your sis, Ruby, shipped boxes of your stuff out by sea and Jenny accompanied me to collect them at the

East Bay docks. I was defensive, even surly, to the customs officer who inquired what was inside, a routine question that made me once again convinced that this was The Event that would expose you and get us reported to the INS. *Hey, sit!* Jenny commanded with a pat on the beam seating. *Let me,* she mouthed, then shuffle-sashayed up to the desk like "Jenny from the Block." Letting her do the talking had become the protocol now that I was not just a gay but a scofflaw-harboring one.

But out there in the Oregonian nothing, even Jenny was spooked. She went silent. Traffic lights hung like vampire bats in repose. Everything that should have looked placid and normal instead signaled that we were in hostile territory.

When "Milkshake" came on the radio, introduced by a *brrrrrand nuuuu trrrrrack!* stinger, I turned it up. We moved along a highway under a blackening sky cut through with stars like spilled crystal meth, occasionally passing the hard glare of gas stations or flicker of standalone stores selling guns, poppers, or laminate flooring. At the sound of the low-end beat, my shoulders didn't exactly untense but began to bop. Kelis sang with little-girl bravado, her voice like sparks over the sawtooth synth.

This sounds great, I proclaimed.

I wanted the song to create a clear distinction between our safety inside the van and the danger lurking outside, like cranking the heat on an icy night.

I turned the radio up further.

Right? I said. *So SCUZZY.*

Each time we came to a stoplight, I couldn't decide if it was a relief to arrive under bright illumination or if it just made us more visible, therefore vulnerable, to whoever pulled up in the next lane. Better to keep on the move.

Finally, now ill at ease with not only the landscape but one another, we parked at an uncomely campsite, basically an unpaved lot adjacent to a Home Depot. I thought I was too tired to be scared anymore, but the place had me on edge again. The whites of eyeballs that glanced from RV windows. The glow of TV screens through mini blinds. A lady of indeterminate age marching across the grounds in a bathrobe holding a bucket of—what?—with grim determination.

Our intention was to avoid snobbery while keeping alert to the signs that indicate someone who might wish us harm. Cash had ceased his usual antagonizing whine. He wasn't even hungry. Cash was always famished. He waved off the idea of finding a place to get fries. *You OK?* I demanded to know. *I don't wanna talk about it,* he said in a meeker version of his trademark flippancy. We all slept uneasily that night, with no particular cause except whatever it was that we couldn't quite make out in the dark.

WE RETURNED TO CALIFORNIA in late June 2003. Those were our last days living in Loveland. On the 26th, we celebrated Mom's birthday with a toast there before heading to Eric's Chinese. Since the whole family was present, we took the opportunity to pose for pictures as if it were an engagement party for you and Jenny. The snapshots were for the record just in case, as we'd discussed over campfires during our trip, we took the plunge and decided the best option was for you two to get hitched. This seemed unlikely. Jenny was ambitious and headed who knows where for grad school. Taking the photos was probably more a way of letting off steam. One more futile gesture to pretend we were doing something about our predicament. Though you marrying my sis seemed a little icky, Mom and Dad gamely posed for photos that suggested you were her fiancé.

It was also the day the Supreme Court issued its decision in *Lawrence v. Texas,* which invalidated state laws prohibiting consensual gay sex.

Unlike the Georgia sodomy law unsuccessfully challenged in *Bowers v. Hardwick,* which officially applied to anyone, the Texas prohibition had been specifically restricted to same-sex partners from 1973, right around the time the state decriminalized not only heterosexual sodomy but a range of other acts, including bestiality.

There'd once been laws proscribing or limiting nonprocreative sex in every state, and punishments could include heavy fines and imprisonment. Illinois was the first to eliminate antisodomy laws; that was in 1962, and it took nearly a decade for another state to follow. In 2001 the United States Court of Appeals for the Eleventh Circuit upheld the state of Alabama's 1998 Anti-Obscenity Enforcement Act, which banned the sale of sex toys, thereby 'discouraging prurient interests in autonomous sex.' By the time of *Lawrence,* in many places intercourse remained regulated as permissible only between one penis and one vagina, both attached to legally wedded spouses, and enacted on private property. At least a dozen states had some version of an antisodomy law on the books. The majority of these applied to straights as well. But historian Marc Stein has remarked that the statutes, even if rarely enforced, had a shadow effect, 'often used to legitimate sexual discrimination.' The implications could be far-reaching, encompassing cases such as employment and child custody; a homosexual could be presumed a criminal and therefore *less than*. Men who were arrested could be expected to keep their heads down and cough up the fine for fear of public exposure.

If the prohibition of homo sodomy was rarely enforced in Texas, legal commentator Dale Carpenter has observed, that 'did not reflect sympathy for gay people, but instead the suspicion that gay men would relish the opportunity to spend time in an all-male prison.' In *Flagrant Conduct,* his expansive study of *Lawrence v. Texas,* Carpenter blows open the case. While it might persist in the popular imagination as a love story, Carpenter reveals that the circumstances actually comprise 'a snarled human story' that was subsequently whittled down to 'a pristine legal argument.'

At the center of the tangle, Carpenter describes an ordinary, if a little seedy, night in September 1998. John Lawrence, a fifty-five-year-old medical technologist, found himself casually hosting at his modest apartment in a sprawling area east of central Houston ringed by freeways and crossed by a bayou. John's lover was out of town. A pair of needy acquaintances, Tyron Garner and his on-and-off boyfriend Robert Eubanks, were over. John had offered to give the two, who sometimes did odd jobs for him, some old furniture. Tyron and Robert, respectively thirty-one and forty, were planning to move in together, which would mark Tyron's first residence that wasn't couch surfing or his family home. They spent the day cleaning, handing over the bulkiest items to a moving company and corralling the rest into the spare bedroom with the plan of packing it into a rental van the next day. The three men unwound at the local branch of Pappasito's Tex-Mex, then returned to John's around nine.

They were not poster boys. When their case rose to national prominence, they would be, to varying degrees, hidden by bigwig gay rights attorneys. That way, the human face on the argument could be imagined, which was likely to be a far cry from the reality. John, a hangdog ex-navy man with a bad habit of drunk driving—convicted in 1967 of 'murder by automobile'—was considered the most presentable of the bunch. Tyron was a poor, softly spoken Black man with, Carpenter observed, 'a slightly bent, hand-on-hips way of standing.' He'd also been arrested for driving intoxicated, as well as pot possession and assaulting an officer. In 1995 he was charged with assaulting Robert, by most accounts the real wild card, a volatile heavy drinker with a job history as uneven and gappy as his teeth.

Robert, who'd been swilling vodka straight that night, went downstairs some time between ten and eleven, supposedly to get a soda from a vending machine. Riled up under the impression that his host was flirting with his boyfriend, he instead phoned the police to report, according to Dale Carpenter's interviews, 'a Black male going crazy with a gun.' Or something along those lines; it wouldn't have been out of character for him to use a far less civilized descriptor, even about his own lover. It seems that with whatever scant presence of mind he retained, Robert figured he could teach Tyron a lesson, fully aware that in this downtrodden, heavily policed jurisdiction, the cop who arrived at the scene could be inclined to racial profiling. In the end, the only incontrovertible arrest that night would be his own, for making a false report.

In response to Robert's bogus claim, four Harris County deputies entered John's apartment in close-stack formation. At the front was a big bald white guy, Joseph Quinn. When Carpenter looked into Quinn's professional profile, he pieced together the picture of a temperamental man known for antics like hauling moms off in cuffs for conducting their school run in a no-parking zone. But Quinn was a little unsure about what to do with the men he found in the apartment. There turned out to be no guns involved, unless you count those wielded by himself and the cops behind him.

According to their own version of events, John was in his underwear, getting ready to hit the hay, while Tyron hung around waiting for his asshole boyfriend to return. Some other guy had shown up and was in the kitchen chatting on the phone; he wouldn't be detained long by the police.

But Quinn claimed he entered the bedroom to find John and Tyron in the midst of doggy-style anal sex, which they continued for, as he said to Carpenter, 'well in excess of a minute' while he and a second policeman, William Lilly, ordered them to cease. Lilly was the only other deputy to report witnessing any sex at all, and later reckoned it was oral. 'I actually saw penis in mouth, way up,' he averred.

The statements are not only contradictory but pretty preposterous on their own. Carpenter lays out how if the two police officers were to be believed, John and Tyron got down to penetration (either anal or oral) within minutes—despite the knowledge that an unhinged, jealous drunkard was due back right away—and kept going while a group of policemen announced themselves loudly, approached with guns drawn, then loomed above, demanding they disengage.

Is it possible that Quinn and Lilly embellished to establish cause for arrest? It was, after all, anal or oral sex (or penetration by an object) that met the criteria for 'deviate sexual intercourse,' which was outlawed in the state under Homosexual Conduct. I guess it wouldn't have been so clear-cut to charge John and Tyron for frotting, fondling, huffing pits, French kissing, face-sitting, sock-sniffing or cuddling, let alone merely hanging out in the same apartment.

If they were indeed not giving an accurate picture, did the deputies deliberately manufacture the story, or had they experienced hallucinations brought on by the febrile experience of being in the presence of gay men? The possibility looms that the deputies were simply triggered by the sight of John's porn stash and, on the wall facing his bed, two pencil sketches depicting James Dean naked with a humongous erection. Deputy Quinn described it to Carpenter as 'extremely oversized.' Apparently farcical banter ensued among the cops regarding the likeness of the actor's face. John Lawrence reckoned to Carpenter that it was only after the cops clocked the James Deans that they 'became agitated and called him a "fuckin' fag."' Meaning it's possible that the two men were essentially arrested for John's homoerotic home decor. Deputy Lilly went on to provide an interviewer with the vaguest of circumstantial evidence—a permeating anal odor: 'That whole apartment smelled of gay.'

Whether actual or fabricated, Quinn wasn't initially sure it was a crime: Could the two men be arrested for a consensual act inside a private home? He phoned an assistant DA, who went through the books and found the state's Homosexual Conduct Law. It made no mention of where the offense took place. Quinn proceeded with the arrests. It probably didn't help that John was irately hurling epithets like 'Gestapo.' Like Michael Hardwick before him, it may be that John was ultimately punished for being uppity. Carpenter describes him being dragged out of his place in only underpants, his skin scraping across concrete as neighbors looked on. Tyron remained quietly cooperative, but still managed to offend Quinn—the deputy described him to Carpenter as 'a naggy little bitch, kind of, you know, "nyah, nyah, nyah."'

Consistent with their story, John and Tyron initially pled not guilty. But then word spread. Carpenter, who spent several years interviewing seemingly everyone involved, has reconstructed this trail of gossip. First, a pair of burly, closeted county employees (a file clerk and a sergeant), alarmed by the charges, confided in each other and then, decompressing in a gay bar, unburdened to a bartender involved in local gay causes. He, as one does, got on the phone with a sagacious bear with a long history of activism and next with a lesbian city councilwoman (who'd go on to become mayor of Houston). Finally he called a local gay attorney, who in turn brought the situation to Lambda Legal on the East Coast. The grapevine had an urgent pulse running through it: Could this be the chance to finally overturn *Bowers* at the Supreme Court?

The two woeful defendants would have to be persuaded to change their plea to no contest as well as waive their right to a trial. John and Tyron seemed to go along with it with a *why-not* shrug, even though John kept insisting to everyone that they hadn't actually been having sex. It seemed that, as lawyer and journalist Dahlia Lithwick summed up Dale Carpenter's findings in *The New Yorker,* John and Tyron 'understood that they were being asked to keep the dirty secret that there was no dirty secret.'

Two weeks later, at their court arraignment, the justice of

the peace fined each of the men a hundred dollars plus court fees. That happened to be exactly one cent below the minimum amount that would qualify them to launch an appeal. So the defense attorney made the unusual move of requesting a higher penalty. The magistrate agreed—just one in a series of nudges and winks seemingly indicating that some state officials were aware of, even sympathetic to, the motive for keeping the case in the court system.

In June 2000 a Texas appeals panel decided 2–1 that the sodomy law was unconstitutional because it violated the state's Equal Rights Amendment, but the decision was reversed by the Fourteenth Court of Appeals in a 7–2 vote. This provided Lambda the chance to send the case to SCOTUS, where it was granted certiorari; that is, accepted for hearing.

In the oral argument in Washington, DC, on the 26th of March 2003, Charles A. Rosenthal Jr., the drawling lawyer from the Harris County DA's office burdened with representing the state of Texas, appeared out of his depth. 'I beg your pardon?' he asked when confused. 'Yessir,' he muttered when chastened.

Rosenthal was considerably outmatched by a battalion of elite lesbian legal minds and enthusiastic interns. The Lawrence team created a narrative of dignity. Their brief barely mentioned anal sex, whereas Carpenter counts sixty uses of the terms *intimate* or *intimacy* and seventy instances of *private* or *privacy*. As Carpenter put it, 'The sex in the *Lawrence* brief was "clothed."'

The fact that John and Tyron were in fact merely acquaintances, each with a boyfriend, was not made known to the justices, who received only the most cursory information about the arrest and those involved. The justices would not have known about Robert, the sketchy third man—let alone that as the case wove its way, he accused Tyron of assault once again. Robert was dead by the time the case got to SCOTUS. The justices would not have known that there might not have been any anal or oral penetration at all, just the James Dean erotica and an unpleasant aroma.

What they did see before them was Paul Smith, a Yale-educated redhead from Salt Lake City representing the Lawrence side in oral argument. Ensconced, institutional, the litigator was nearly perfectly cast. He did not look like a second-class citizen or behave like an activist. He was gay but, as Carpenter describes the necessary requirement, 'not *too* gay.' Smith politely reasoned that a law only pertaining to a certain classification of people amounted to 'mere disapproval or hostility.' Smith had been yet another of the clerks working for Lewis Powell, the justice who infamously switched his vote in *Bowers* and seemed forever ignorant of the numerous homosexuals around him. Considering that historical misstep, the sure-footed Smith was highly motivated to get this right.

Meanwhile, the squirming lawyer from Texas struggled to articulate a coherent argument, or even find one. 'So what is the justification for this statute?' Justice Stephen G. Breyer asked with some mix of bemusement and exasperation. If immorality was all Rosenthal had, Breyer asked, 'What about the statute which this Court I think once had to grapple with: People felt during World War I that it was immoral to teach German in the public schools. So then would you say that the State has every right to do that, parents want their children to learn German, but the schools forbid it? See, the hard question here is can the State, in fact, pass anything it wants at all, because they believe it's immoral. If you were going to draw the line somewhere, I guess you might begin to draw it when the person is involved inside his own bedroom and not hurting anybody else.'

On the 26th of June 2003, in humid Washington, DC, sometime before Mom's birthday toast—doubling as "the engagement party" for you and my sister—SCOTUS announced its *Lawrence* opinion. Happy birthday! Sodomy wins! It wouldn't be an association Mom bragged about—she'd save that for *Obergefell*, the gay marriage decision announced on the same date in 2015, one of four gay rights victories issued by the Supreme Court on her birthday.

The majority opinion was authored by Anthony Kennedy, the very same who thwarted Richard Adams and Tony Sullivan's long legal struggle against separation. In his public announcement, Kennedy stated that *Bowers* was now overruled: 'not correct when it was decided and it is not correct today.' He averred, 'It is the promise of the Constitution that there is a realm of personal liberty which the government may not enter.'

Dissenting justice Antonin Scalia took the microphone to speak up for the democratic rights of those 'protecting themselves and their families against a lifestyle they believe to be immoral and destructive.' While the opinion claimed it made no move toward gay marriage, Scalia warned, 'Do not believe it. Today's opinion dismantles the structure of constitutional law that has permitted a distinction to be made between heterosexual and homosexual unions.'

By omitting the many unsavory and odd details of the *Lawrence* case, the Lambda legal team successfully provided a blank canvas onto which justices could sentimentally paint their own image of a committed couple. In his opinion, Kennedy affirms sexuality with strings attached: 'The conduct can be but one element in a personal bond that is more enduring.' His opinion uses the word *relationship* eleven times.

In this way, *Lawrence* rebranded two fuckups who didn't necessarily mean a whole lot to each other as an ideal couple. Ironically, years before, Kennedy had been given the chance to help protect an actual pair of lovebirds—Richard and Tony—but didn't.

The *Lawrence* opinion opens: 'Liberty protects the person from unwarranted government intrusion into a dwelling or other private places.' Kennedy and his concurring justices decided the disputed laws 'have more far-reaching consequences, touching upon the most private human conduct, sexual behavior, and in the most private of places, the home.'

Because of the emphasis on privacy, historian Stephen A. Allen complained, 'This is actually a step backward for the Supreme Court.' Legal scholar Katherine Franke wrote that in the opinion, liberty is domesticated, 'not the synonym of a robust liberal concept of freedom.' It encloses rights in a private home, based on values she tentatively termed 'domestinormative.' She intuitively called out the court for taking it 'as given' that John and Tyron were in a relationship: 'Did they even know each other's name . . . ?'

Marc Stein notes how just prior to the *Lawrence* decision, North Dakota politicians voted not to repeal a law, on the books since its statehood was established in 1889, that criminalized unmarried couples living together 'openly and notoriously.' A clutch of states would continue to outlaw shacked-up unwed lovers for years after *Lawrence*. Michigan kept a 1931 law against 'lewd and lascivious cohabitation' on the books until 2023, and as I write these words, the act still falls under Crimes against Public Morals and Decency in Mississippi. (Also by my time of writing, Texas has never managed to take the Homosexual Conduct Law off its books, though the words 'declared unconstitutional' have been added, one might suspect begrudgingly.)

Stein has described how queer scholars found that 'Kennedy's opinion portrayed the individual who engaged in sex with another person as aspiring to respect and dignity, not as engaging in physical exercise, enjoying libido and lust, exploring shame and debasement, experiencing power and powerlessness, or experimenting with transgression and subversion.'

Having painstakingly documented *Lawrence,* Dale Carpenter arrived at a position that might be called realpolitik: 'From the beginning, *Lawrence* was about more than constitutional theories and doctrines. It was about lives.' Carpenter became not only an authority on the case but the narrator of a rebel tale: 'We have the law, deformed by ignorance, pressing into the lives of marginalized people,' he wrote near the start of his book. 'We have resistance, generated not by abstractions but by experience.'

ANY TIME QUITE SO many queers file into the chambers of the Supreme Court, opportunities present themselves for moments of high camp.

At one point during *Lawrence*, Justice Scalia attempted to describe anal sex as a social whim rather than a right worthy of constitutional protection—by comparing it with pole sitting, a craze from the 1920s that entailed, exactly as it sounds, perching atop a flagpole or other post. Was Scalia being snarky, or just clueless? 'Suppose all the States had laws against flagpole sitting at one time,' Scalia hypothesized. In his premise, people were annoyed and passed laws against the act, then got used to it eventually, and so repealed their prohibitions. And yet, he pressed: 'Does that make flagpole sitting a fundamental right?'

In another instance, Justice Breyer demanded of the floundering Texas lawyer Rosenthal that he give 'your *straight answer* to these points.' The crowd broke into laughter, and eventually Breyer seemed to get it—with a helpful whisper from Clarence Thomas, Dale Carpenter notes.

It was, Carpenter writes, 'as close as one could get in the august confines of the Supreme Court to the combination of sophistication and humor one might encounter at a screening of *All About Eve* to a gay audience at the Castro Theater in San Francisco.'

In a kind of reverse ritual, in the Castro district on the day the *Lawrence* opinion was announced, the rainbow flag that normally flies above Harvey Milk Plaza was swapped out for the Old Glory. A crowd gathered there—the go-to meeting point whenever some big gay thing happens. The San Francisco Gay Men's Chorus led a rendition of the national anthem.

It was all a little obedient. How quickly we become docile, switching from indignation to allegiance. How about someone sitting on the flagpole? Climbing up naked to be fisted by the mast? That's more in the spirit of the San Francisco I'd come to know.

But who were we to pass judgment on respectability politics and the private family unit? We were up the street with my parents at Eric's restaurant, feasting on Buddha's Delight and kung pao prawns, pleasantly making plans for your wedding to my sister.

14
WATERFALLS

The day after the *Lawrence* decision was announced, Deb Price and Joyce Murdoch got hitched in Toronto, Canada. Same-sex marriage had been legalized throughout the province of Ontario less than three weeks before. Murdoch noted that it was 'the first place on the planet that non-resident American gay couples could marry.'

The two journalists met in 1985 when they both worked for the *Washington Post*. They had previously registered a civil union in Vermont, and before that a 'legally meaningless but important nevertheless' partnership in Takoma Park, Maryland.

Deb Price is known as the first nationally syndicated lesbian columnist, a chronicler of domesticity who believed that sharing aspects of her personal life was political. For example: 'We watch our siblings get eight silver trays, 12 pickle forks, a fondue pot and a trip to Hawaii for settling down. And then our relatives give us a hard time or nothing at all.'

I can only imagine that the couple welcomed the opinion in *Lawrence*, but also that the timing must have burned. They had published their book *Courting Justice: Gay Men and Lesbians v. the Supreme Court* the year before; the landmark decision came just a little too late to be included.

But that's the thing with nonfiction. There will always be omissions, including what happens later.

A COUPLE MONTHS EARLIER, on the 12th of April 2003, Clive Boutilier passed away at the age of sixty-nine in a rest home in Welland, a city in Ontario not far from Niagara Falls. Clive was the hazel-eyed Canadian who was removed from the United States in 1968 on the basis of his "psychopathic personality." He'd left the country a very different person, having been struck by a vehicle days before the opinion was issued in the Supreme Court case that bore his name and made him—or some version of him—into history.

In what appears to be an anomaly, Joyce Murdoch was able to speak, albeit briefly, with Clive. The phone call took place a few years back, when she was coauthoring *Courting Justice*. By then, Clive was already residing in the Welland facility. He spoke 'haltingly,' she observed in the book, and what information she gleaned was in small, broken pieces. His feelings on the case: "No comment!"

Meanwhile, historian Marc Stein was developing an unequaled devotion to the *Boutilier* case. An academic whose appointments led him across the border to Canada from the States, Stein was himself subject to an FBI check, which thankfully did not turn up any breach of antediluvian laws against cohabitation or sodomy, nor his act of civil disobedience in peacefully marching on the Supreme Court in the wake of the asinine *Bowers v. Hardwick* decision. Then Canadian immigration authorities required he take an HIV/AIDS test as a part of his permanent residency application, Stein suspects because he disclosed involvement with advocacy groups. 'For these and many other reasons,' Stein wrote in the preface to his book *Sexual Injustice*, he 'was profoundly moved' by Clive's challenges and 'the related stories of thousands of people excluded unjustly from the United States.'

Despite his investigative zeal, Stein was never able to make contact with Clive himself. 'Deported from US territorial space,' Stein muses, 'he was also deported from US collective memory.' But Stein has been valiant in preserving what tatters remain. He dug up scraps of information about Clive's accident in an old newsletter of the Mattachine Society, the gay rights organization, from December 1968. Stein read:

> According to a reliable source, he walked in front of a bus (whether attempted suicide or accident we don't know) and was hospitalized for three months. He's out now, collected a large settlement from an insurance company and is living back in Canada with his mother in a brand new house.

Through records accessed via Freedom of Information Act requests, Stein then assembled a far more troubling and far less resolved chain of events.

After being struck by the bus—or car, other sources maintain—Clive was in a coma for at least three weeks. Meaning that when the Supreme Court ruled against him in May 1967, he was in critical condition. In July the INS wrote to Clive. Their office had already informed the Royal Canadian Mounted Police about his imminent deportation. But Clive was, said his doctor, 'barely able to speak and was not oriented as to time and space.'

In the autumn, the INS sought an update. A medical report diagnosed Clive as suffering memory loss, confusion and 'paranoid ideation concerning his parents.' He could be 'explosive, suddenly showing a hostile attitude without apparent provocation.' His condition was characterized as 'post-traumatic psychosis.' In an irony upon irony, not only does it seem that the case over whether Clive could be classified as psychopathic led him to this actual state of psychosis, the condition was now being given as the reason to delay his deportation.

Clive was finally deported about a year later, in November 1968. His mother and stepfather accompanied him to Canada because he required full-time care. His little brother Andrew appears to have gone to Canada, too, and died there in 1969. Clive told Joyce Murdoch that he was aware that his roommate Eugene had also passed away, but nobody has ever come forward with more details, and it remains unknown to what extent the two kept in touch. Stein has tried, but Eugene O'Rourke is just too common a name to get anywhere.

Murdoch explained to Stein that once she finally got in touch with Clive, he was in no condition to be properly interviewed. He appeared to be severely debilitated, and pushing him 'would have been taking unfair advantage.' Murdoch relayed that Clive had come to consider disclosing his sexuality a mistake, but that was in regard to his earlier statement to the US military rather than the citizenship application that led to his deportation. What's more, did he mean his mistake was his self-understanding, or his willingness to go on the record?

After Murdoch's brief interview with Clive, any further contact of the sort was forbidden by his mother. Stein located Clive's niece through a genealogical website. There wasn't much she could do to facilitate an interview through Clive's mother, her grandmother. The niece believed that she 'drummed it into his head' that their experiences were 'never to be brought into the light of day ever again.'

Clive's niece wasn't familiar with many of the details of the case, but she expressed a sensitive curiosity about her family history. She emailed back to Stein that she'd ascertained that when

Clive was tragically struck in traffic, the person behind the wheel happened to be a customs officer.

In the 1990s, after his mother was no longer capable of providing care, Clive was moved into the group home. He looked drunk when he walked, his niece explained, but managed to get dressed on his own. He once said of a young gay man in the family, 'He has the problem too, doesn't he?'

After his yearslong devotion to the case, Stein has been left to wonder if he'd have been able to uncover more dimensions if he'd been able to reach Clive—to sit with him in person, perhaps, rather than by phone. But Clive's mother's moratorium on interviews was likely insurmountable; anyway, his niece said, 'Clive tells her everything.'

I am left with questions that overlap with those that have plagued Stein for years. How at ease was Clive in his sexual life as a youth in Canada? What did Eugene mean to him, exactly? Did Clive have any connection to gay social scenes? Did he intend to be hit by a car? Was it true he collected a payout? Some, Stein relays, have the impression that Clive developed a relationship with a woman through his final period at the home. And his mother—was she driven by protectiveness, riddled with shame? Tyrannical, or merely cautious? Did Clive experience any happiness whatsoever in the three and a half decades between his deportation and death?

A conscientious historian, Stein is mindful not to project current-day terminology and context onto Clive's experiences. He acknowledges 'the complicated connections and disconnections between Boutilier's world and ours.' In his essay "Crossing the Border to Memory: In Search of Clive Michael Boutilier (1933–2003)," Stein wrote that 'memorializing queers' is one thing, as in paying homage to past figures identified as such, whereas 'the notion of queering remembrance more usefully refers to the process of remembering in queer ways.'

I suppose the act of *queering remembrance* could have myriad manifestations. To allow in some degree of speculation to fill gaps; or, alternatively, to just let those gaps—what Gary Ferguson, writing of the executed men of the Latin Gate, called the 'many holes'—be. To think prismatically—always bearing in mind that a given civil rights concern is not isolated but intersectional, with implications that affect those apart from a singular identity group. To consider the role of passivity in social change. To refrain from judgment and assumptions. To accept love as a nuanced, expansive, unquantifiable thing. In this way, for instance, it's not just that the potential revelation of a commitment to Eugene should have justified Clive's right to remain, but rather that the mechanisms that validate interpersonal relationships, govern sexual identity and decree citizenship could be reassessed altogether. Clive did not deliberately set out to challenge the status quo; rather, his very existence, his complex choices, bring into question legal and ethical standards so often taken to be self-evident.

You and I, to be frank, weren't actively *queering* much. We took authority for granted. Saw systems as just the way things are. We were focused on the loopholes and the workarounds.

Clive lived for many years after being struck down by both a vehicle and the Supreme Court. He was worn down by too much attention and categorized according to other people's frameworks. We inherit Clive's disappointments and stress. That, too, is a queerness that needs to be known. Whenever people talk of queer joy (all the time), I think: Yes, but also the lows.

Clive died at sixty-nine from issues of the heart. His niece informed Stein by email. She never had the chance to speak with him about what he went through, but felt sure he was at peace after such a difficult life. He requested a cremation without fuss. Stein asked about the obituary; there was none.

In Fairview Cemetery, Niagara Falls, Clive's name shares a family headstone with his American stepfather and his mother, Joseph and Mary McKenna. Joseph had died in 1980; Mary outlived Clive by another two years. The headstone is engraved with their three names and dates, and the words:

IF I COULD HAVE LOVED YOU BETTER AND BY DOING SO MADE YOU STAY I WOULD HAVE…

15
A LITTLE COSMOS

Once I figured out I was a vulture, I could really spread my wings. Like when an acquaintance struggled to find the right person to share her open-plan rental, and I swooped in. She was upping sticks to Oakland. I asked her to put forward our interest in taking over the impressive space.

This would be our final residence in the city—the ground floor of a corner house constructed in a local vernacular: residential quarters upstairs from what would have once been a small dry goods store or dairy. We inhabited the former shop, with concrete floors and a recessed double-door entrance. Light came through from both north and west.

Upstairs, Stephanie Greenwalls dwelled in louche bohemian rooms that opened onto an operatic balcony. She was the de facto landlord while the elusive owner whiled away his advanced years "on safari." From our brief interactions at Video Hut, I pegged Stephanie as the kind of ass-kicker who would plow down a jaywalker and complain about the song playing on the radio. But

I came to know that she would also take that pedestrian in and nurse them back to health. She dotted her politics around the property in decoupage and gold leaf. *No More War. Free Tibet.*

Stephanie had spiky hair and wore spike heels. Her one stipulation: *You can't complain that I strut in stilettos around the house.* She struck me as a cross between 'Mother of Us All' Mrs. Madrigal from *Tales of the City* and Sigourney Weaver after being possessed by Zuul in *Ghostbusters*. Wrapped in a Fendi shawl, dripping with Peruvian jewelry, taut and blunt, she told us we could do whatever we wished downstairs, which she probably regretted as you proceeded to paint the place like a psychedelic preschool.

You did one wall in cerulean blue that rounded the corner and then broke up into a flock of birds. A red column dissolved into bugs scattering across the cement floor. The former chimney breast was filled with the profile of an elephant, to which I added the text *l'éléphant* to appeal to Stephanie's francophile sensibilities. She would periodically poke her head in and grimace, disappointed we hadn't turned out to be a better class of gay.

I painted the kitchen butter yellow and the bathroom Jamaica green. The cats came and went through the window over the toilet, which was on the level of a small, lovely garden, lit after dark by Moroccan lanterns. The sharklike face of Marie Antoinette, Stephanie's bull terrier, would snout into the bathroom. Marie Antoinette meant no harm, but her lurking struck fear into Clementine and Isabel, karmic retribution for all their terrorizing of Leonora the cockatoo.

At the rear was our wood-paneled bedroom, then a storage space that, after a single peer into the blackness and whiff of mold, I could never bring myself to enter again. The main room and kitchen were arranged in a capacious L shape, the inside corner of which had been fitted with a partition wall by a former tenant. In the resulting nook, another past renter had constructed a loft bed. A place for guests with whom we weren't currently having sex.

You despaired at the awkwardness of a bulky cabinet drilled randomly into the middle of the longest wall, so began connecting planks of pine in order to integrate it into a larger shelving system. When you raised yourself up, absorbed in your work, an open cabinet door gashed your forehead. It wouldn't stop bleeding. A group strolled by and peeked in, which was the norm when the front doors were left open; the place looked like it could be a junk shop or lowbrow gallery.

Does anyone know what to do? I begged, pointing at the blood-saturated paper towel you held to your forehead.

I think you should take yourself to the hospital, said one of the women, who told us she was a nurse.

What would a normal person do—*a real person?* Our first thought every time something like this happened: What about the forms? Having no Social Security number? We were convinced a small cut could lead to you being found out and deported. I was overcome with dread while waiting in the emergency room, not about the injury but whether the administrative nurse was in there asking about your immigration status.

The last time we'd been in such a panic, we'd been drinking beer in front of a "street art" exhibition opening in the Lower Haight. The small gallery was full of cartoonish paintings; we were distracted by the jostling saggers. The drinks had run out, so we procured some cans from a corner store. Two cops pulled up and taunted us with the possibilities of issuing a ticket. *We could cite you for public drinking,* one said. *And we could also get you for jaywalking.* I'd forgotten the paper bag rule. I was usually so strict with you about the law against openly drinking alcohol, which you found inconceivable: we'd have a picnic in the park, but your libation had to be concealed from view. *How uncivilized,* you'd tut. But in that moment you did not speak, lest the cops pick up on the incriminating accent. Eventually a few Black boys cycling on the sidewalk took their attention away.

It turns out that going to the hospital was indeed a mistake, only because we were guileless enough to walk into an emergency room uninsured. Your forehead was stapled back together. We followed the instruction to return the following week and have the staples removed. That meant a second instance of crossing the emergency room threshold. We were now out thousands of dollars.

I was regaling a new part-timer at Video Hut with this tale, or the one about being caught with beer on the street. I sat cross-legged on the floor, stickering the week's delivery of DVDs. A regular customer, a beloved civic employee, absent-mindedly joined in. *You'll probably be all right,* he said, leching over the cover of *Ten Things I Hate About You.* Then he said something that sounded monumentally important. I shot up from the floor.

Wait! Can you repeat what you just said?

He raised his eyes from Heath Ledger's tight T-shirt. *That's the law here,* he shrugged. *I wouldn't worry too much in a hospital, or even a police station. We live in a City of Refuge.*

In 1985, San Francisco had declared itself a City of Refuge to protect asylum seekers from El Salvador and Guatemala; in 1989 voters passed the Sanctuary City Ordinance, which extended to all immigrants, prohibiting the use of municipal funds and resources to enforce federal immigration laws. Berkeley had been the first US city to enact sanctuary legislation when it did so in 1971. In May 2002, amid the the post-9/11 "war on terror," the San Francisco Board of Supervisors passed a resolution reaffirming its status as a City and County of Refuge as well as an "INS Raid-Free Zone." Such places have generally come to be called sanctuary cities.

There is no precise legal definition of a sanctuary city, but in one form or another over the following decades, there would come to be over five hundred sanctuary jurisdictions in the United States, including municipalities, counties, and whole states. These can be places in which undocumented people are able to report crimes (or commit a misdemeanor themselves), utilize health services and enroll their children in school with less fear of being forced to disclose their residency status.

The 1996 Illegal Immigration Reform and Immigrant Responsibility Act (IIRIRA) outlawed citywide bans on reporting undocumented denizens to federal authorities. So some cities enacted laws that prohibited public officials from *inquiring* about immigration status in the first place. One rationale for sanctuary legislation is that if undocumented residents are not keeping healthy and safe through civic services, everyone around them is worse off.

The religious intimation of the word *sanctuary* is not incidental. Berkeley's initial legislation followed on from actions taken by the local Universal Lutheran Chapel to protect conscientious objectors. In the Southwest in the 1980s, it was faith-based groups that organized to assist asylum seekers from Central America.

The Hebrew Bible describes the provision of six cities of refuge, three on each side of the Jordan River. These were sites of asylum for those who committed accidental manslaughter, as they were elsewhere vulnerable to blood vengeance by a clan member of the dead.

According to the Talmud, the roads that led into these cities were double the regulation width, especially smooth and sign-posted REFUGE—all to enable safe arrival. Classical rabbinical scholars have distinguished the cities of refuge as sites of atonement rather than protection. Because God would never allow a human to die at an innocent's hand, the person who somehow committed manslaughter must have previously sinned. Atonement for these past transgressions was only achieved when the local high priest died. If a refugee died first, he should be interred at that site until the priest passed away in order to achieve posthumous atonement.

Scholars have found that ancient territories of asylum, sometimes extending past town boundaries, could become a hotbed of crime. In modern-day America, contrary to common perception, this isn't the case; studies have shown no effect, or in fact lower crime rates and stronger economies, in places that enact sanctuary policies.

I suspected that the common practice of under-the-table employment in San Francisco was another, tacit motivation. Plus, I solipsistically concluded, the policy was also meant to allow cutie-pies like you—for which there was no exact word; a *gaylien,* I guess—to dwell in the city as you wished.

We were warmed by the news; once again, a customer had dropped some intel that seemed otherwise impossible to access.

By then you had been to see two different lawyers. The chic one who said *There is nothing I can do for you now* after you spilled your guts about overstaying. We thought that was the way it worked: one handed over the truth for a lawyer to massage into a lie. Not so. She collected a few hundred dollars in fees, which I kept imagining she put toward a Jil Sander blouse. Then Frank took you to a Joe Pesci type he somehow knew. Sitting in his sordid storefront office with its American flag and framed picture of the pope, you were confident he was more likely to get you deported, or damned, than help you stay.

Learning about the sanctuary law was a weight lifted. But the assurances were precarious, hazy, and also lulled us into a false sense of security, or at least complacency, as with other aspects of life in San Francisco. Our routes to denial, our routines: the weekly shops at Rainbow Groceries, the scrambled eggs with sweet corn at Chloe's Cafe, the late-night pasta in some nameless cabaret, the jukeboxes, the neon signs of dive bars that promised refuge within refuge.

You did not go through with marrying Jenny, who'd begun to move around a lot according to her studies and professional commitments. Instead we'd just settled into a fiction, hoping the wrong person would not open it up and read the pages.

Having something to protect, we were prone to take cover. Michael Warner has written that 'the notion of pure love' associated with the push for legal marriage is 'an image of sentimental privacy.' He argued 'that a politics based on such a sentimental rhetoric of privacy is not only a false idealization of love and coupling; it is an increasingly powerful way of distracting citizens from the real, conflicted, and unequal conditions governing their lives, and one that reinforces the privilege of those who already find it easiest to imagine their lives as private.'

Like other aspects of San Francisco, the City of Refuge thing sounded a little flaky to us. We didn't quite trust that you'd be fine if, for instance, you were arrested in a protest. We did attend a march against the war on Iraq. But the more anarchic participants—the skinny youngsters in balaclavas—made such action seem a little too risky. We could end up kettled. Like how our pal Naya was arrested at a demonstration when she thought she'd just drunkenly joined a parade. (She wound up spending the night in jail, and phoned me the next day to let me know she was pretty sure she was now a lesbian.)

The next time an antiwar protest was announced, we couldn't bear to put you in harm's way. Instead we rode our bikes through the aftermath, tooling around the discarded placards and other debris of public life, attempting proximity to the action but utterly failing to contribute to the collective political statement.

Some of the young protesters were a part of Gay Shame, which agitated against same-sex (or any) marriage. We were ashamed we couldn't take that position. We were too desperate. Neither could we campaign *for* same-sex marriage for risk of exposure. Anyway, although I didn't know anyone who would have benefited more from accessing the same rights as a straight married couple, it never felt like our cause. I'd always thought any cause worth fighting for must be about someone else.

So we'd become *idiots*—in the archaic sense that Hannah Arendt wrote about, meaning away from public life. To be private, Arendt postulated, is to be deprived. With simply too much to lose, we kept our heads down. Yours was a disobedient but subjugated body. Previously we had followed the law and, separated from each other, relied on imaginary world-building. After you took the step that allowed you to be with me for real, we separated ourselves from the world. These were our *apart-ment* years—as in the condition of being apart, when we were together but closed off from the rest.

YOU WERE WORKING THE day when, making the rounds in his 2003 mayoral campaign, Gavin Newsom greeted local residents in front of Video Hut. With lacquered hair and waxwork features, Newsom carried himself as though he were running not just for mayor but for president of the United States. His hand freaked you out. It seemed robotic or frozen. You did not shake it, though you stood nearby. As usual, you did not come forward or speak. A couple of trailing photographers took shots that made the Democratic candidate appear admired by all those he encountered.

Newsom was too slick, too pedigreed. We despaired at the ways in which he steered the city in dealing with its unhoused population. As a city supervisor, he'd just gotten through a proposition euphemistically nicknamed Care Not Cash, in which funds once paid out directly to those on the streets would be diverted to subsidize landlords, theoretically for use in providing shelter.

We were supporting Green Party candidate Matt Gonzalez, whose screen-printed campaign posters looked like rock-and-roll handbills.

I have to say, though, his schlumpy suits, complained Frank when he agreed to let us put a MATT sign in the window. Having come to better know his customer base, Frank had buried his historical Republicanism.

Top brass in the Democratic Party—Clinton, Gore, Feinstein, Pelosi, and so on—all came out in support of Newsom, sensing that a Green Party victory had the potential of an irrevocable shift away from their embedded centrism. Newsom took a commanding lead in the primary, garnering over twice as many votes as Gonzalez, who came in second. But because Newsom hadn't won an outright majority, there would be a runoff between the two. Because Gonzalez was such an underdog, for a brief period it was all very groovy and exciting. Supporters of other first-round contenders rallied behind the Green upsetter. We were hopeful this coalition might just manage a swing left. In the end, Gonzalez lost, but only by a little more than five percent. We took it personally. In a city that basically operated on a left-to-center spectrum, Newsom was more foe than friend. We didn't *want* a mayor that looked like the president of the United States.

I bet Frank did vote for Newsom—he loved that tidy look; he was always telling us we should groom our beards at the neck. In turn, maybe Newsom felt he owed his victory to gays like Frank. Not much more than a month after he moved into the mayor's office in early 2004, in probably the most casual yet revolutionary act on the road to same-sex marriage, Newsom authorized City Hall to begin issuing licenses to gay and lesbian couples.

It was two days before Valentine's Day and four days before your twenty-eighth birthday. Was this our moment? We held back. What were the repercussions of all this? We'd been looking for our in but were unconvinced by one quite so unprecedented. It'd be exchanging vows on shaky ground.

Newsom stated that he was inspired by the State of the Union address in January, when President Bush stopped short of endorsing a constitutional ban on same-sex marriages: 'If judges insist on forcing their arbitrary will upon the people, the only alternative left to the people would be the constitutional process.'

This was a reaction to recent state advances like how the Massachusetts Supreme Judicial Court declared it unconstitutional to deny marriage to same-sex couples. The first legal lesbian marriage would be performed in Cambridge, Massachusetts, at 9:15 in the morning on the 17th of May, followed by hundreds more. Not to be outdone, Newsom eclipsed all states and cities in spectacular fashion.

San Francisco City Hall squealed with excitement. Shoes squeaked and click-clacked through the newly renovated marble lobby. One local documentarian interviewed a mature Asian man who'd served as a state-appointed deputy marriage commissioner for five years. He'd married some thirty couples so far on the day. 'Many happy couples,' he beamed. And not just gay, the man with the camera interjected. 'No,' the deputy concurred. 'Well, we do boy and girl marriage, we do two girls, and we do two boys.' He rang out, 'Come to San Francisco and get married!'

Perhaps the most joyful-looking queue in the history of municipal bureaucracy snaked through the building, though fatigue was setting in. Over two hundred volunteers were being quickly trained to handle the flood of couples. Flights were booked by gays and lesbians around the country. Comedian Rosie O'Donnell and her partner got their ticket.

State Assembly member Mark Leno pointed to the news story of a recently released serial rapist who was about to wed a female pen pal he had yet to meet in person. 'And to think that that is legal in the eyes of George Bush, but that two eighty-year-old women who've been living together as domestic partners for fifty-one years is an illegal act... So this makes no sense. What's going on here today at City Hall makes great sense, and makes great sense of the heart as well.'

Leno would have been referring to the first same-sex couple to be solemnized, Del Martin and Phyllis Lyon, respectively eighty-three and seventy-nine years old. Del and Phyllis first met in 1950 and moved in together on Valentine's Day three years later. (Phyllis: 'We really only had problems our first year together. Del would leave her shoes in the middle of the room, and I'd throw them out the window.' Del: 'You'd have an argument with me and try to storm out the door. I had to teach you to fight back.')

The two went on to cofound the Daughters of Bilitis, the first lesbian political organization in the country, which eventually counted some two hundred chapters. Del and Phyllis were active in groups including the Council on Religion and the Homosexual at Glide Memorial Church, the Alice B. Toklas Democratic Club and Old Lesbians Organizing for Change. The *Washington Post* described them as the bride who wore lavender and the bride carrying a gold-chained purse. Though they'd never been particularly motivated to enter into the institution of marriage, when Newsom invited them to be the first, the *Post* reported, 'the couple understood perfectly their role as chess pieces in a larger strategy.'

On the morning of the 12th of February, they were wed by the city's assessor-recorder Mabel Teng, using the first of the revised licenses that city staff members had worked through the night scrubbing of references to *husband* and *wife*. Those gathered were crying. Teng briefly mixed up the names of the spouses-to-be, and the goof lightened the mood. They were pronounced 'spouses for life.'

Ninety-five same-sex marriage licenses were issued that first day, with estimates in the hundreds the next. Ten of Teng's staff members were deputized as marriage commissioners to help cope with the influx.

ON THE 24TH OF February, Bush held a press conference in which he ramped up the call to go further than the Defense of Marriage Act and 'protect the institution of marriage' in the US Constitution. Bush disparaged the 'activist judges and local officials' who, despite overwhelming public opinion to the contrary, had recently 'made an aggressive attempt to redefine marriage,' referring to Massachusetts and San Francisco as well as a half day of same-sex marriages in Sandoval County, New Mexico.

Proclaiming that the time had come to take decisive action, Bush called on Congress to pass the Federal Marriage Amendment and promptly deliver it to the states for ratification. (The most recent of the twenty-seven amendments to the US Constitution, which concerns congressional salary, was ratified in 1992, having been originally introduced in 1789 alongside those that came to be known as the Bill of Rights.)

'The union of a man and woman is the most enduring human institution, honored and encouraged in all cultures and by every religious faith,' Bush said, delivering his lines like a sixth grader bullshitting a social studies report.

Bush then slowly, haltingly asserted that the freedom of all people and exclusion of some did not amount to a contradiction. He muttered that the debate could play out 'without bitterness or anger,' but instead with 'kindness and goodwill and decency.' He exited robotically.

Is he coming back? reporters asked one another.

Class is over, one sniffed.

Dismissed, said another.

I've never felt so used in my life, said a journalist as he rose. *Except for last week.*

'Within hours,' reported the *Washington Post*, 'the backlash to the backlash begins. A florist arrives with 40 bouquets sent from anonymous supporters across the country. Each card says, "To any gay couple, C/O City Hall, San Francisco, CA."'

A young town mayor in New York began issuing licenses. Commissioners in Multnomah County, Oregon, granted thousands. Chicago's mayor signaled he might do the same. Meanwhile, the vows exchanged in San Francisco were headed to trial through the state court system. 'This was all done to victimize marriage, voters and state law,' said Randy Thomasson, the executive director of Campaign for California Families, one of two conservative organizations filing suit against the mayor.

By the end of February some three and a half thousand same-sex couples had been married in San Francisco, with more people arriving in the wake of Bush's announcement, panicking that the whole thing would be shut down for good.

FRANK ARRANGED FOR ME to go with him to City Hall for a less romantic reason. He was reorganizing the business to give me (so, really, *us*) a small share of the company. We had run the required public announcement in the legal notices of some suburban newspaper with inexpensive rates. We now had to bring the paperwork down to City Hall to get the whole thing registered. There was no sign the crowds there were abating. Should we put it off?

No, no—we have to do this, Frank insisted irritably. He had been a bit of a party-pooper. Was it a Catholic thing? Newsom was Catholic, too, but Frank seemed uncomfortable about the iconoclastic move. Late one weekday morning, he drove me into a parking garage adjacent to City Hall; the weddings were still very much happening.

Frank mostly griped about the traffic jam. His jeremiad was peppered with an occasional *Weee-heee!*, briefly giving in to the celebratory sight of so many rainbow flags.

He was back to peevish as we entered the building.

No, no, he explained to staff members with frozen grins. *We need the Office of the Treasurer. We're here on BUSINESS.*

Frank carried himself purposefully through the atrium, as if he belonged there more than everyone else. This is about real life and real money, he telegraphed with his short-legged stride. This isn't about your fantasy.

As we proceeded, getting turned around once or twice, the sight of the two of us strutting through rather than waiting in line gave people the impression that we had already undergone the rites and were Just Married.

Congratulations! queuing gays and lesbians shouted.

No! Frank snapped.

A reporter with a ridiculously big camera approached for a snapshot of the newlyweds. Frank covered his face like a celebrity ducking paparazzi.

Congratulations! more people rang out.

No! cried Frank, determined to shut this down. *He's my son.*

IN MARCH, GAVIN NEWSOM was on *The Charlie Rose Show*. Yet again, he came across as if he were running for POTUS.

'Y'better believe it—1849,' he said of his Irish-Catholic family's five generations in San Francisco.

'It's got a ninety-six-point rating,' he said of his Napa Valley vineyard, with a fist pump. 'We're proud!'

Newsom revealed that when he ran for mayor, every single one of the twenty-one candidates said they supported gay marriage, but that lack of controversy around the issue also meant that none felt compelled to put forward a plan, let alone one so dramatic.

Rose surmised Newsom's take. 'Civil union is the escape route.'

Newsom made each word its own sentence: 'Separate. But. Unequal.'

He was able to play the role of a rebel uncowed by public opinion. Rose affirmed that the mayor's popularity in a regional poll was at an impressive sixty-nine or seventy percent. Not a single Democratic presidential contender was as gung-ho for gay marriage. 'The end of the day, you can either make a difference or you can make a career,' Newsom preached. He was, of course, doing both.

The youngest mayor of San Francisco in a century and a half, born the year of *Loving v. Virginia*, had made the gay marriage question into a daytime soap. Newsom had pulled one of the most astounding stunts in the history of the debate.

The San Francisco weddings were halted within a month. That summer, the same-sex marriage licenses issued in the state—nearly four thousand of them—were invalidated by California's supreme court. But an underlying constitutional question remained open. Six lawsuits that challenged the cessation would be consolidated into one, known as *In re Marriage Cases.* It would take nearly a decade, but the ensuing legal challenges would go all the way to the Supreme Court. In the meantime, Newsom's shenanigans could cost the Democrats the White House.

CARA, A CUSTOMER WHO reminded me of Rachel from *Friends,* had decided enough was enough. At once matter-of-fact and winsome, she was perpetually in a rush yet prone to lingering. Her lustrous hair was capable of a range of gestures: it paced, playfully shrugged, gave a coy *who me?* Cara was obviously intelligent and a little spaced-out. I could tell from her hands that she was older than she looked; the significant rocks on her simple rings suggested she came from money.

At first, I couldn't get my head around what Cara was suggesting. It seemed far outside my impression of her as bougie and self-contained. But, she said, she had to *do something.* She was inviting us to accompany her to Reno to help get out the vote for John Kerry among registered Democrats on the day of the presidential election. Nevada was a pivotal swing state. An old friend of hers would drive. You and I could sit in the back seat.

I consulted you, and we decided we couldn't any longer duck out of the political realm due to self-protection. So it was that you found yourself heading to Reno, not a citizen of the state or even the country, trying to convince Americans to get to the polling booth.

I wasn't surprised that Cara's friend's car was a Volvo, but his level of neurosis exceeded expectations. Every minor task involved pontification. Then he began to explain to glowingly pretty Cara why she found herself over forty and single. (Basically, because she hadn't settled for him.)

Sideways, I whispered to you, nicknaming him in reference to Paul Giamatti's fragile character in the newly released movie about midlife crisis and wine tasting.

It wasn't that far to Reno, but the atmosphere in the car was suffocating, like being driven by a friend's uptight parents. We listened to Brahms, Chet Baker, *A Prairie Home Companion,* then nothing at all.

We checked into a generic hotel, then ate at a vegetarian café that served nothing stiffer than carrot juice.

At least I wasn't hungover in the morning. Sideways pulled up in front of a repurposed church hall, where the four of us plunged into a semicircle of volunteers. Their organization was called something like America United Forever. Young grandmothers, recovering alcoholics, aging Edie Brickell types, undergrads who'd surely once been in marching band. Each was given a clipboard with a list of addresses, a xeroxed section of a local map and key phrases to remind voters how tight the election was and how high the stakes. We could arrange a ride for any Democrat with mobility impairments. The leader came across like a field hockey coach on the verge of firing off shaming invectives. When you and I refused to take separate address assignments, she scoffed.

We have to do it together, I insisted.

Everyone seemed embarrassed on our behalf. I resented being made to feel like an underachiever, like a Girl Scout who isn't hustling enough Thin Mints. Did the leader know if Reno was a sanctuary city? I didn't. But I stayed silent. If we couldn't bring ourselves to broach our situation with a local coordinator of America United Forever, we certainly couldn't testify door-to-door about how a marriage amendment would affect a couple like us. We were not there to win over unsure individuals. We were there to cheer assured Democrat voters on.

The Bush-endorsed Federal Marriage Amendment had just failed in the House that September, as it did in the Senate in July. Nevada's own Senator Harry Reid, the Democratic whip, stated ahead of that vote: 'We are ready to rock and roll on the debate on this issue.' John Kerry and his running mate, John Edwards, senators from Massachusetts and North Carolina respectively, both sat the filibuster vote out, presumably attempting to avoid the divisive, distracting issue. Kerry remained a domestic partnership kind of guy. Bush continued to fan the flames, enjoining 'defenders of traditional marriage' to not 'flag in their efforts'—if only because, as the *New York Times* wrote, it was 'a top priority of many of his socially conservative supporters.' The president of the Family Research Council stated ominously: 'We know which senators are for traditional marriage and which are not, and by November, so will voters in every state.'

You and I were from a city that commenced gay marriages chaotically. Kerry was from a state that had sanctioned it formally. Obviously, we knew we should tamp down our swishiness and omit our life experience, lest we put wavering Democrats in mind of those flagrant San Francisco weddings and make them squeamish about their party's libertine contingent. We had backfire written all over us.

We set off on foot through the residential area we'd been assigned. There were very few people around. We tried to predict the type of locals we'd be encountering. We figured university students, strippers, and *Roseanne*-esque working families.

A slick van pulled up and a bunch of youngsters spilled out, looking like the staff of an Abercrombie & Fitch.

We're MoveOn.org! they sang. *You guys gettin' out the vote, too?* They were armed with glossy pamphlets and wore branded merch.

We're... America United Forever, I mumbled with a humiliated thumbs-up.

In truth, we were having no luck, which we maybe cultivated to some extent. People weren't home. Or didn't answer the door.

Or had a KEEP OUT—GUARD DOGS ON PATROL sign on the chain-link fence. The most successful we'd been so far was catching a hot straight couple in their driveway. I fantasized they were a pole dancer and a croupier after a night shift.

Yeah. The girlfriend sighed.

Somebody's been already, the boyfriend added, as if on the verge of staying home due to the pestering.

We kept running into gaggles of golden MoveOn youth; I resented their being on our turf.

Hey! shouted a young woman who looked like a volleyball powerhouse. *MoveOn!*

Hey, I uttered feebly. *America United Forever.* Why was I more annoyed than if she were campaigning for the Republicans?

Oh gawd, you said. *This is like school.* I knew your stories by then. How when you moved to England, the other kids had new A-Team or Transformers lunch boxes, while your mum packed your food in a margarine tub.

Look! Starbucks! I yelled, pointing at a strip mall like it was the Emerald City. I had no affinity for Starbucks, but pictured comfy chairs and a clean bathroom. *Let's go!*

I got a Frappuccino. You ordered tea. We chose baguette sandwiches. After we scarfed it all down, we laid our heads on the table. I was half asleep and deeply ashamed.

Yeah... You sighed. *We should probably knock on more doors.*

They're all protected by guns and dogs, I complained. If the two of us were at all indicative, I figured John Kerry was doomed.

We reconvened with Cara and Sideways at dusk in the hall that had been taken over by America United Forever. We hung our heads amid the exchange of high fives and the last of the morning's complimentary doughnuts.

No thanks, I said. *We had Starbucks.*

Cara grimaced. Sideways chomped on a bear claw, which somehow made him look even more affluent, as if he were an aristocrat slumming it.

We returned our lanyards and clipboard. Very few ticks on the address list, just a few measly excuses in the margins, as if it made any difference. *Dog. Gun?? Not home. PRETENDED not home.*

The others traded stories about making heartfelt connections and discovering the Real America. I kept mum. You never looked less like a citizen.

On the drive back, Cara said, *Let's just take advantage of Nat's offer.*

Definitely yes, agreed Sideways.

Cara turned to us. *We'll spend the night at Nat's family's chalet, OK?*

We first stopped at an Italian restaurant somewhere west of Lake Tahoe. Sideways softened over a glass of zinfandel.

Not long after, we pulled into an enclave of ski chalets belonging to the clans of tycoons with familiar names. Cara pointed to telltale symbols in the eaves of their properties. *Ooof,* Cara said once we were inside Nat's parents' kitchen. *We forgot to get wine.* I looked through the selection of paperbacks. A lot of fat John Irving novels. I wasn't in the state to read. We slept in a lower-floor bedroom. It smelled nice, of the surrounding woods and clean sheets.

When we woke, snow was fluttering down. It grew faster and became a flurry. We turned on the TV: Bush wins. Strange to watch the news from an unfamiliar bed. Outside, branches were becoming heavy with white. I hadn't seen snow in ages. The sky was silver. Nevada: Bush, by some twenty-two thousand votes, a victory of less than three percent.

Cara beckoned us out. *While we're here, might as well!* She showed us how to walk on the racket-like wooden snowshoes.

We threw snowballs. You made a snow angel.

Sideways told us to stow the equipment just as we'd found it in the mudroom. Before we left, Cara reminded us to replace the toilet rolls with the paper hanging over, not under. That's how we'd found it. Everything just as we'd found it. I had a bad attitude, embittered that I didn't know the Waspy ways. Cara and Sideways had stopped talking politics. We were preoccupied with not offending Nat's parents. Cara plumped cushions.

Won't there be a cleaner? I whined.

Let's not make any extra work for her, Cara clarified.

We weren't to disturb the way things are meant to be. We were to make it look like we'd never been there.

ON THE DAY AFTER the election, California senator Dianne Feinstein plainly answered a question about the San Francisco weddings at a press conference in front of her home in the city: 'I believe it did energize a very conservative vote.' She added, 'So I think that whole issue has been too much, too fast, too soon. And people aren't ready for it.'

The *New York Times* wrote that Karl Rove, Bush's chief political adviser, 'appeared to stifle a grin when asked whether he was "indebted"' to Gavin Newsom and the Supreme Judicial Court in Massachusetts. Another *Times* article, entitled "Some Democrats Blame One of Their Own," reported that Barney Frank, the openly gay representative from Massachusetts, had been against Gavin Newsom's anarchic move 'from the start.' Frank thought people should do it the Massachusetts way—properly, through the courts. There, the *Times* confirmed, 'every state legislator on the ballot who supported gay rights won another term.'

Also in that election, eleven states passed amendments against gay marriage. Kerry did win in Oregon and Michigan, where such initiatives passed. But he lost by a two percent margin in the battleground of Ohio, another place to enshrine marriage as 'a union between one man and one woman' in its constitution, even prohibiting anything that 'intends to approximate' the institution. If Kerry had taken Ohio, he'd have won the Presidency. Such a loss was in part, Barney Frank seemed to suggest, 'because of the "spectacle weddings" in San Francisco.'

THEN YOUR MUM WAS having her lymph nodes removed. Then she was going through chemo.

Your parents had visited just once. They stayed in a small hotel in the Haight. We took them to a piano bar in the Castro, which may have been a little disconcerting, although that kind of gay sensibility—very "I Am What I Am"—often seems to register with parents as just pleasantly nostalgic.

Your dad rented a car, and we accompanied them to Big Sur. I burned whenever my opinion differed from his regarding which route to take and where to stop. He didn't think of me as his guide to California like you did; I was the guest on his trip.

We got through it, listening to *On the Beach* by Neil Young.

Before they returned to England, your mum and I spent an hour or so alone at our place. That was when we were briefly renting a cheerless apartment above a lovable queer dive bar—a rebound after Loveland. Murphy's law, they came to visit while we were slumming it there. Your mum and I stayed back while you accompanied your dad to return the car. We were mostly quiet. And that was all right. I tidied up, rearranged some things on a shelf. She leafed through a real estate magazine she'd picked up in Carmel-by-the-Sea.

After that, when she phoned, her voice like honey, I was a little less ashamed than before, but still passed the receiver to you quickly.

You'd still never exactly come out. Their impressions of you were atomized: the bold choice to move to America, great taste in finding this wonderful city, against-the-odds devotion to an unlikely mate. You were a nonconformist. Your parents did perceive us as a unit, recognized it as solid and mutually supportive. Sort of the way people would call homo partners "friends" in the fifties. And some still did. My grandparents on the Chinese side would say it cutely: *Your friend.* Ni Ni smiled at you with very little worry and no condemnation.

Happy? she'd ask.

We'd nod and *mm-hm*.

We could be seen as a good match, an admirable connection, up against outside interference, fighting to maintain privacy. Ruggedly individualist, like *Brokeback Mountain.* That way, it could stay out there in the wild, inside tents. Nobody had to think about both your balls in my mouth or all my toes in yours. What's more, if people did want to give it any thought, they could project onto this male-male relationship a certain strength. Two men could be considered fuss-free, with their dual sets of extroverted genitalia. Better not to be confronted with gender fluidity, to consider the actual nuances and changeability between two individuals of the "same sex."

So it was ironic in several different ways to see your image in a British newspaper with a headline that read something like DOES YOUR MOTHER KNOW? A friend in London clipped and mailed it to us. On the cover of the Family section, there you were, in an image so big it was on both sides of the fold. It was one of the pictures the fashion photographer had taken of you and your housemate in his bed with the spray-painted pillowcases. In the picture, you read as a couple, and the verité style suggested a *real* one at that, though you never were, and he never self-identified as gay. In the picture, you both are shirtless and winsome. But you radiate, and one can almost detect a future wisdom forming on your brow. *DOES she know?*, we joked. *She does and she doesn't. She does now.*

It was sometime soon after that your mum was diagnosed

with cancer. You received the updates in dribs and drabs—parceled out with the intention of not causing you worry. Suddenly the distance between you and your family seemed vast. All the meds, the wait-and-see, the pending lab results. Them dreading the telephone ringing in rural England. You dreading their call to share the update.

MAYBE AROUND THEN YOU became quiet in a new way, different from the combination of shyness and refinement I'd long known. This seemed more like fragmentation or fading.

You'd always been drawn to the imagery of tumbleweeds, but a tumbleweed can only tumble so far. You were stuck. And what's more, standing still revealed the hollow spaces. I perceived your sadness, the see-through parts, as if you were a tangle but not quite coalesced. As if you were less than solid. I think after years without legal status, you sometimes considered yourself to be insubstantial.

But others did notice you—and saw you in motion. The track from the Magnetic Fields album *69 Love Songs* that made friends think of you most was "When My Boy Walks Down the Street." In the lyrics, completely new forms of weather herald the presence of this precious creature. The deep male voice proclaims he will make the boy his wife.

Through my blogs and zines, you were now known to strangers as the Famous Blue Raincoat, or Famous for short. Among other things, it was an inversion of your furtive status.

But in life, I called you Bird.

By then you'd renewed your UK passport. The new one had no telltale stamp of entry. But it had no stamp at all, meaning there was no story on its pages. Where did you come from, exactly? And when? We had no idea what kinds of records were actually kept. The specter lingered of a border official who'd interrogated your sister, Ruby, when she connected flights in Saint Louis on her first trip out to visit. This bully claimed to know every detail of your overstay, down to the return flight seat on which you failed to plant your bony butt.

Since then, your ass was getting plumper, fuzzier. You had arrived in 1999. A year passed, then five, and days kept going.

You could not fly back to see your mum without the risk of being forbidden reentry. You could be banned for a decade. Maybe you'd sail through based on your air of innocuousness. *You know what I do when I'm nervous in front of someone in power?* you once told me. *I lie, or I flirt.* Either way, it comes across as squirming. You couldn't bear to think about all that. Each new day had become another period of procrastination. And I was racked with guilt that every day you stayed with me, as we waited (for what, exactly?), you were choosing me over your family.

Since the Twin Towers crumbled, you'd even been hesitant to fly domestically. Then we gave ourselves the confidence to do that. Flew to Hawaii finally, where we watched a sunset from a heap of lava rocks, roaches flying around our burnt, dazzled faces. The registration on our rental car was stolen by local meth heads. We went snorkeling in Kealakekua Bay. Bubbled *wow* at each other. You loved canoeing on the open water. I was terrified. You relished making me even more scared. Pretending to see a shark fin. Or suggesting: *Why don't we just drift for a while?* I demanded we muscle back to shore.

You could be fearless. Like the time I fell asleep on a low rock in the desert and woke up to the sound of your voice right beside me. But you'd scrambled up a precipitous boulder some five or six stories high. In an acoustical trick, the sound carried through the unpeopled valley so that you didn't have to raise your volume to tickle my ear with my name. I looked up, squinting, my hand blocking the sun. You were tiny and gleeful, up there in the stratosphere, sure of your balance, taking delight in my fear you would fall.

But the risk of being permanently separated from me was one you were unwilling to take. So you told your mum on the phone, and wrote to her in letters, how much you wanted to be there, but couldn't. You sent her objects decorated with robins or otters. I knitted her a scarf, in which I ostentatiously alternated between every stitch I could do. We sent her Burt's Bees lip balm and nettle tea. You assured her you were happy.

IN JULY 2006 THE New York Court of Appeals ruled that there was no constitutional right to same-sex marriage in that state. Between this announcement and a similar opinion issued by the Washington Supreme Court twenty days later, historian John D'Emilio penned a frustrated article in the *Gay & Lesbian Review* entitled "The Marriage Fight Is Setting Us Back."

D'Emilio asked rhetorically, 'Please, can we speak the truth? The campaign for same-sex marriage has been an unmitigated disaster. Never in the history of organized queerdom have we seen defeats of this magnitude. The battle to win marriage equality through the courts has done something that no other campaign or issue in our movement has done: it has created a vast body of *new* antigay law.'

D'Emilio viewed marriage equality activists as prone to 'tactical stupidity.' More profoundly, he argued their campaign 'runs *against history.*' He described remarkable changes over half a century, from the prevailing impression that 'faggots and dykes were beyond the pale, regarded as deviant and dangerous' to pluralistic ways of living in which '*the lives of many, many heterosexuals have become much more like the imagined lives of homosexuals.*' The shift, D'Emilio posited, doesn't result from gays demonstrating that they're just like straights, but rather that 'many of them have become so much like us that they find us less threatening, less dangerous, less strange.' For decades, without gay marriage and before the push for it, gays and lesbians had been 'swimming with history, not against it.' What could have followed was a push to decenter the institution of marriage. Instead, 'along come some yearning couples, plus a band of activists to support them' who 'confuse ordinarily intelligent queers by purveying the line that full dignity, full respect, and full citizenship will only come when gays and lesbians have achieved unobstructed access to marriage.'

If, for instance, health insurance is one of the most significant benefits of marriage, why not push for universal health care? That, D'Emilio perceived, was a state-by-state fight that might actually be won. D'Emilio insisted national gay and lesbian leaders stop 'racing into the wind against history.' The time had come to 'make a major course correction.'

Around that time, the open letter "Beyond Same-Sex Marriage: A New Strategic Vision for All Our Families & Relationships" was published online and eventually signed by over two hundred writers, intellectuals, activists and legal scholars. D'Emilio signed, as did feminist Gloria Steinem and queer theory legends Lisa Duggan (credited with popularizing the term *homonormativity*), Judith Butler and Lauren Berlant of the University of Chicago. Some signatories, including Armistead Maupin and legal scholar Nancy Polikoff, author of *Beyond (Straight and Gay) Marriage*, later got married themselves.

The letter softened the corners of an *anti-* position. It read more along the lines of: Fine, marriage, but also. As with D'Emilio's analysis, the letter put forward that the new norm had already become no norm. The majority of Americans were no longer nuclear. Multigenerational immigrant families, *Golden Girls*–esque senior roommates, throuples, blended families, queer co-parenting arrangements.... Why should these lives outside of marriage be considered 'less socially, economically, and spiritually worthy?' Marriage is only one option, while 'LGBT communities have ample reason to recognize that families and relationships know no borders and will never slot narrowly into a single existing template.'

It was an expansive letter, demonstrating how this array of living arrangements responded to a time of economic hardship and corporate greed, in which a shift of public funds to the military, police and prisons widened the wealth gap. The emphasis on winning marriage equality in order to access a partner's corporate benefits, for instance, neglected the fact of such benefits being shredded by the state.

Many arguments echoed those advanced by Michael Warner at the turn of the century. 'No discussion of the issue can occur without some idea of what would count as progress,' Warner wrote. 'To take a view on same-sex marriage, pro or con, is implicitly to imagine movement toward some future: Whither America? Whither faggotry?'

REALLY, WE'D TAKE ANY solution. A partnership by another name, even an immigration concession, would do. In fact, those versions seemed cooler—irreligious and unburdened by the proprietary baggage. *Husband* can be a sexy word in a gross way, conjuring some alpha yuppie; *husband* sounds kind of hot when it means sleeping with somebody else's. But it's not a title we particularly longed to use for each other. *Boyfriend* was cuter, as if we were ever new.

The aspiration of marriage rights arrived with the image of double-groom or double-bride figurines on a wedding cake. Already dated before its time, like nostalgia for a parallel universe that had gay marriage all along.

But the bureaucratic fact was that marriage would sort out a number of obstacles in a relatively centralized and affordable manner. If more nations legalized marriage, it would facilitate transnational recognition. While marriage may have been the most regressive solution, it was also the most resolute. I was constantly drafting my own open letter, something like: *Dear Queer Theory—Please help. What else can we do?*

We used to worry that the birdsong would come, heralding the morn and our separation. Now we worried that the noise at dawn would be immigration officers. In fact, enough time had passed that we were already using an outdated term, calling the agency INS even though it was now ICE. I pictured them arriving with human-sized nets.

Something about the position of our new apartment meant I frequently heard the foghorn. This wasn't just a matter of distance, but of where we were located uphill in relation to other wrinkles and bends in the city's topography. We hadn't ever lived anywhere else in town where I heard the foghorn so clearly. It made me feel hopeful, even safe. It wasn't intended for my guidance or protection, but I could imagine it was.

We could pretend our mattress was a raft that braved open waters. We could pretend it was its own floating nation. I could convince myself we were self-governed. Roland Barthes: 'What I want is a little cosmos (with its own time, its own logic) inhabited only by "the two of us." Everything from outside is a threat.'

Isabel and Clementine ignored or swatted each other all day, but at night they came into bed with us, united in a reluctant sisterhood thrust onto them by their two daddies, whose combined stink they knew and trusted. They would sleep against the backs of our shins. Sometimes they would knead us—thighs, butts, backs. Sometimes they'd plop down on our heads. They hung out elsewhere when there was another boy in the bed.

It didn't matter to our two cats that we were just playing house. They had come to know our familiar positions and voices. Everyone in the room fell into the same rhythmic breathing. You could see the heaving of their breath clearly, especially with Clementine's skinny middle. We adapted to their feline way of perceiving. They required no paperwork from us. We were real to them. We were, at least, all breathing. The rise and fall of cat bellies, calming but vulnerable, two more bodies woven into a never-quite-settled life, becoming atmosphere.

It didn't matter to friends that we were just renting, or that you were in the country on borrowed—stolen—time. We were hosts. We fed them. We made a welcoming space.

Records. Songs from other eras. Aural travel. "Helplessly Hoping." Ballads. Sung through rough history and sweat, released by Atlantic Records. "Ballad of Easy Rider." "Ballad of El Goodo." Slide guitar. Vinyl, scratched and embedded with cat crumbs.

The jackets still musty from our basement years. Tindersticks. Round, layered sound, soaring yet chuggy, magnificent, intimate. "Waitin' for a Superman." Music I played for you and our friends and lovers while you cooked, always burning the pine nuts. *He's going to burn the pine nuts,* our pal Jesse would stage-whisper while massaging my ass. The Thirteenth Floor Elevators played. You smoked the kitchen. *There he goes,* Jesse teased. We all, in concert, made the place into a mood.

Songs by Joan Armatrading brought our connection down to earth and into the room, shaped it into sound, almost like a harness, yet unraveling. Isn't it funny how even while our bodies bring music *in* when we listen, it's rather as if it's bringing something *out*—something to vibrate between us? We become an atmosphere, a part of the air, releasing the notion that we are separate selves. We are inside the sound, and of it. Aretha Franklin. I once said *Her voice is a whole room,* and someone replied, *A whole cathedral.* True, but what I meant was: a space one can call home. I understood clearly through those days that I was living a feeling. And when I remember now, I am still living that; it has been folded into me and continues to resonate. On some level, we knew then that we were creating this feeling to be taken along from then on.

16
RENTERS

Whoever invented Christmas, you said, *oughta be crucified.*

It was the festive season once again, and we were on duty for other people's time off. Some Video Hut customers were hogging new releases. The reservations list would build up, so you and I would drive to BestBuy to get more copies. *The Incredibles; The Bourne Supremacy; Mean Girls; Shaun of the Dead; Eternal Sunshine of the Spotless Mind.*

After Lydia departed, we were required to not only replace her but bring in more staff members until we were at any given time roughly the size of a baseball team. We tried to always include youngsters who'd grown up locally. A baby dyke who'd dropped out of art school and moved back to her family home. Leanne, a soulful mezzo-soprano, just seventeen, with whom I would rewind and rewatch the stretch limo scene in *Romy & Michele's High School Reunion.* The handsome sons of lesbians. An acoustic guitarist who spent his days off doing errands barefoot and fingerpicking on his rooftop. The sole employee of Celebrity Video across the street, which had finally folded.

For a while anyway, there always seemed to be one woebegone elderly gay, brought on by Frank because *he just needs a little boost.* Once Frank began devoting the bulk of his time to Crispin, the new hires more closely mirrored me and you. We coaxed our pal Bobby into a position. He worked the early shift, managing to foster a chic ambience while at the same time catering to the parents of young children by playing vintage Hayley Mills films with the sound off, rescored by Stereolab and Blonde Redhead. Then came the wave of recent Wesleyan grads, who arrived in San Francisco to continue reading Walter Benjamin and spin Modern Lovers records while sipping Pabst Blue Ribbon. Also in their early twenties but a world apart from the Little Ivy alumni, Chrissy and Anthony were two streetwise troublemakers from Seattle. Anthony was an orphan and an enabler. *Ohmygoodness, ohmygosh,* he would say about each next drink. We renamed him Antoine. *Loveyoulongtime* was his usual sign-off. Anthony had sold himself to us at his interview by insisting *You won't need to worry about me,* delivered in an offhand, believable way. A few months later, you and I were being driven by Antoine, totally sloshed, from dive bar to club, screaming our way through ten lawless minutes of near-collisions. We had become friends, and probably didn't worry about him enough.

That Christmas when you were at your wit's end, the rest of my family had gone abroad. So instead of spending the holidays with them as usual, we bought our first Christmas tree. A very adult thing to do. We figured we'd invite the staff over to party around it. Frank showed up wearing a Santa suit, a sack of bonus checks slung over his shoulder.

He couldn't stay long. Crispin was now going through dialysis. It was messy. He'd been put on a waiting list to receive kidney and liver transplants as part of a clinical trial. The meds had debilitating side effects. Who knew what else might arise when a new organ was introduced into his fragile system. So Frank was rarely around. He had to drive Crispin to a thousand appointments and deal with his fatigue afterward. Their day-to-day had become brittle and their outlook heavy-lidded. But for just a few minutes, Frank turned it on.

Ho, ho, ho! he cried out, in more of a squeal than a bellow.

He announced each name, distributing the checks one by one. That night everyone adored Frank. The occasion justified his infantilizing tone. He left with his empty sack after a swift, bittersweet toast.

I ARRIVED AT THE store one gray morning to find the pavement around the doorway strewn with barely there items, the contents from inside a pocket: torn rolling paper, lint, dime. Just enough more than the usual debris to give me pause.

Then I got a call from Dru—one of our wild-card hires, an aspiring game designer who was always in some scrape. The night before, on the way home from his regular dive, Dru had been jumped and mugged, and in his concussed state had walked not home but to the store. In his socks—they'd stolen his sneakers. He came to at the shop door. By the time I spoke with him, Dru had been in and out of the hospital. Obviously relieved about his recovery, I was also touched that his homing instinct had brought him to us.

I knew we could never be everything to everyone. But also that to many people, we offered some kind of refuge. Some customers, many elderly, fell apart as they confided their unsolvable troubles to Frank. Once a preteen asked to use the tiny bathroom, where she proceeded to smear her shit across the wall. It was Lydia who dutifully cleaned that up, revealing an innate empathy. It had been a cry for help; Lydia recognized that. The girl was long gone, but it struck me that on some level she supposed this might be a place where that message, whatever it was, stood a chance of being read.

As the staff changed guard and grew in size, some were sleeping with each other. Some had decided to experiment with heterosexuality. Some betrayed others right under our noses. Antoine moved back to Seattle. I felt we'd never been enough for this young man who'd lost both his parents as a child. But what more could we have been? His replacement, Alistair, another one from Wesleyan, was a minx who didn't believe in labels. We began to fool around with him. I'd already been intimate with Bobby, but that was before he worked with us, and it was just the kind of fumbling that fags do as they become better friends. With Alistair, too, it was only ever fumbling—and we too were forming a kinship. But I burned with guilt. I was pretty convinced I was a creep. Was there a *law* about this kind of thing? My catastrophizing meant that Alistair additionally took on an undue burden of offering assurances. *We'll take it step by step,* he chirped like a twink Jiminy Cricket. We took him to the IKEA in Emeryville, where we walked through the showrooms pretending to be a family. Which surely smacked of favoritism, so we invented other, less perverse field trips for the other staff members, too.

Leanne, the young singer, converted to Islam, the faith her estranged father had all but left behind. She wore a headscarf and, when December came around again, a homemade badge that read I'M MUSLIM to prevent customers from bestowing inapt greetings. She asked me not to put my hand on her shoulder when I passed her behind the till, which was absolutely correct, but still I was hurt. I'd become that most pathetic of things—a boss desperate to be liked. I had come to identify as someone who crossed borders, but slowly understood that adult life had to involve the creation and maintenance of boundaries, a matter of recognizing that the world is not just one's own.

THE PROBLEM WITH MOVING to California, Margaret Wilhelm said, *is that there are no seasons. And because there are no seasons I have no sense of time passing. And so I can't place my memories. There's no: That was the snowy winter when the dog died. Or: That was the summer that came late and hard, when our older son turned ten. Now I just look back at a blur.*

Margaret Wilhelm was one of our most elegant customers, tall and sturdy, identifiably East Coast, reassuringly plain like an L.L.Bean raincoat. She had two sons who looked like they modeled wristwatches that cost an average annual salary. She was one of the first to win the *New Yorker* cartoon caption contest; when I enthused about it, she was dismissive. *Well, it wasn't actually a very good caption, was it?*

It was fucking brilliant, I thought, defensive of my taste for her talent. And, for that matter—what do we need seasons for? Who needs time? But I had to admit I wanted to experience this heightened capacity to remember that she suggested was possible. Was it true that my experiences blurred together? The city was gray with splashes of cake-icing pastel, never stark wintry white or bright high-summer blue. Surely in my case, the blur was just the booze. But which came first?

And then the thoughts arrived, as they do to pretty much everyone living in San Francisco: Is this it? When do I leave?

For us, yet more questions: When would we be found out? And were we just killing time until then?

People make fun of San Franciscans for being slackers, but it made sense to coast while we were in this holding pattern. You were not native but had become a fixture, as with those palm trees on the slopes of Dolores Street like hipsters lining up for a gig.

Bobby drew us a delicate psychedelic owl with a rectangle cut out in the middle so that it could be placed over a light-switch plate. A gentle addition to a home that I think he and others considered part theirs. It was one of many things that people gave us to make us feel that we belonged.

Clementine and Isabel sat on the windowsill. As different as they were, they'd developed a kind of parallelism. They perched like silly sphinxes. They were absorbing the sunlight through the glass, but as one approached the house, it appeared as if they were radiating the warmth of the place.

CRISPIN WAS NO LONGER just Frank's lover but his patient. Death was not just a threat but an option. The doctors had begun to advise Crispin on hospice. Crispin would decide to stop taking his medication, in which case his doctor predicted he would die within a month. Then he'd change his mind.

I got the news in the morning while at the bakery ordering my usual iced coffee and chive muffin. I was behind schedule and would have to sweep the sidewalk after opening the shop. The phone in my pocket rang. The little Nokia you and I shared so that staff members could tell us they were running late. I expected that's what this was about. But it was one of Frank's daughters.

My dad died, she whispered, as if inhaling.

You mean Crispin, I corrected gently.

No, she said.

The week before, as we were tallying up, Frank had stopped moving receipts between piles and looked at me with a kind of intense blankness.

If Crispin keeps U-turning about the meds, he sighed, *it'll kill me.*

Crispin would think he was ready to relieve himself of the side effects, until it hit home that meant relieving his body of its life force altogether. Within weeks, the end. That's what he had to think about. How soon it would come, and how painful. How chaotically would that last darkness arrive? He was scared. He'd lash out with an unreasonableness that matched the unreasonable circumstances.

Frank hadn't been back since that closing. Not even to make the bank deposits, his final tether to the store's daily operations. Then the night came when Crispin was in the hospital and Frank, alone, sat down with a Manhattan at the large kitchen table where he did the payroll and once hosted dinner parties. He lit up a B&H Gold Special Filter, and his heart quit.

I went to Jan, who owned the bookstore across the street. She'd seen some things. She was the one who happened to show up just after Frank and I were held up at gunpoint. She'd glimpsed behind the curtain already.

No. You must mean . . .

Crispin?

Crispin.

Yeah—but, no. It was Frank.

Holy shit, she said. *Frank.* Jan had the countenance of an open prairie, so I could see her process the information.

What should I do? I asked.

She advised me to keep the store closed that day. Put up a polite sign that didn't yet give the reason. As if we should allow for the denial phase.

Person by person, we told the staff. I showed up at Leanne's door; she lived with her mom just a block from the shop. She was blank. Days later, she explained that when I delivered the news, she didn't feel anything. Still didn't. That she knew how adults were supposed to respond, but couldn't access that yet. As if she was, in the J. M. Barrie way, heartless. I learned on the spot not to pass judgment. Now everything was learned on the spot.

I was immediately in charge of payroll. It had always been just the fun stuff for me and you—writing the newsletter, constructing the Totoro-shaped returns slot. Frank did all of the accounts in a massive hardbound ledger with pages that unfolded across the table. I swapped over to an online payroll service. Payday was Friday. This first time, I'd missed the cutoff, so the checks would be issued by the company on Monday instead. I apologized to the staff, and said we could offer an advance out of the till.

Leanne was annoyed. *This really messes with my weekend, though,* she complained.

She seemed to be acting out, detecting in her own way that boundaries needed to be drawn. So I drew them. *You'll deal,* I said firmly. Was that treating her like a child, which I'd tried to avoid for two years? Or was a boundary an equalizing apparatus? *As I said, you can borrow money out of the till. So it makes no difference. And— I'm doing my best.*

Not long after that, I couldn't figure out how to do that anymore. One afternoon, I left you and Alistair at the store, poured myself a Jameson, went into the shower, and my legs gave out. Soon enough, you appeared.

This seems kind of like a nervous breakdown, right? I wondered.

Verge, you said. You may have been slightly resentful that my emotions were so externalized. Or annoyed with how that can read like a performance. *What do you need?*

Grits and crab, I said. It was a signature dish that Dahlia, one of your British guardian angels, served down the street at her restaurant, the Bayou. Like you, Dahlia had embraced Americana in her own way.

The Bayou maybe doesn't really do takeout, you said.

Can you ask?

Yeah. Yeah, I'll ask.

Tell them it's for me.

I dried off and wrapped myself in the quilt we'd found in a tiny thrift store when we first moved in together, a fabric history put together by someone else's grandma. I knocked more whiskey back.

You returned before long with a soggy box in your hands.

Dahlia confirmed that she doesn't do takeout, you intoned, slightly irritated on her behalf. *But anyway, she said just this time.*

The grits steamed—comfort food. I felt I deserved this, and the whiskey, and taking the afternoon off. I felt entitled to secondary gains.

Just for me, I suggested, *because of all that we're going through.*

Sure, you said.

You may have been feeling very far away from your mum. She had been going through another round of chemo. I felt you sometimes thought you weren't entitled to anything at all. Like too much whiskey, a day off; like *going home.* You went back to Video Hut to finish the shift with Alistair, and when you returned, I was out front smoking under the starless sky.

Weren't things somehow more broken apart after that? Like all I was experiencing were the details, so many accumulated over a decade, all the figurative and real mementos, which for a while seemed to puzzle together but no longer quite locked into place.

I VOLUNTEERED TO SAY something at Frank's funeral. His daughters said yes, they'd already been thinking that was a good idea. I didn't know how one did this, exactly, but had been reading Eileen Myles, who convinced me one can write anything. Like a text I loved—a poem that is a commencement speech, or commencement speech that is a poem. It is *present.* Funny, dark, unafraid to acknowledge its own form.

I considered whether I should write about that time we were held up at gunpoint.

This was back when Frank was still working shifts and coming up with new entrepreneurial ideas. The addition of frozen pizzas. A delivery service. A rental kiosk that would burn a movie onto a disk on demand. We pooh-poohed most of these notions and let some, like the frozen pizzas, hover on the horizon until they faded away. Frank was forever planning where the freezer would go.

He also made executive decisions, like extending the shop's closing to ten. This struck me as unnecessary, considering the neighborhood was so sleepy. I stated my objections; Frank thought I was condescending. He had a high threshold for differing views, but found certain small rebellions infuriating.

I returned home having left the tension unresolved. You'd already opened the night's bottle of Les Jamelles, and we watched an episode of *Buffy*. I was still miffed. Should I quit?

Less than a week later, Frank and I were on the brand-new late shift together. After eight, the former closing time, no more customers came. I knew better than to say I told you so. It was cold. The windows revealed nothing of the street, only reflected back our brightly lit shelves of thousands of movies.

We both thought the loner who wandered in and asked for *Die Hard 3* was sketchy but left it at that.

It passed nine.

The guy returned, shaking and boozy. *Gimme Die. Hard. Three.*

I told you, we don't have it... I began.

He revealed a gun, held low. *All the cash.*

He'd probably worked up his liquid courage at the Irish tavern. You were down the street at the lesbian bar. You were with Dylan, which gave me some comfort. I wished I could send a telepathic message: *I'm in danger. Call the cops.* But also: *Do NOT come here.*

Don't point the gun at him, Frank said. *Point it at me.* Which the man did.

Frank handed over the money from the drawer, remarkably steady, giving the impression that he was in charge. The man shooed us into the back, demanding we get down on the floor.

Frank did a sort of gestural squat.

ALL THE WAY DOWN, the robber demanded.

Dagburnit, Frank scowled. *My knees...!*

The man swatted the gun in our direction. *Now count to one hundred—slowly.*

I couldn't be sure whether I was pissing. Now my only telepathic message to you was a dumb, frantic *I love you.*

After he'd backed out the door, and we were still slowly counting, or pretending to, Jan from the bookstore came in. She'd been in retail for years, so she understood not only that we were freaked, but how none of us particularly wanted word of the incident out on the street. Frank said, *Let's just keep this between us,* and she nodded calmly.

Need anything? she added.

No. I'll just call the police.

As we waited for the cops to turn up, Frank showed me how at some point on the shift he'd slipped most of the day's cash takings into his front pocket. Was that something he regularly did?

Maybe it was a new precaution because he was less convinced about the later closing time than he'd let on.

I called the bar and asked the staff to find you. You arrived swiftly, looking pale and tiny.

Frank and I attempted to describe the robber's beanie to the cop.

Maroon, I said.

Frank suggested burgundy. He added, *I can tell you, he has very hairy legs. I know this because he was wearing shorts, and he made us get ALL THE WAY DOWN on the floor.*

The cop paused taking notes and shot us a look.

For the eulogy, I decided, no. That was a good story. But it wasn't *feel-good.* Nor was it a tearjerker. It was tense and counterintuitive. Choosing an anecdote for a funeral was like recommending a movie: I couldn't give them *Fargo* when they wanted *Beaches.*

On the day, I looked over the enormous crowd, standing room only, extending all the way out the door of St. Rita Catholic Church. At the front were Frank's daughters and his ex-wife, looking stunned that his new life was so highly populated.

I told the City Hall story instead. How people jubilantly called out, *Congratulations!,* to which Frank snapped back, *He's my son.* There was absolutely no reason why he shouldn't explain we were there to complete small-business paperwork. I'll never know why he said what he did. Maybe he didn't want to be seen as the type to jump on the marriage bandwagon with a twink. But I figured I would've said the same thing. There was something so gay about his response—as if, in order to live up to the sense of occasion, the thing to do was to present as some kind of family.

I told the mourners how strong he was. Once I arrived at the store, shocked to find that he'd moved a massive wooden shelving unit on his own. *Small but mighty,* he panted.

I had learned a business term from Don, the Santa Claus–like traveling salesman from Santa Cruz who sold us our videos. *Perceived value.* Don was explaining the industry's challenge of communicating the worth of loaning a movie—a commodity of experience and time, merely and yet so much more than a flimsy disk. At our place, I reckoned, the *perceived value* was the exchange itself. It was how Frank required his staff to sweep the sidewalk—to understand keeping shop as a responsibility to the place where it stood. People took refuge there—came in to unburden or stage a dirty protest.

Frank helped make this avenue, I said, only realizing it was a crescendo as I spoke the words, *the closest I've experienced to Sesame Street.*

The crowd laughed, which grew into cheers and clapping. For a moment I took the applause as a compliment.

At a small wake we held for the staff at our place, some things dawned on me. I understood the speech wasn't about my own observations per se. I'd just rented them some *feel-good*.

The neighbors could border on self-congratulatory. It was the kind of neighborhood with a mural celebrating diversity. But a good place, somewhere people felt part of. The locals welcomed you and me into the fold. But this was their *home,* whereas you and I, even after all that time, we were just tenants. We'd rented four different apartments over the period in which we rented the neighbors their movies. We swapped germs through those tapes and disks. We kept wiping their grape (or blackberry) jam off the returns—slightly repulsed as we surmised, *I suppose that's community.* But we were only ever renting.

IN THE UK UNDER Tony Blair, civil partnerships had been in effect for over a year. On the 5th of December 2005, hours after the new law went into effect, Christopher Cramp and Matthew Roche were the first to be registered. The usual fifteen-day waiting period had been waived because Matthew was terminally ill. The ceremony was held at a hospice in the coastal town of Worthing, and Matthew died the following day. Two weeks later, the next couple, Shannon Sickels and Grainne Close, registered their partnership with media gathered outside their ceremony in Belfast, Northern Ireland.

'For us, this is about making a choice to...' Grainne began stating to the press.

Shannon picked up the thread: '...have our rights, our civil rights, acknowledged and respected and protected as any human being.'

Shannon is, like me, American and half Chinese. One reason she'd become civil partnered, *The Guardian* reported, was in hopes that Grainne could eventually emigrate to the States more easily.

A few spiteful protesters had gathered that day, but I got the impression that the British transition seemed to occur without much fanfare or fallout. Just stuff here and there, like a woman who wrote a stiff letter to the BBC saying that man and lady parts clearly fit together, so everything else is an abomination.

In the UK, rather than dithering and endlessly debating, the civil partnership law preserved the old ways of marriage while affording the same rights to gays and lesbians. Nearly two thousand couples were legally partnered in December 2005, followed by over sixteen thousand pairs the next year. We began to look into what the process involved. Did it include me? It did. If we decided to move there, Mom and Dad agreed to take on the cats.

CRISPIN DIED ABOUT A week after Frank did. Frank's mother died, too. It was like Frank was their oxygen, and he'd been switched off. His two daughters were warm and quietly tough. We maintained trust, which was a way of holding one another up. What was my role? What was I to them, to you, to the staff, to the customers? How could I be there for others, but not be their air?

We helped sell the business with the daughters. And we also started to sell off most of our possessions. A chunk of our book collection went to Jan's store; normally unsentimental, Jan told me that she cried when she was doing the buy, because some of the books contained inscriptions between us. A Pierre et Gilles monograph. *The Unbearable Lightness of Being.* A book of Nan Goldin photographs. The book about Sophie Calle stalking some guy. *City of Quartz.* A guide to oak trees. *Winesburg, Ohio.* Baudelaire. Rimbaud. *The Heart Is a Lonely Hunter.*

By then, half the mixtapes we mailed to each other were already gone. They'd been on the floor of a problematic old Saab that I'd purchased on a whim. When the car was stolen, it was frankly a relief to have it taken off my hands. Days later I got a call. The Saab had been ground down even more than it already was on a joyride. It would be destroyed. I had the opportunity to claim the various personal items in it. I lamented relinquishing the tapes, yet couldn't muster the energy to take a train out to Oakland to rescue them. Now that we were moving, I was in a taxonomical frame of mind, and came to the decision that the incomplete set that remained only drew attention to those that were absent. So I put the surviving tapes out with the trash.

I don't see the logic, you protested, but stopped short of insisting. You didn't want to be accused of being nostalgic or a hoarder. So, reluctantly, you let the tapes go.

I'm a completionist, I shrugged. *We're not even bringing a tape player anyway. Let's move on.*

The cats tarried around the cassettes, in a dusty Vans shoebox alongside the trash can on the sidewalk. The tapes half glimmered, forlorn and hairline cracked.

We're so much more than the songs, I said. But we've been trying to recall what tracks were on those tapes ever since.

We had a garage sale. Everything must go. The hot pink Mexican blanket. A Murano glass vase my sis brought back from Venice. The Alessi cheese grater. The *Deep Throat* VHS. Strangers and acquaintances went off with miraculous objects, or just bought kitchenware in support of our move.

As we began to pack up in the late afternoon, a customer, Sue Yamamoto, showed up and handed me twenty dollars before picking out a purchase. She grabbed a pepper mill.

This is my thank you, she said. *My daughter was the one who came in and asked you if there was a movie version of* Catcher in the Rye.

But there isn't a movie, I said, recalling my line to her daughter at the time. She'd been running behind in her assignment to read it for school.

No, there isn't. And you told her to read it.

I'd told her that maybe the reason there wasn't a movie yet was because it would be too hard to make. Because of its interiority, the way it sees from within being young. And for that very reason, I figured she might actually like it. Either way, I'd said, you can read it in a day.

And she read it.

Yeah?

She loved it.

That's great.

Because of you, she loved a book.

Well . . .

She left with the pepper mill.

A boy slowly pedaled off with your bicycle, his father keeping him steady by holding on to the top tube. The son would grow into it. *Thanks—good luck with the move!* the dad sang out.

The dusk closed in, pinkish gray and hazy. No longer the overture of a naughty night to come, like it used to be for us in this city. Just a murmuring, unspectacular end.

17

THE HAPPENING

Apart from the whisky, there was little ceremony to speak of. It was doing the paperwork. We signed the register at the Historic Guildhall in Exeter, a Roman city in Devon, southwest England.

We had arrived a few weeks prior, in the middle of May 2007. Following an excruciating wait, my passport, with a UK visa clearing me to enter Britain with the intention of getting hitched, arrived the day before we were booked to leave California. At the airport, your departure didn't raise an eyebrow. It was me who received the questioning: Why the one-way ticket? I turned to the visa page with some pride.

England's West Country was fragrant and bright but, that summer, especially wet. Pastoral rolling hills gave way to a rugged edge at the sea. But compared with California, the coastline was tame, like a neatly trimmed pubic bush. The meadows buzzed and bleated with well-mannered wildlife.

We dragged our giant suitcases into your parents' teeny

cottage on a sloping plot of land near Dartmoor, where wild ponies roam and drink from shallow streams. Your mum, who'd finished her latest course of chemo, beamed in your presence. This time her hair had grown back in shiny ringlets, and she shook them girlishly. Her smile turned gently judgmental when I attempted to help out in the garden.

The gay neighbors brought over sloe gin. I thought they said *slow gin*. Their existence probably eased your parents into all this. They say it helps to know one or two personally. An aristocratic air emanated from the couple's antiques collection and Rudolf Nureyev gossip.

There were almost as many insects on the guest bedroom ceiling as stars in the sky. Your mum kissed you briskly on the lips each night before bed.

On the July day we became legal partners, she was radiant in a folksy red dress ordered from a Scandinavian catalog, and disappointed in our nearly complete lack of ceremony.

We reminded her about the big reception we were throwing—on their property—in September. But a party at a months-long lag probably struck her as too late, and too much; unimaginably ambitious. Friends would be arriving at their cherished smallholding not only from London but New York, San Francisco and Los Angeles.

We wanted to get the legal stuff out of the way pretty much as soon as we could. We chose to perform the civil partnership on 07/07/07, a date that sounded auspicious, memorable, and funny.

You should have seen the people who showed up last year on 06/06/06, the registrar said.

We had nothing on last year's goths. We didn't even have music, rice or bouquets. We did exchange rings—a pair of "undulating" silver bands purchased from a hippie jeweler in Bristol. We were careful about the signatures. Being required to list an occupation, we decided to both write down Business Owner. I guess to make a record of our respectability. Your parents were the witnesses. They kept calling it marriage, and we mostly didn't correct them.

Your dad took a photo of you, me and your mum sitting in three plain chairs that had been arranged one on each side of a rectangular pillar. We look choreographed in a melancholy mise-en-scène, three people looking in three different directions. But our expressions are peaceful. Your mum was trying to hide how let down she was by our flippancy, while we were relieved there was no extra fuss. Opposite to how she saw it, proceeding perfunctorily made the whole thing feel more real to us.

Back outside, under the intense, rare sunlight, you lamented writing Business Owner under your name.

I'll regret that for the rest of my life, you said.

I announced that one day I'd have my loose ring resized. Instead, years later, on an uneventful evening at a pizza parlor in Peckham, I would put forward the idea that we could just take them off. To which you would agree without hesitation. Relieved, we would slip both into my backpack. *Ringfinger:* what a heteronormative word.

Newly *civil-ized,* we were taken out by your parents for lunch at a dark, nearly empty but not disreputable pub. I had fish stew and local ale followed by a single malt whisky. I had learned to never say "Scotch" in front of your dad, who was raised in Scotland and claimed the only stuff that counted came from his homeland, so the term was redundant. I queasily boarded the train to London. We were stopping off there before a continental honeymoon.

At Waterloo station, I was vocally relieved to behold some diversity again. Down where we were staying, it was something like ninety-eight percent white. We decided then and there that we should probably move to the capital city.

First, we were to travel to Paris and Berlin, then return to your parents' property to prepare for our party there just before autumn. We headed to your sister Ruby's place in north London, where we would spend the night before heading off on the honeymoon.

Ruby's housemates went: *Oh, shit! The brother! Finally!*

Now I was the supporting character.

OUR HONEYMOON WAS JUST me and you. And Dylan, who'd settled in Berlin with his boyish wife, plus their friends and friends of friends, as well as the lovers we encountered briefly in the bars and saunas.

We first slept in a sad little room on the second floor of a hotel in the Marais, from which we peered into the windows of Parisians who occupied far superior spaces. They lifted art deco goblets with limbs like vines. They glided between rooms, performing each little task artfully. Now that I was *European*, could I too become sophisticated?

It dawned on us that one day we could be counted among the earliest wave of gay honeymooners. A waiter would ask if I'd like to taste the wine because I somehow presented as more husbandlike.

I adored being with you in front of each monument. I was gaga for you in museums. Having been living in the countryside with you—where, after each dinner with your parents, we ambled between hedgerows amid the scent of manure, which seemed weirdly not icky to step on—I knew you more than ever as a country boy. Though you resented this image, it sent me head over heels: the trajectory of you moving yourself into city life. In the pristine, shiny Musée d'Orsay, you seemed to bring the tall grass and bees with you.

I pictured young men arriving from the provinces in the hundreds to dig up Parisian streets during Haussmann's renovation. They are the ghosts of each dusk over the Seine, laying down tools, cruising wealthy men. The frisson of evening in the city is escalated by the presence of newcomers. Theirs are the stories about to begin.

We went to the gay bars—the kind that could be anywhere in the world. Arrive in some new city where all the men are gorgeous (in Paris, big-haired and big-nosed), but in those bars, where did they all go? The men inside cluster in closed circles, emitting complaints and cologne.

On the second night, we tried a different sort of place. My guidebook promised it would be "alternative" and "popular with students." The bar comprised a long hall and mezzanine full of young punters, some chatting with older men, whom I liked to imagine as their professors.

We swiftly spotted a likely pair to partner up with. And indeed each of them attached to one of us as if instructed by a casting director. We adjourned upstairs, swooping in on a settee in a cavernous corner as soon as it freed up. I offered to buy a round. Your boy's choice was vodka and apple juice. I went down with my boy to the bar, where I offended the gruff bartender by asking for a vodka *a-pelle,* forgetting the word *pomme*. My boy came to my rescue, ordering the rest of our drinks. I paid, and we joined you upstairs. Your boy had his hand on your knee as you engaged in one of those broken-English conversations. Life experience reduced to plot points. Issuing opinions without the capaciousness for nuance. We lay back on the settee, frotting side by side like four horny breadsticks.

Clearly, we were going to need a room. The clerk at our hotel stood sentinel; we could never sneak two more gays up. And the garçons lived way out in some banlieue; it sounded like a drag to travel there and back. We were all trying to ensure the decision-making didn't take so long that someone would start desiring a good night's sleep more than sex.

There's this sex dungeon near to the river . . . one of them suggested.

I think I know it, I confessed.

We walked through courtyards lined with shuttered luxury shops. When the Seine came into view, how could we resist going down to the bank? Plus, maybe we could just get off there in the shadows, a sex club without a cover fee. Such derelict public sex surely fell in a grand homosexual tradition. As we stood ready to cross the Quai de l'Hôtel-de-Ville, cars, vans and motorbikes whizzed by. After nightfall, the avenue no longer clogged bumper-to-bumper and crossed by throngs of tourists, drivers went at higher speeds.

Our group jolted and came asunder. Two or three young men in black hoods had infiltrated. They'd zeroed in on you—your bounce, your slender limbs flailing at the curb—and one shoved the center of your back. You careened into the street, nearly falling over yourself in a somersault. You landed on one palm. For a split second, before the boys and I could get a handle and hoist you up, we beheld the excruciating sight of your humiliation. With you safely back on the curb, we became angry, but the youths were gone, their cackles bouncing off the walls of elegant buildings.

A surge of traffic came. You'd been lucky enough to be pushed in a moment of pause. We still did cross the street to the river, but now an air of aftermath hung around us. We sat there a short while like a double date just out from the cinema, with nobody volunteering to give the first review.

BERLIN WAS MORE LIKE a honeymoon should be, in that we had better group sex. First some stroking in the back room of a leather bar, where they scan each guest at the door to ensure not so much that you're a gay man but the right kind. No limp wrists, no excessive perfume. We bottled up our fizziness—the same excitable quality that can alert gay-bashers can repel a leather-bar bouncer.

In the center of the labyrinth, we joined a circle jerk. A towering man became greedy for you. Why such violence from all sides? His slimy penis seemed to seek you out like a hungry eel.

The next day in a clean, bright sauna, we ogled a handsome hunk as he showered, looking like a stallion on hind legs under a waterfall. He swaggered over to the hot tub where we bobbed, overheating. Was he in charge? Had we broken a rule, and he was about to correct us? Instead, he dropped the white towel around his waist and lowered himself into the steaming water. He sat across from us, silent and swarthy, then floated between, brushing calf, thigh, back of the hand.

We had little work to do to find his erection. So this is swooning, I thought, wrapping my fist around that girthy, veiny thing with its enormous head like a fireman's hat. We could both grasp the shaft at once, my hand on top of yours. His dick had a personality, like Magnum P.I., who fought crime but also offered damsels a supportive hug. And were we now *kissing* this beast? Back and forth. He bit my lip. I wanted to bite his head off. He smelled of tobacco, not like the stale, rank traces on a chain smoker, but the aroma of a freshly opened pouch of Golden Virginia. His stubble was reassuring and made me feel softer. And yet he would not try to turn me into a bottom. Instead, he rose, wet fur slicked down his massive thighs and chest-plate chest, and wordlessly led us both into the cubicles, pushing us back onto a sticky vinyl bed. He served us like a god bestowing apotheosis on two mortals.

I paid little mind to whatever porno was on the video monitors, though I detected that it seemed actually quite good. He worked our dicks with masterful skill, using mouth and both hands elegantly. He grinned at the climax, giving us a brawny ceremonial milking, until we erupted, no longer new deities, just two googly-eyed, open-mouthed Muppets. He gave us each a double pat on the thigh. I blurted, *Thank you.* He smiled in a gentlemanly way, then sauntered off, his still-hard dick as thick as *Infinite Jest.*

Should we move to Berlin? We wondered how complicated that would be and to what extent my right to be in the UK was transferable to other European countries. We were tempted to move for the saunas, for the penis. But putting all the work into my British visa applications compelled us to stay there awhile—the first place to receive us as a couple. When my next letter arrived from the UK Home Office, with a visa that established my leave to remain, it was genuinely welcoming, almost chipper. But less than five years later, Home Secretary Theresa May would usher in the Hostile Environment Policy, a brutally monikered set of measures intended to drive out undocumented denizens that would send ripples of malice toward foreign nationals and minority groups more generally.

Upon returning to England, we made our life decisions in your parents' thatched-roof cottage and in the countryside around it. We sat on a hay bale by a reservoir and agreed we would move to London. It would be the first time I lived in a capital city. The rest of the summer played out like a bildungsroman. We made wedding plans slumped against trees as if daydreaming, but we'd begun to receive real RSVPs.

THE YURT ARRIVED. YOUR mum was taken with the young hippie couple who put it up. Next came two portaloos, so that guests didn't tread through your parents' cottage to their single small bathroom. We decorated the plastic walls of the loos with cartoons of British pop icons of the moment. Lily Allen. Amy Winehouse. Simon Amstell. We rented two holiday homes down the lane for guests. Anyone who didn't nab a bed there could camp in the yurt. We created a label reminiscent of a seventies folk rock album for the bottles of your dad's home-brewed ale. We purchased a croquet set, not knowing it would lead to a tournament among the more competitive guests and nearly hijack the whole event. We made a batch of vegetarian chili every night for a week while watching *EastEnders* on the small TV in the kitchen, then stored it in a chest freezer in the barn. We planned it to be a simple meal lovingly made.

We chose the 1975 song "Canto do povo de um lugar" by Caetano Veloso for a processional. The Portuguese lyrics are about people living in tandem, following rural circadian rhythms. Morning gives way to afternoon, in turn to a moonlit dance, exalting the night before the following day. It may also be political, a riposte to the elitist urban wealth accumulated during years of fierce military rule.

It wasn't a love song exactly. But as a veneration of nature and community, it seemed right. We wanted the ceremony to be about us being part of everything else. We planned to walk down the aisle, meaning across the lawn, carrying a cherry tree to be ceremoniously planted. A small, perhaps arrogant gesture: to create a ritual around something that will outlive us—not parented, not even *authored*, just something we were once near, a young tree going into the earth after being briefly in our hands.

Maybe the only way I could cope with the omnipresent,

overwhelming fear of one day losing you was to perform a reminder of our inconsequentiality. Our smallness compared with a tree, with the earth we put it in. As if the only way I am able to love you is to accept, even embrace, oblivion. If I think of us both as fleeting—two little accidents who will one day disappear—I am able to think of our love being not just between but around us.

'Following legalization of same-sex marriage and a couple of other things,' Andrew Sullivan said in 1997, 'I think we should have a party and close down the gay rights movement for good.' This vision of liberty as sequestered seems to me misguided. We lay down roots so that we can nurture and shelter the life that is near us.

Dad, Mom and Jenny arrived the day before everyone else. Our combined families suppered in a pub on Dartmoor. My mom and your mum seemed at ease in each other's company. They took up whispering. We posed for a group photo in the parking lot.

International guests would be arriving via London then train to Exeter, which was still an hour's drive from our spot. This meant Jenny had to keep ferrying Americans in a rental SUV. I considered this a generous wedding present.

I'd been checking the forecast obsessively. We'd been through weeks of rain. On the morning of the big day, dew glistened on the spiderwebs in the grass. But that was it—a last little wet kiss. It was sunny and nearly cloudless; those that did drift by were the fluffy stuff of reverie.

Londoners pulled up in carpools.

Then Jenny would reappear with her latest cargo: Xuan, who was present when we first met, from Los Angeles. Matt and Carl from New York; we'd met them online somehow, the way that queers had begun to, and become close as cousins. Cash and his on-off boyfriend Theo from San Francisco. Alistair, the former Video Hut employee with whom we'd had that ill-advised semi-fling. I tried not to count how many of the fags present we'd had sex with. They stepped onto the gravel of the drive, jet-lagged and happily disoriented.

Matt and Carl had barely shaken off their journey when the ceremony was about to begin. They snuck me away to a pile of stones to smoke. Everyone else was getting ready for the nuptials. Jenny and Ruby were struggling with the daisy chains. You, looking heavenly, were chatting away with old friends. From what I could tell, you were nowhere near as nervous as I was. *Of course you're nervous,* Carl said gently as he lit my cigarette.

We wore white tunics over wide dark trousers and hoisted the tree between us. Our sisters walked first, dropping petals, adult flower girls, and it all went so quickly that the Caetano Veloso song never quite reached its choral climax. I hoped the more cynical present would indulge us. I glanced shyly at the guests. Did Xuan just want to get back to the croquet championship? One or two people I wouldn't have expected were wiping tears from their faces. Mom was officiating.

Finally! her speech began, to which everyone hoorayed.

So far, so good: very publike. She said our union must have been *written in the stars.* I'd long ago made up my mind not to believe in such things. Then thinking about this contradiction, I flushed with shame, like Holden Caulfield confronting his own brattiness over his mother buying him the wrong kind of skates. Mom was giving the people what they wanted to hear. Sure, some may not have quite gone along with her remark that the setting was so magical she could be convinced she might see an actual *piskie,* the fairylike creature of Devon folklore. We'd used piskies as a decorative motif, and she was prone to bestow such curiosities with supernatural meaning. But she was comforting, informal, lovely—exactly why we asked her to speak.

Mom suddenly seemed so young, so American. This person who had managed to transform so much of her childhood trauma into sunshine. But there was a sadness to her smile. She was losing us to England. At least she saw it as a genteel place.

We sat facing everyone, wearing the daisy chains around our foreheads. Yours looked perfect in your wavy locks. You glowed. Mine looked discordant against my buzz cut and blunt features, like a mainland politician donning a lei in Waikiki.

We placed the tree in the pre-dug hole and did some performative planting, not totally unlike throwing dirt on a casket at a funeral. I cued up the recessional track on your dad's boom box, and the two of us withdrew up the hill accompanied by the drama of "The Happening" by the Supremes, a firm family favorite that I'd heard countless times from *my* dad's boom box.

As dusk approached, it became clear we should have begun defrosting the chili much sooner. Each Ziploc-bagged batch was a brick, forcing me to make several trips to a neighbor's kitchen to defrost in her microwave. Your parents were not microwave people. When finally enough of the brown goop was warmed, it was combined in a big ceramic pot. Everyone was waiting under the canopy. I gave a quick speech saying we wanted the day to be about togetherness and sharing, as partly inspired by artist Rirkrit Tiravanija, who fed gallery visitors hot bowls of curry in one of his exhibitions. Jenny, who was on her way to a PhD in art history, later razzed me about the extraneous reference. Maybe it was more apt to think of the canopy as akin to a chuppah in the Jewish wedding tradition. The structure harkens to Abraham's tent—an open house—and posits marriage as a starting point for hospitality. Not just turning inward but welcoming in. Despite the religious conventions not relevant to our own situation, something resonates in this symbol of a home without walls.

I hoped nobody would get food poisoning.

After dinner, there was supposed to be dancing, but only a few joined in. Then the sound system failed, and an even smaller group of us stepped side to side around the boom box playing "Where Are You Baby?"

The rest were lounging in small clusters on lawn chairs, exchanging bemused revelations of early middle age.

I don't really enjoy listening to Björk, Xuan announced, relishing the unpopular opinion. *It's just not relaxing to play around the house.*

Theo, Cash's currently-on boyfriend, was indignant, bordering on angry: *Björk is a genius.*

Then the sky lit up over the wide black horizon of Dartmoor. Nobody could think of any reason for the fireworks display. Colorful light and trails of smoke noisily patterned the normally eventless night sky.

Can you believe this? people said to one another of the synchronicity. I found my mom and tapped her shoulder. We watched the spectacle together, and maybe it was your dad's home brew, but I found myself willing to believe in fate.

Later, your mum and some of her friends from Folk Club stood in a circle, singing one of those witchypoo, morose English traditional ballads. They were tipsy and feeling tied to the soil of Albion, which annoyed me because I thought it had little to do with the shared identity of me and you. But your mum looked so content. She'd finally gotten her ceremony.

She would die two years later, in 2009. Your dad would then sell the property and move. I wonder how "our" cherry tree has fared. There could still be a little plaque at its base with our names on it, rusted from rain.

Your mum would not live to see the law change so that same-sex couples had the option to be not just civil-partnered, but married. The first same-sex marriage ceremonies in the UK would take place in the spring of 2014. At first we wouldn't see any reason to swap out our civil partnership. But marriage is an international term, so after same-sex marriage was finally legalized in the United States in 2015, we would go ahead and do the paperwork. We would "convert" our UK civil partnership into marriage, therefore also deemed valid in the US. It would just take our signatures and a small fee.

Your mum would've been even less impressed with the lack of fanfare that day. Afterward, we would treat ourselves to breakfast at the South London Gallery. We would briefly argue about nothing. We would do a selfie that I would post to Instagram with a Nashville filter. You'd go to work. I would take a bus back home and masturbate, the first time I'd be ashamed of the act in ages.

The UK government's policy would be that a "conversion" to marriage does not supplement but *replaces* a civil partnership. So literally on that day in 2016, we would leave the civic office with a marriage certificate backdated as 2007.

A weird twist on queer temporality we could not have seen coming. In this revised version of things, your mum did indeed witness us not only partnered but married back then in 2007.

MOST WERE APPROPRIATELY HUNGOVER the next morning. Especially Theo. The story began to circulate over coffee that after Cash dragged Theo away from the reception, they'd forgotten the way to their guesthouse. It was really quite simple: five minutes down the lane, hang a left at the red phone box, pass the creepy barn. But they kept walking. They lumbered down the long, narrow route between tall hedgerows.

Then, almost as abnormally as the fireworks display had been out there in the middle of nowhere, a cab drove past.

Taxi! Theo called, waving his arm as if hailing a ride in San Francisco.

The driver slowed. He took one look at the pair, rolled the window back up and drove away.

Somehow Cash and Theo found the house before dawn, but it involved turning back and retracing their steps for miles. They'd given everyone a new wedding story to spread around.

Just as we made our big move to England, the issue of gay marriage was really heating up in America. Agitated and expensive, it would proceed incrementally, state by state and couple by couple. California was in the throes of turbulent legal and political battles. Just days before our wedding party, the state legislature approved a bill legalizing same-sex marriage, which it had also done two years prior. But, as before, it was vetoed by Governor Arnold Schwarzenegger. Not exactly terminated; he reasoned that there was a need to wait for a decision over Proposition 22, the state's constitutional amendment banning same-sex marriage, from California's supreme court. It had been headed there since it passed all those years ago, in 2000, when we were living in the musty basement with the newly replaced front door.

A year after we left the state, in May 2008, the Supreme Court of California would finally overturn Proposition 22, and gay marriage would subsequently resume in San Francisco and elsewhere. Cash and Theo would get married that summer. Then in November 2008, California voters would approve yet another bill—Proposition 8—that superseded the ruling and banned gay marriage again. The state's supreme court, however, would confirm that this did not invalidate the existing marriages. In a bizarre way, this clarified the arbitrariness of all the back-and-forth. A couple could be legally gay-married if they had managed to sneak it in during the intervening months. Some time around then, American Apparel released T-shirts that read *Legalize Gay!*

Author Armistead Maupin would be one of those to get married in California during the brief period of legality there. Also Maggie Nelson, who would later write in *The Argonauts* of spontaneously tying the knot just before Prop 8 passed. She and her partner, Harry Dodge, got the gist from a preelection report on the radio that a majority were likely to vote for Prop 8, meaning the ban on same-sex marriage would once again resume. 'We were surprised at our shock, as it revealed a passive, naive trust that the arc of the moral universe, however long, tends toward justice. But really justice has no coordinates, no teleology.' So they googled how to get married in Los Angeles. As Maggie would later put it in an interview, 'I completely believe in abolishing marriage, and I also got married—it's that kind of paradigm.'

Amid a dizzying sequence of lawsuits, Prop 8 would be ruled unconstitutional in district court. The bill's sponsors would appeal, like a dog with a bone, spending time and money, ostensibly aggrieved at the disregard for voters as well as irked that the case was decided by a gay judge. But in 2012 the Ninth Circuit Court of Appeals would affirm Prop 8 to be invalid.

The next year, the US Supreme Court would hold in *Holling-*

sworth v. Perry that opponents in California did not have the standing to intervene with same-sex marriages that had been ruled constitutional by the courts. The *Hollingsworth* decision would be announced on the 26th of June 2013—the same day that SCOTUS would issue another opinion, *United States v. Windsor,* which would declare Section 3 (the definition of marriage) of the Defense of Marriage Act unconstitutional. So that would be two more advances to land on Mom's birthday. The national legalization of same-sex marriage would arrive with the *Obergefell* decision exactly two years later.

The fact that a string of landmark gay rights decisions all happened to be announced on Mom's birthday is treated in my family as auspicious. But it's not just that we receive news of these decisions sentimentally. They are arrived at subjectively. Former SCOTUS justice William O. Douglas wrote of how he was advised by his chief justice, Charles Evans Hughes: 'Ninety percent of any decision is emotional. The rational part of us supplies the reasons for supporting our predilections.'

Together legally across the pond, we would find ourselves paying less and less attention to the cases. Our issue, it turned out, had never really been marriage, but borders.

OUR FRIENDS DEPARTED. WE packed up the wedding piece by piece. The portaloos were trucked back out via the narrow gravel road. The young hippie couple returned to disassemble the yurt.

It was time for another sort of honeymoon, briefly touring the West Country with my whole family plus, pretty awkwardly, Alistair during the first leg of the journey. We figured he must have become intimate with your sister Ruby in the yurt over the weekend. For such a mild-mannered guy, Alistair had turned out to be quite the player. *Wait, how do you know him again?* Jenny quizzed us, then changed the subject, deciding she didn't want to know.

In St Ives, Alistair, who hadn't packed trunks, went into the sea in his little black briefs. It was always just *there,* unmistakable, his blond-fragranced bisexuality. We dropped him off in Penzance and didn't mention him again.

We were heading to Bath via the Cheddar Gorge. In Bath, we would admire the limestone Georgian buildings, one after the other, elegantly same-ish. Then we would finish in London, where you and I would begin to look for a flat. From there, my family would depart back to California. They would take care of Clementine. Isabel had gone missing the day we left the country—probably in search of her former life with us in San Francisco. Three years later, though, she would be found. Having been fed in the meantime by who knows how many households several miles away. *She's gained weight,* Mom would report. *We call her Isabella now.* And for several years after that, both cats would continue to live with my parents—our needy, drooling, feline surrogates.

You and I would go on to make a life for ourselves in London. Around the time of our arrival, a rainbow of words would be installed on the brutalist concrete exterior of the Hayward Gallery:

DOG DAYS ARE OVER.

We would see it often. I wouldn't become aware until many years later that its creator also shared a love transcending borders. The European artist met an American poet one year after we did, in 1997. They became a thing two years later, would be married following its legalization, and would be together in New York City until the poet's death in 2019. We'd have no reason to read a transnational, homosexual aspect into the artwork—not any more than any other rainbow—but the words would sing out as if just for us: a symbol of hope, marking the end of over a decade without legal status and welcoming us to a new place.

What *are* dog days? The hottest days of the summer, as marked by the heliacal rising of the Dog Star, Sirius, the brightest in the sky; thought to bring drought, thunderstorms and bad luck; to send dogs mad; to incur lethargy and fever. When the dog days are over, things cool down. It gets colder still. The following year will bring new dog days. Those too will pass, and temperatures will drop again. With yet more dog days to come.

This was the rainbow that awaited us.

For now, we descended with my family in their rented SUV into the magnificent chasm of the Cheddar Gorge. On the speakers was the mix CD that we'd burned to hand out to guests—ten or twelve songs selected because they expressed something of our life together and reflected the spirit of the weekend.

Our recessional, "The Happening," came on.

Perhaps because I was more relaxed after weeks of preparation and days of hosting, I finally took in the lyrics. I yelped.

What? What, Jeremy?

It's a breakup song!

So!? Dad shouted, having been sure I was alerting him to a flat tire or other such urgent matter.

We marched out to this at the wedding! It was our big triumphant moment!

It does sound triumphant, Mom said.

I told Jenny, who was driving, to press the back arrow to play the track from the start.

But, I commanded. *Listen!*

Huh, Mom said. *Never really thought about it.*

Obviously we didn't either, I whimpered. *Diana Ross is left with a burst balloon*—that's *what is "happening." She's left alone.*

You're sure that's not a metaphor?

Well, it is, yes—but a burst balloon.

Hmmm, yeah, Mom said. *Not great.*

Is it bad luck?! I whined.

Maybe in some cultures it's actually good luck, someone said. A member of the Lin family always says something like that.

I sat wondering who in attendance might have noticed, and how badly they would have judged us.

The late-summer air came in through the windows, wet and fresh. Your face was calm and beautiful. You were on the verge of your new life in London, with both of us fully legal, officially belonging. And for now you were carried along, a content passenger, into a majestic, verdant valley.

Look, you said. We'd begun winding through the Cheddar Gorge. We were surrounded by lush greenery and damp stone. We came under the shadow of ancient peaks. It was as if we glided across the palm of a giant's hand, and could at any minute be picked up, enveloped by curling limestone fingers.

You don't care, I complained.

No, you agreed. *About the song? Don't care.*

I harrumphed and looked out the window. Begrudgingly, I began to take in the landscape. In the face of such prehistoric grandeur, I had little choice but to surrender.

It doesn't make a difference, you said. *Nobody cares about the words.*

ACKNOWLEDGMENTS

Jamie Atherton
Ka Bradley
Vivian Lee
Laura Macdougall
Elliot Martin
Arik Hardin
Miranda Ottewell
Pamela Marshall
Katherine Isaacs
Marie Mundaca
Jean Garnett
Morgan Wu
Ben Allen
Juliette Morrison
Gabrielle Leporati
Eleanor Horn
Olivia Davies

Carl George
Jacs Rodriguez | Visual AIDS
Kyle Croft | Visual AIDS
Virginia Fowler & Nikki
Giovanni
Marc Stein
Wesley Gryk
Mark Watson
Gary Ferguson
Luke O'Sullivan
Eileen Chow
Kristie Lu Stout
Sam Ashby
Dale Carpenter
Carolyn Levin
Steph Miller
Paul Flynn

Stuart Comer
Julie Ayoob
Kelly Rancatore
Tara McDowell
Peter, Jean & Jenny Lin
Euan & Heron Macdonald
Brandon Johnson
Rainbow Migration
Thomas Miller
Joel Gibb
Coco Cole
Jack Rollo & Elaine Tierney
Howard Gertler
Chris Power
Shon Faye
Melissa Febos
Callie Garnett
Jennifer Thomas
Georgina Le Grice
+ all at United Agents
Mikaël Demets
Carmela Chergui
The Hastings Bookshop
The Hastings Queer Book Festival
The Hastings Writers Workshop
Marieska Luzada
Rosie Brown
Emma Littel-Jensen
Kayleigh George
Kirin Diemont
Daniele Roa
Richard Clesham
Nico Blackstock
Jack Pierson
Birk Thomassen

To all these and the many others who helped make this book, I'm enormously grateful.

NOTES

Epigraph excerpted from "My House" (1972) by Nikki Giovanni. By permission of author.

1. SHUT THE FRONT DOOR

For information on Hawaii's supreme court and the Defense of Marriage Act, I drew on Sasha Issenberg, The Engagement: America's Quarter-Century Struggle over Same-Sex Marriage *(Vintage Books, 2021), along with records at congress.gov, C-SPAN footage, and various news media.*

WORKS CITED

4 'the most painfully': Michael Warner, *The Trouble with Normal: Sex, Politics, and the Ethics of Queer Life* (Harvard University Press, 2000), 52.

8 "Japo-Swiss": Robert Winter, *The California Bungalow* (Hennessy + Ingalls, 1980), 67.
Note: For information on bungalow courts, I referred to this book generally; for cinematic depictions, see John Schlesinger, dir., The Day of the

Locust, *1975, and David Lynch, dir.,* Mulholland Drive, *2002.*

Note on "buggery" laws: Whereas sodomy offenses had previously been addressed by ecclesiastical courts, the Buggery Act 1533 (or An Acte for the punishment of the vice of Buggerie) established "buggery" as a capital offense in civil law, regardless of the sex of participants, and remained officially punishable by death until 1861. The Criminal Law Act of 1885, which set the age of consent for heterosex at sixteen, also expanded the criminalization of sex between men to proscribe the vague realm of "gross indecency." The changes to "buggery" laws in 1994 were an amendment to the Sexual Offences Act of 1956.

17 'State-by-state skirmishes': David W. Dunlap, "Congressional Bills Withhold Sanction of Same-Sex Unions," *New York Times,* 9 May 1996.

17 'licking whipped cream': Lloyd Grove, "Rep. Barr's New Quest: Impeachment," *Washington Post,* 10 February 1998.

Note: The Respect for Marriage Act, codifying the legal status of same-sex marriage, was finally passed through Congress and signed into law by President Joe Biden in 2022. It was originally proposed in 2009 as a repeal of the Defense of Marriage Act. The act was supported by Bob Barr, the very same who authored the Defense of Marriage Act, as well as Bill Clinton, who signed DOMA into law.

17 'neckline': Libby Copeland, "Bob Barr: The Master of a Curious Universe," *Washington Post,* 18 August 2018.

Note: Gail Barr, Bob Barr's second wife, made statements about his familial relations in an affidavit to Hustler, *8 January 1999, in an apparent attempt by the publisher to highlight the politician's hypocrisy.*

18 'As a general rule,' etc.: Andrew Koppelman, "No Fantasy Island," *New Republic,* 7 August 1995.

19 'wooing homosexual voters': Paul Bedard, "Clinton Offers New Promises," *Washington Times,* 18 April 1996.

19 'Not something we intend to espouse': Bedard.

19 'do everything we can to support': Bedard.

19 'against same-sex marriage': Dunlap, "Congressional Bills Withhold Sanction."

19 'a homosexual group': Bedard, "Clinton Offers New Promises."

19 'find ways to ensure' . . . 'vehicle': Bedard.
20 'Interesting story in the *Washington Times*': Sasha Issenberg, *The Engagement* (Vintage Books, 2021), 156.
20 'Sounds like an opportunity': Issenberg.
22 'He believes this is a time': Todd S. Purdum, "White House Is Avoiding Gay Marriage as an Issue," *New York Times*, 16 May 1996.
22 'I don't think there's any question': Purdum.
22 'It is a ridiculous statement': Purdum.
23 'immature and inappropriate behavior': Evelyn Lieberman, quoted in "Lewinsky's Transfer to Pentagon Troubled Clinton," *Tampa Bay Times*, 3 September 1998.
23 'White House officials say they engineered': Jeff Leen, "Lewinsky: Two Coasts, Many Lives, Many Images," *Washington Post*, 24 January 1998.
23 'values agenda': Issenberg, *Engagement*, 12.
See also: Dick Morris, Behind the Oval Office: Getting Reelected Against All Odds *(New York: Random House, 1997); Joe Klein, "The Consultant,"* The New Yorker, *19 January 1997.*
23 'an overarching, pre-emptive metaphor': Memo ascribed to Naomi Wolf via the *Washington Post*, quoted in "Worrying About Women," *Newsweek*, 11 February 1996.
23 'The Good Father': Wolf.
23 'building a house together': Wolf.
23 'negotiate about the shape of the house': Wolf.
24 'a lone holding in an alien forest-world': Robert Duncan notebook no. 37, 27 April 1966, Robert Duncan Collection, The Poetry Collection of the University Libraries, University at Buffalo, State University of New York, cited in Tara McDowell, *The Householders: Robert Duncan and Jess* (MIT Press, 2019), 17.

2. BETWEEN TWO FAGGOTS

For information on Richard + Tony, I drew on the documentary film Limited Partnership, *directed by Thomas Miller, and the podcast* Lost

Highways, *written by Noel Black and produced by Tyler Hill, along with various news media.*

For details about Clela Rorex, I drew on Neil Genzlinger, "Clela Rorex, Clerk Who Broke a Gay-Marriage Barrier, Dies at 78," New York Times, *20 June 2022.*

For information on Jack + Michael, I drew on Michael McConnell with Jack Baker, as told to Gail Langer Karwoski, The Wedding Heard 'Round the World: America's First Gay Marriage *(University of Minnesota Press, 2016); Joyce Murdoch and Deb Price,* Courting Justice: Gay Men and Lesbians v. the Supreme Court *(Basic Books, 2001); and various news media.*

WORKS CITED

26 'Now, you can make up your own jokes . . .': Johnny Carson on *The Tonight Show* (1975), via Thomas Miller, dir., *Limited Partnership*, ITVS International/Tesseract Films/Treehouse Moving Images, 2014.

26 'Y'know, this could be the first time': Johnny Carson on *The Tonight Show* (1975), via "Clela Rorex, the Clerk Who Issued Some of the 1st Same Sex Marriage Licenses, Dies," *All Things Considered*, NPR, 23 June 2022.

27 'a mini-Nevada for homosexual couples': Grace Lichtenstein, "Homosexual Weddings Stir Controversy in Colorado," *New York Times*, 27 April 1975.

27 'He had a line all prepared,' etc.: Miller, *Limited Partnership*.

28 'Everything was going along blissfully fine,' etc.: Noel Black and Tyler Hill, "Six Gay Weddings," *Lost Highways*, History Colorado, September 2019.

30 'matched pair': Gail Langer Karwoski, *The Wedding Heard 'Round the World* (University of Minnesota Press, 2016), 18.

30 'Legally': Karwoski, 21.

30 'a sparkling new house': Karwoski, 20.

30 'We outfoxed them': Jack Baker interviewed by Erik Eckholm, "The Same-Sex Couple Who Got a Marriage License in 1971," *New York Times*, 16 May 2015.

31 'Not all homosexual life': Jack Star, "The Homosexual Couple," *Look*, 26 January 1971, in *The Wedding Heard 'Round the World* (University of Minnesota Press, 2016).
31 'We love each other': Karwoski, *Wedding Heard 'Round the World*, 39.
31 'usually the evening's entertainment': Karwoski, 38.
31 'just enjoyed feasting their eyes': Karwoski.
32 'just as friendly as she could be': Karwoski, 120.
32 'sensible reading,' 'as old as the book of Genesis': *Baker v. Nelson*, Supreme Court of Minnesota, 191 N.W.2d 185 (1971).
32 'about love, not sex': Joyce Murdoch and Deb Price, *Courting Justice: Gay Men and Lesbians v. the Supreme Court* (Basic Books, 2001), 163.
32 'landmark indecision': Karwoski, *Wedding Heard 'Round the World*, 150.
33 'in all respects valid,' State of Minnesota County of Blue Earth, Fifth Judicial Court, no. 07-CV-16-4559.
34 *I can endure no more*: Personal correspondence, in Miller, *Limited Partnership*.
34 YOU HAVE FAILED TO ESTABLISH: Robert Barnes, "40 Years Later, Story of a Same-Sex Marriage in Colo. Remains Remarkable," *Washington Post*, 18 April 2015.
34 'can perform the female functions': Paul John Caña, "Remembering Richard Adams: Filipino-American Rights Activist," *Esquire*, 17 December 2021.
34 'Right from the beginning, Richard and I': Black and Hill, "Six Gay Weddings."
34 'When people get married in the US': Bella DePaulo, "Unearned Privilege: 1000+ Laws Benefit Only Married People," *Psychology Today*, 2 April 2018.

Note on Adams v. Howerton: *Judge Irving Hall's opinion in the 1980 district court decision cites the ruling in yet another failed lawsuit brought by two would-be same-sex spouses, Paul Barwick and John Singer, who based their 1974 case on the newly implemented Equal Rights Amendment in the State of Washington.*

35 the term 'spouse': *Adams v. Howerton*, 673 F.2d 1036 (9th Cir. 1982), cert. denied, 458 U.S. 1111 (1982).
36 'extreme hardship': *Sullivan v. INS*, 772 F. 2d 609 (1985).
36 'a qualifying relative': *Sullivan v. INS*.
36 'a cap like someone from Bakersfield': Tony Sullivan, in Miller, *Limited Partnership*.

37 'The nature of injustice': Justice Anthony Kennedy, in *Obergefell v. Hodges,* 576 U.S. 64 (2015).

Note: In her book The Tie Goes to Freedom: Justice Anthony M. Kennedy on Liberty *(Rowman & Littlefield, 2009), author Helen J. Knowles-Gardner describes Kennedy's jurisprudence as 'modestly libertarian.' Kennedy authored significant SCOTUS rulings widely held to be victories for gay rights:* Romer v. Evans, *517 U.S. 620 (1996);* Lawrence v. Texas, *539 U.S. 558 (2003);* United States v. Windsor, *570 U.S. 744 (2013);* Obergefell v. Hodges, *576 U.S. 64 (2015). But he also went with the 5–4 majority in* Boy Scouts of America v. Dale, *530 U.S. 640 (2000), which upheld the right to ban homosexuals from serving as scoutmasters; and penned the majority opinion in* Masterpiece Cakeshop v. Colorado Civil Rights Commission, *584 U.S. 617 (2018), which avoided ruling whether business owners have a First Amendment right to refuse a service (like baking a gay wedding cake) based on religious beliefs. Besides speculation that Tony and Richard's case informed Kennedy's jurisprudence to some extent, other analysis mentions the possible impact of his early period working with legal scholar Gordon Schaber, who acquaintances claim was gay. See Sheryl Gay Stolberg, "Justice Anthony Kennedy's Tolerance Is Seen in His Sacramento Roots,"* New York Times, *21 June 2015; Mark Sherman, "Gay Mentor, Belief in Dignity at Roots of Kennedy's Views,"* APNews, *26 April 2015.*

3. HOMOSTUPID

For queer critiques of same-sex marriage, I drew on Michael Warner, The Trouble with Normal: Sex, Politics, and the Ethics of Queer Life *(Harvard University Press, 2000), along with relevant works by theorists including Lisa Duggan, Katherine Franke, Nancy Polikoff, John D'Emilio, and Lauren Berlant.*

Historical context on same-sex marriage as a civil rights issue comes from George Chauncey, Why Marriage? The History Shaping Today's Debate over Gay Equality *(Basic Books, 2004), along with other texts.*

WORKS CITED

39 'Presidential election years are the time': Todd S. Purdum, "White House Is Avoiding Gay Marriage as an Issue," *New York Times*, 16 May 1996.

40 'crude sexual advances': Alison Mitchell, "Clinton Drops Military Issue in Request for Suit Delay," *New York Times*, 29 May 1996.

40 'frontal attack on the institution of marriage': Hearing on H.R. 3396, the Defense of Marriage Act, before the Subcommittee on the Constitution of the House Committee on the Judiciary, 104th Cong., 2d Sess., 15 May 1996.

40 'elephant stick': Hearing on H.R. 3396.

41 'Aloha,' 'The people of Hawaii': Hearing on H.R. 3396.

41 'uphold an anti-gay status quo': Joyce Murdoch and Deb Price, *Courting Justice* (Basic Books, 2001), 219.

41 'the N word . . . that special kind of significance': Hearing on H.R. 3396.

42 'the transgendered': Hadley Arkes, "A Morally Empty Jurisprudence," *First Things*, 17 June 2020.

42 'We do not seek equality': Hearing on H.R. 3396.

42 'As it has become more acceptable': Andrew Sullivan, "Here Comes the Groom: A (Conservative) Case for Gay Marriage," *New Republic*, 27 August 1989.

43 'self-civilization': William Eskridge, *The Case for Same-Sex Marriage* (New York: Free Press, 1996), 58.

43 'Never mind that many gay men . . . it was precisely': Michael Warner, *The Trouble With Normal* (Harvard University Press, 2000), 94.

44 'to channel the polymorphous,' etc.: Hearing on H.R. 3396.

44 'everything was decided': Hannah Arendt, *The Human Condition* (University of Chicago Press, 1958), 26.

44 'where the household head ruled': Arendt, 27.

44 'society always demands': Arendt, 39–40.

45 'a deeper and harder-to-extract-yourself-from': Sullivan, "Here Comes the Groom."

45 'I am a talk show host': Hearing on H.R. 3396.

46 'Boy you've got a different set': Hearing on H.R. 3396.

46 'We live in a house divided,' etc.: Hearing on H.R. 3396.

47 'Let's tell the truth,' etc.: Hearing on H.R. 3396.
47 'It offends me tremendously': Hearing on H.R. 3396.
48 'A full set of documents': George Chauncey, *Why Marriage?* (Basic Books, 2004), 113.
48 'Erasing the history of gay political disenfranchisement': Chauncey, 12.
48 'seen as the proper place for the provision': Lisa Duggan, "Freak Flags and Freedom Fighters: Love, Hate, and the Limits of Law Reform," presented at the Fourth Annual Barbara L. and Norman C. Tanner Center for Nonviolent Human Rights Advocacy Forum, 25 February 2010.
48 'the loss of the plural statuses': Duggan.
49 'Marriage bans': Chauncey, *Why Marriage?*, 161.
49 'between the late nineteenth century': Chauncey.
49 'The fact is... I know': Hearing on H.R. 3396.
50 'What would the world be like?': C. G. Jung, "The Tavistock Lectures," Lecture III, 1935, in *The Collected Works, Volumes I–XX* (1953; repr., Routledge, 2014), 7946.
57 'Conservative activists in nine states': Chauncey, *Why Marriage?*, 51.
57 'the amendment seems inexplicable': Justice Anthony Kennedy, *Romer v. Evans*, 517 U.S. 620 (1996).
57 'Gay activists seem to understand': Hadley Arkes, "The End of Democracy? A Culture Corrupted," *First Things*, 1 November 1996.
58 'Mr. President': President Clinton and German chancellor Kohl, press conference, 23 May 1996, Clinton Presidential Materials Project.
58 'as I understand it': Clinton and Kohl, press conference.
58 'molded by its handling of gay marriage': Sasha Issenberg, *The Engagement* (Vintage Books, 2021), 15.
60 'unofficial envoy... I just wish the straight white boys': Francis X. Clines, "Weary Aide Is Buffeted in Gay-Marriage Storm," *New York Times*, 29 May 1996.

Note on same-sex marriage debate: This book does not extend to the discussion of partnerships with transgender individual(s). Relevant cases worthy of attention include: Vecchione v. Vecchione *(1997);* Littleton v. Orange *(1999);* In re Estate of Gardiner *(2002), and* In re Jose Mauricio Lovo-Lara and Gia Teresa Lovo-Ciccone *(2005).*

4. THE APHOTIC ZONE

WORKS CITED

62 'the ballet of the good city sidewalk': Jane Jacobs, *The Death and Life of Great American Cities* (Random House, 1961), 65.

64 'Don't come': "S.F. Mayor Puts Out Unwelcome Mat for Clinton," Associated Press, 7 June 1996.

64 'I remain opposed to same-sex marriage': J. Jennings Moss, "Bill Clinton: The Advocate Interview," *The Advocate*, 25 June 1996.

64 'would like to be legally married': David W. Dunlap, "Some Gay Rights Advocates Question Drive to Defend Same-Sex Marriage," *New York Times*, 7 June 1996.

64 'Why should three couples': Dunlap.

64 'Mad vow disease': Dunlap.

64 'One thing our community': Dunlap.

65 'We're going to fight it': Dunlap.

65 'We want it defined under God': Dunlap.

66 'ill-named': Congressional debate on Defense of Marriage Act, US House of Representatives, 11 July 1996, via *The Last Word with Lawrence O'Donnell*, MSNBC, 29 March 2013.

66 'moral disapproval': Committee on the Judiciary Report 104-664, 9 July 1996.

66 'Defense of Mean-Spirited Bigots Act': Congressional debate on the Defense of Marriage Act, US House of Representatives, 11 July 1996, via C-SPAN.

Note: John Lewis's rousing 'one house' speech puts me in mind of tracks like "Can You Feel It" (lyric version, 1988) by Mr. Fingers (a project of Larry Heard), featuring a sample of the Chuck Roberts vocal on "My House" (a cappella version, 1987) by Rhythm Controll. Various aspects of house music obliquely inspired the title of this book, including the movement between private and public embedded in the disputed etymology of the term house. *Does it reference The Warehouse, the legendary club held in a converted factory in Chicago? Or does it summon the concept of producers using synthesizers in their own homes? Furthermore, the process of assembling the book is inspired by sampling and mixing. In these ways, the title* Deep House *is not completely disconnected from the music genre.*

74 'great consort': "America and West Indies: June 1699, 12–20," *Calendar of State Papers, Colonial America and West Indies: Volume 17, 1699 and Addenda 1621–1698*, ed. Cecil Headlam (London, 1908).

74 'the island of pirates': "The Pirates Cemetery," *Atlas Obscura*, 23 November 2015.

83 'It may, finally, be in the gay man's rectum': Leo Bersani, "Is the Rectum a Grave?," *October*, no. 43 (Winter 1987); reprinted in Bersani, *Is the Rectum a Grave? and Other Essays* (University of Chicago Press, 2010), 29.

84 'a line or a law,' etc.: Maggie Nelson, "Porousness, Perversity, Pharmacopornographia: On Matthew Barney's OTTO Trilogy" (2016), in *Like Love* (Graywolf Press, 2024), 79.

Note: Maggie Nelson here references Creativity and Perversion *(1984) by Janine Chasseguet-Smirgel.*

84 'Why did it take me so long': Maggie Nelson, *The Argonauts* (Melville House, 2015), 87.

Note: Maggie Nelson continues, 'Really, though, it's more than a perfect match, as that implies a kind of stasis. Whereas we're always moving, shape-shifting. No matter what we do, it always feels dirty without feeling lousy.'

87 'is killed, or rather extinguished': Hannah Arendt, *The Human Condition* (University of Chicago Press, 1958), 51.

87 'can only become false': Arendt, 52.

Note: Hannah Arendt took a different view from that of James Baldwin, who wrote in The New Yorker *(9 November 1962) that, in an attempt to 'end the racial nightmare, and achieve our country, and change the history of the world,' he and other 'relatively conscious' people 'must, like lovers, insist on, or create, the consciousness of the others.' Arendt responded to Baldwin in an open letter: 'In politics, love is a stranger, and when it intrudes upon it nothing is being achieved except hypocrisy.' Via* The Book Haven *blog (2 October, 2019), stanford.edu.*

5. LOST WEEKEND

For information on Boutilier v. Immigration and Naturalization Service, *I drew on Marc Stein,* Sexual Injustice: Supreme Court

Decisions from Griswold to Roe *(University of North Carolina Press, 2010); Stein, "Crossing the Border to Memory: In Search of Clive Michael Boutilier (1933–2003)," among other texts; the online archive that Stein organized at outhistory.org; email correspondence with Stein; case documents, via oyez.org; Joyce Murdoch and Deb Price,* Courting Justice: Gay Men and Lesbians v. the Supreme Court *(Basic Books, 2001); and various news media.*

WORKS CITED

90 'A male and a male walk in': Justice James S. Burns, quoted in Sasha Issenberg, *The Engagement* (Vintage Books, 2021), 81.

90 'permissible discrimination': Sonia Faust, quoted in Issenberg, 82.

90 'not quite right': Hadley Arkes, "The End of Democracy? A Culture Corrupted," *First Things,* 1 November 1996.

Note on Honolulu media coverage: The headline STATE: KIDS NEED MOM, DAD from Honolulu Star-Bulletin, *10 September 1996, via sashaissenberg .com.*

90 'I don't categorize myself': Harris Wofford, "Finding Love Again, This Time with a Man," *New York Times,* 23 April 2016.

91 'He signed the bill in the wee hours': Associated Press, "Clinton Faces More Censure for Same-Sex Marriage Law," *Deseret News,* 23 September 1996.

Note on the Church of Latter-Day Saints: The LDS more recently supported the Respect for Marriage Act, safeguarding same-sex marriages, as a form of reconciliation with the gay and lesbian population, while apparently maintaining its own religious doctrine regarding the sin of acting on homosexual urges. For more on LDS property ownership in Hawaii, see Issenberg.

92 'malicious hooliganism with exceptional cynicism': William Branigin, "Gays' Cases Help to Expand Immigration Rights," *Washington Post,* 16 December 1996.

93 'a new area of immigration law': Branigin.

93 'particular social group': Branigin.

93 'We're telling HIV-positive people': Branigin.

94 'sociopathic personality disturbance': American Psychiatric Association, *Diagnostic and Statistical Manual of Mental Disorders* (American Psychiatric Association Mental Hospital Service, 1952), 38–39.

95 'complainant': Marc Stein, "Forgetting and Remembering a Deported Alien," *History News Network*, 3 November 2003.

95 'I am an officer of the United States Immigration and Naturalization Service': James B. Sarsfield, *In re Clive Michael Boutilier*, record of sworn statement before the Immigration and Naturalization Service, 13 January 1964 [fol. 1], in *Boutilier v. Immigration and Naturalization Service*, 387 U.S. 118 (1967).

95 Q: This charge of sodomy... A: I'm homosexual: Clive Michael Boutilier, *In re Clive Michael Boutilier*.

97 'the alien was afflicted with a class A condition': Paul G. Smith, MD, and Maria Sarrigiannis, MD, of the US Public Health Service Hospital to District Director, Immigration & Naturalization Service, 17 January 1964 [fol. 11], Exhibit 4—Certification of USPHS, in *Boutilier v. Immigration and Naturalization Service*.

98 'He is not psychotic... potential for frank criminal activity': Edward F. Falsey, MD, to Robert P. Brown, 2 March 1964 [fol. 12]: Exhibit 6—Report of Dr. Falsey, in *Boutilier v. Immigration and Naturalization Service*.

98 'initial spontaneous outburst... What emerged out of the interview': Montague Ullman, MD, Director of Psychiatric Services, Maimonides Hospital of Brooklyn, clinical abstract, 30 March 1965 [fol. 14]: Exhibit 7—Report of Dr. Ullman, in *Boutilier v. Immigration and Naturalization Service*.

100 'In such case to which country': *Colloquy between Special Inquiry Officer and Counsel*, before the Immigration and Naturalization Service, 26 July 1965 [fol. 16], in *Boutilier v. Immigration and Naturalization Service*.

100 'Canada... No, sir': *Colloquy between Special Inquiry Officer and Counsel*.

100 'Whatever the phrase "psychopathic personality"': Ira Fieldsteel, *Decision of the Special Inquiry Officer*, US Department of Justice, Immigration and Naturalization Service, *In re Clive Michael Boutilier*, respondent, in deportation proceedings, 5 August 1965 [fol. 23], in *Boutilier v. Immigration and Naturalization Service*.

101 'a term of art': Chairman, Order and Decision of Board of Immigration Appeals, US Department of Justice, Immigration and

Naturalization Service, *In re Boutilier*, deportation proceedings appeal, 12 January 1966 [fol. 29], in *Boutilier v. Immigration and Naturalization Service.*

101 "The Case of the Elusive Euphemism": "Immigration: The Case of the Elusive Euphemism," *Time*, 22 July 1966.

101 'We do not quarrel with Boutilier's contention': Irving Kaufman, *Clive Michael Boutilier, Petitioner, v. The Immigration and Naturalization Service*, United States Court of Appeals for the Second Circuit, 8 July 1965 [fol. 31], in *Boutilier v. Immigration and Naturalization Service.*

101 'To label a group so large,' etc.: Leonard P. Moore, *Boutilier, Petitioner*, 8 July 1965.

101 'the house of horrors erected by': Kaufman, *Boutilier, Petitioner*, 8 July 1965.

101 'habitually misbehave': Moore, citing *Flores-Rodriguez* (1956), in *Boutilier, Petitioner*, 8 July 1965.

101 'challenged popular stereotypes': Marc Stein, *Sexual Injustice: Supreme Court Decisions from Griswold to Roe* (University of North Carolina Press, 2010), 83.

102 'a red-head': Blanch Freedman and Robert Brown, brief for petitioner, 30 December 1966, *Boutilier v. Immigration and Naturalization Service.*

102 'It has long been held that the Congress': Justice Tom C. Clark, majority opinion, *Boutilier v. Immigration and Naturalization Service.*

103 'aliens afflicted with dandruff': Justice William J. Brennan Jr., oral argument, *Boutilier v. Immigration and Naturalization Service.*

103 'as clear as mud to me': Justice Abe Fortas, oral argument, *Boutilier v. Immigration and Naturalization Service.*

103 'ordinarily a homo is a psycho': Conference note on *Boutilier* attributed to Justice William O. Douglas, quoting Justice Abe Fortas, cited in Joyce Murdoch and Deb Price, *Courting Justice: Gay Men and Lesbians v. the Supreme Court* (Basic Books, 2001), 114.

103 'so broad and vague': Justice William O. Douglas, dissenting opinion, *Boutilier v. Immigration and Naturalization Service.*

104 'as impersonal as if the court': Murdoch and Price, *Courting Justice*, 117.

104 'downplaying its significance': Stein, *Sexual Injustice,* 243.
Note on SCOTUS certiorari: The Supreme Court would not hear oral arguments in a queer-related case until 1984. In the intervening years, over two dozen such cases reached the court but were denied or dismissed. See also: In re Petition for Naturalization of Olga Schmidt, *289 N.Y.S.2d 89 (1968).*
Note on the Coney Island photograph: Details and text from image uploaded to findagrave.com.

106 'post-traumatic psychosis': Dr. Alan E. Joseph, medical certificate for Clive Michael Boutilier, 27 November 1967, in Stein, *Sexual Injustice,* 276.

6. OTHER PEOPLE'S INVITATIONS

WORKS CITED

113 'lover of universal life': Charles Baudelaire, "The Painter of Modern Life" (1863), in *The Painter of Modern Life,* trans. Jonathan Mayne (1964; repr., Phaidon, 2010), 9–10.

113 'When one is left out': Adam Phillips, "On Being Left Out," *London Review of Books,* 20 May 2021.

114 'What new unbounded spatiality?': Judith Butler, "Imitation and Gender Insubordination," in *The New Social Theory Reader* (Routledge, 2001).

114 "The third doorkeeper": Franz Kafka, "Before the Law" (1915), trans. Willa and Edwin Muir in *The Complete Stories* (1971; repr., Schocken Books, 1995), 3.

118 'a sexual authority': Joan Didion, "John Wayne: A Love Song" (1965), in *Slouching Towards Bethlehem* (1968; repr., Farrar, Straus and Giroux, 2008), 30.

118 'the house shelters daydreaming': Gaston Bachelard, *The Poetics of Space,* trans. Etienne Gilson (1958; repr., Beacon Press, 1969), 6.

120 'Your children are not your children': Kahlil Gibran, "On Children," in *The Prophet* (Knopf, 1923), 17.

121 'Indian-Rappahannock': Arica L. Coleman, "What You Didn't Know About *Loving v. Virginia,*" *Time,* 10 June 2016.

121 'claiming descent from Pocahontas and John Rolfe': Coleman.

122 'who have no ascertainable trace': Georgia legislature (1927) cited by Hrishi Karthikeyan and Gabriel J. Chin, "Anti-Miscegenation Statutes and Asian-Americans," *Race, Racism and the Law,* 5 August 2011.

123 'I support the freedom to marry': "Mildred Loving, 40 Years Later," *The Atlantic*, 18 June 2007.

124 'Sharp distinctions persisted,': Nancy F. Cott, "Justice for All? Marriage and Deprivation of Citizenship in the United States," in *Justice and Injustice in Law and Legal Theory* (University of Michigan Press, 1998), 90.

124 'Mary K.... illegal and void': Cott, 77.

124 'not a "white person"': *United States v. Bhagat Singh Thind,* 261 U.S. 204 (1923).

124 'while American authorities': Cott, "Justice for All?," 77.

124 'Has the American Government': Mary K. Das, "A Woman Without a Country," *The Nation,* no. 123 (4 August 1926), cited in Candice Lewis Bredbenner, *A Nationality of Her Own: Women, Marriage and the Law of Citizenship* (Berkeley: University of California Press, 1998), 135.

125 'hope of widowhood': Mary Sumner Boyd, "Have You Been Enfranchised Lately? Naturalization," *Woman Citizen*, no. 2 (5 January 1918), cited in Bredbenner, *A Nationality of Her Own*.

125 'unaware that she'd irretrievably': Bredbrenner, *A Nationality of Her Own*, 136.

126 '... and thus it will go on': J. M. Barrie, *Peter Pan* (1911; repr., Puffin/Penguin Books, 1967), 220.

126 'is about the undeveloped nature': Grant Barrett, "A Different Meaning of Heartless in Peter Pan," in *A Way with Words,* podcast (28 July 2018), waywordradio.org.

126 'It is only the gay and innocent and heartless': Barrie, *Peter Pan,* 213.

126 'children don't experience': Barrett, "A Different Meaning."

126 'Being boy eternal': Carol Mavor, *Reading Boyishly: Roland Barthes, J. M. Barrie, Jacques Henri Lartigue, Marcel Proust, and D. W. Winnicott* (Duke University Press, 2007), 174.
Note: Mavor is referencing the phrase 'boy eternal' from The Winter's Tale *by William Shakespeare.*

126 'with nothing to do and nothing to spend': J. R. Ackerley, *My Father and Myself* (1968; repr., New York Review of Books, 1999), 175. *Note on colonial sodomy laws: Political researcher Enze Han has observed that such laws were demonstrative of a 'Victorian, Christian puritanical concept of sex.' Han describes a British rulership that 'wanted to protect innocent British soldiers from the "exotic, mystical Orient"—there was this very orientalized view of Asia and the Middle East that they were overly erotic. They thought if there were no regulations, the soldiers would be easily led astray.' Enze Han, interview by Tessa Wong, "377: The British Colonial Law That Left an Anti-LGBTQ Legacy in Asia," BBC, 29 June 2021.*

130 'Children who need to be taught': Margaret Thatcher, speech to Conservative Party Conference, 9 October 1987, margaretthatcher.org.

130 'Quite right too... quite prepared to affirm': Elaine Kellett-Bowman remarks cited in "Are LGBT People Safe with the Tories?," *Attitude*, 7 September 2017.

132 'Why, when there are so many people': Lauren Berlant, "Intimacy: A Special Issue," *Critical Inquiry* 24, no. 2 (Winter 1998): 286.

7. LEAVE TO REMAIN

For information on Mark + Ander, I drew on the BBC documentary episode "Compelling Circumstances" (BBC), along with Wesley Gryk, "LGBT+ History Month and the 'Coming of Age' of Same-Sex Relationship Immigration Rights," and email correspondence with Gryk.

WORKS CITED

135 'You wander around the house': Mark Watson interviewed in "Compelling Circumstances," *The Day That Changed My Life*, BBC (21 July 1999).

135 'This was a time': Wesley Gryk, "LGBT+ History Month and the 'Coming of Age' of Same-Sex Relationship Immigration Rights" (7 February 2020), gryklaw.com.

136 'we love each other, and all we want': Watson, "Compelling Circumstances."

136 'who were almost sort of shining': Watson.

137 'incidentally created an army': Gryk, "Same-Sex Relationship Immigration Rights."

138 'The perceived frequency': Carl F. Stychin, "A Stranger to Its Laws: Sovereign Bodies, Global Sexualities, and Transnational Citizens," *Journal of Law and Society* 27, no. 4 (December 2000).

138 'the sense of feeling cheated': James Baldwin interviewed by Richard Goldstein, "Go the Way Your Blood Beats," *Village Voice* (26 June 1984) reprinted in *James Baldwin: The Last Interview and Other Conversations* (Melville House, 2015), 67.

138 'a homogeneity and familiarity . . . both migration and homosexuality': Stychin, "Stranger to Its Laws."

140 'no doubt an historical': Gryk, "Same-Sex Relationship Immigration Rights."

149 'Why not? . . . cultivated unprecedented kinds': Michael Warner, "Normal and Normaller: Beyond Gay Marriage," *GLQ* 5, no. 2 (1999): 122–23.

Note: Historian George Chauncey writes that 'support for gay marriage was a distinctly minority position in the lesbian and gay movement' in the 1970s. He describes liberationists constructing new relational modes and patterns, and qualifies: 'We shouldn't overstate the strength of any of these cultural or political tendencies in the 1970s. They were especially characteristic of young white lesbians and gay men living in certain places, although they had disproportionate political significance because those same people formed the core of the organized gay movement. The sexual revolution in San Francisco, New York, and a few other cities far outpaced that occurring in most of America. Most lesbians and gay men still looked for a steady relationship.' George Chauncey, Why Marriage? *(Basic Books, 2004), 93–94.*

149 'The 1950s made all of us realize': George Rimmey, "When I Come Back, I'm Going to Be Gay," unpublished ms., cited in Dale Carpenter, *Flagrant Conduct* (W. W. Norton, 2012), 21.

149 'such areas of law as probate': Warner, "Normal and Normaller," 144.

149 'thinking creatively about other ways': Michael Warner in conversation with Harry Kreisler, "Publics and Counterpublics," *Conversations with History*, 21 March 2018.

150 'To speak of marriage as merely one choice . . . The state merely certifies a love': Warner, "Normal and Normaller," 128, 130, 136.

Note on UK unmarried partner concessions: As of 2024, Britain has established a much different standard for sponsoring a foreign partner; an unmarried couple does not need to prove prior cohabitation of two years but rather that they have been in a 'durable relationship' that is 'akin to a marriage or civil partnership' for at least two years.

8. SAFEWAY

For information on Bowers v. Hardwick, *I drew on Joyce Murdoch and Deb Price,* Courting Justice: Gay Men and Lesbians v. the Supreme Court *(Basic Books, 2001), along with case documents at oyez.org, the* Washington Post *article "The Unintended Battle of Michael Hardwick" by Art Harris, and various essays and news media.*

Information on Yamataya v. Fisher *comes from historylink.org and frontporch.seattle.gov articles by public historian Eleanor Boba.*

WORKS CITED

161 'illegals': Cesar Chavez to *San Francisco Examiner*, 27 November 1974, cited in "The 1974 Letter to the Editor Where César Chávez and the UFW Promoted Amnesty and Legal Residency for Undocumented Workers," *Latino Rebels*, 1 April 2021.

161 'wets': Gustavo Arellano, "Woke California Pays Homage This Week to Another American Hero with a Complex Legacy," *Los Angeles Times*, 29 March 2021.

161 'wetbacks': Cesar Chavez, interview, KQED, cited in Sean Saldana, "The Complicated Legacy of Cesar Chavez," *KUT News*, 17 October 2022.

161 'wet line': Oscar Raymundo, "Cesar Chavez and UFW's Questionable Tactics," *Huffington Post*, 31 March 2014.

161 'our brothers and sisters': Chavez to *San Francisco Examiner*.

Note: Further examination of Cesar Chavez's views on undocumented workers can be found in The Crusades of Cesar Chavez *by Miriam Pawel, on the United Farm Workers website at ufw.org and in various articles and essays. Additionally, the intersection of Chavez's activism with gay and lesbian populations has been discussed in articles including Mike Spradley, "Cesar Chavez: LGBT Rights Activist?,"* Huffington Post, *3 May 2012, and Doug Smith, "Cesar Chavez Tells Gays How to Woo Corporate Funds: Boycott,"* Los Angeles Times, *31 March 1983.*

162 'They have been able to travel freely': Justice Clarence Thomas, dissenting opinion, *Obergefell v. Hodges*, 576 U.S. 64 (2015).

169 'The private individual': Walter Benjamin, *The Arcades Project* (repr., Belknap Press of Harvard University Press, 1999), 8, 9.

169 'The only efficient way to guarantee': Hannah Arendt, *The Human Condition* (University of Chicago Press, 1958), 71.

172 'oxymoron': Justice Clarence Thomas, concurring opinion, *Dobbs v. Jackson Women's Health Organization*, 597 U.S. 215 (2022).

172 'legal fiction': Thomas, concurring opinion, *Dobbs*; citing his concurring opinion, *McDonald v. Chicago*, 561 U.S. 742 (2010).

172 'in future cases,' etc.: Thomas, concurring opinion, *Dobbs*.

172 'demonstrably erroneous': Thomas, concurring opinion, *Ramos v. Louisiana*, 590 U.S. 83 (2020).

172 'correct the error': Thomas, concurring opinion, *Gamble v. United States*, 587 U.S. 678 (2019).

173 'He must have stared... Ranting and raving': Art Harris, "The Unintended Battle of Michael Hardwick," *Washington Post*, 20 August 1986.

174 'cocksucking': Elizabeth Sheyn, "The Shot Heard Around the LGBT World: *Bowers v. Hardwick* as a Mobilizing Force for the National Gay and Lesbian Task Force," *Touro Law Center Journal of Race, Gender and Ethnicity* 4, no. 1 (May 2009).

174 'from a gay... doesn't remember his father': Harris, "Unintended Battle."

175 'chilling effect': Paraphrased in Joyce Murdoch and Deb Price, *Courting Justice* (Basic Books, 2001), 279.

175 'a married couple interested in variety': Murdoch and Price.

175 'Personally, I think it's disgusting': Murdoch and Price, 281.

176 'As far as sodomy is concerned': "To Right a Wrong," *Tampa Bay Times*, 16 December 2002.

176 'focused a spotlight on the penis': Murdoch and Price, *Courting Justice*, 287.

176 'I must say that when Professor Tribe': Murdoch and Price, 295.

176 'The principle that we champion': Laurence Tribe, oral argument, *Bowers v. Hardwick*, 478 U.S. 186 (1986).

176 'Home is the place': Tribe, *Bowers v. Hardwick*.

Note: The correct line is 'Home is the place where when you have to go there, they have to take you in.' Robert Frost, "The Death of the Hired Man," 1914.

176 'Concededly, there are certain kinds . . . personal bonds': Michael E. Hobbs, oral argument, *Bowers v. Hardwick*.

177 'We had this unbelievably romantic day . . . Powell's unbroken string': Murdoch and Price, *Courting Justice*, 304.

Note: While Powell insisted that he never interacted with homosexuals, Murdoch and Price reported that he actually did so with British codebreaker Alan Turing during World War II.

Note: Wolfson went on to found Freedom to Marry in 2003, and is considered (along with lawyers including Mary Bonauto) to be 'a chief architect of the political quest for same-sex marriage.' Frank Bruni, "Gay Marriage's Moment," New York Times, *20 June 2015.*

178 'I think it is somewhat broader': Tribe, *Bowers v. Hardwick*.

178 '4½–4½!': Murdoch and Price, *Courting Justice*, 314.

178 'of "deeper malignity"': Justice William Burger, concurring opinion, *Bowers v. Hardwick*.

179 'Homosexual orientation . . . no real choice': Justice Harry Blackmun, dissenting opinion, *Bowers v. Hardwick*.

179 'train of painful imaginings': Eve Kosofsky Sedgwick, *Epistemology of the Closet* (1990; repr., University of California Press, 2008), 75.

179 'The question kept coming up . . . this ruling': Sedgwick, 74–75.

179 'to take the most aggressive measures': Murdoch and Price, *Courting Justice*, 306.

179 'I think I probably made a mistake': Linda Greenhouse, "Black Robes Don't Make the Justice, but the Rest of the Closet Just Might," *New York Times*, 4 December 2002.

180 'We cannot think of any': *Powell v. The State*, 270 Ga. 327, 510 S.E. 2d 18 (1998).

Note: This 1998 Georgia ruling overturned the conviction of a man who was at the time serving a five-year sentence. He had been accused of raping his wife's seventeen-year-old niece in his apartment. Though she testified she'd been forced, he was acquitted. Instead, he was convicted of sodomy, having described how he performed oral sex on her in what he insisted was a consensual act. See: Gregory K. Smith, "Powell v. State: The Demise of Georgia's Consensual Sodomy Statute," Mercer Law Review *51 (2000).*

181 'In decisions spanning more than a century': "The Rights of Immigrants: ACLU Position Paper," 8 September 2000, aclu.org.

181 'protect... infamous crime': Justice George Shiras Jr., *Wong Wing v. United States,* 163 U.S. 228 (1896).

182 'It is not a "banishment"... is not imprisonment': Shiras.

182 'the rights of the petitioners': Justice Stanley Matthews, *Yick Wo v. Hopkins,* 118 U.S. 356 (1886).

183 'an aristocrat from the top': "Pretty Japanese Girl with Romantic Past Is Not to Be Found," *Seattle Star* (11 April 1903) via Eleanor Boba, "Supreme Court Rules in the Japanese Immigrant Case, *Yamataya v. Fisher,* on April 6, 1903" (3 July 2018), historylink.org.

183 'prosecutor, judge and jury': Boba, "Supreme Court Rules."

Note on INS/ICE home raids: Through the time of editing this book, immigration officials are generally only allowed to enter a private residence with consent or a judicial warrant.

186 'bombshell ruling': Carey Goldberg, "The Nation; Redefining a Marriage Made New in Vermont," *New York Times,* 26 December 1999.

187 'aesthetics of horror vacui... clutter, ornament, jewelry': Rebecca Solnit, "Rattlesnake in Mailbox" (2010), in *The Encyclopedia of Trouble and Spaciousness* (Trinity University Press, 2014), 32.

9. A DELICATE DANCE

For information on Felix + Ross, I drew on email correspondence with Carl George, cross-referenced with the Carl George, Felix Gonzalez-Torres and Ross Laycock Archive (on loan to Visual AIDS at the time of consultation) as well as Shawn Diamond's interview with Carl George, 31 July 2017, visualaids.org. Also: Jonathan Katz, remarks on "Hide/Seek" (2010–2011), National Portrait Gallery.

For depictions of New York Gay Pride 1989, see also: "Amnesia at Gay Pride 1989," 25 June 1989, by Nelson Sullivan, archived by 5NinthAvenue-Project; and Sarah Lyall, "Thousands March to Commemorate 20 Years of Gay Pride," New York Times, *26 June 1989.*

WORKS CITED

189 'could literally sit on my stoop': Sarah Schulman, *The Gentrification of the Mind* (University of California Press, 2012), 26.

189 'homosexuals cannot yet . . . traditional, legally': *Braschi v. Stahl Assoc. Co.*, 543 N.E.2d 49 (1989), cited in "We Are Family? Not If Non-Traditional," *ABA Journal* (1 November 1988): 96.

190 'particular resonance in the age . . . and Manhattan landlords': "We Are Family?," 96.

190 'a more realistic, and certainly': Judge Vito J. Titone, *Braschi v. Stahl Assoc. Co.*, cited in Philip S. Gutis, "New York Court Defines Family to Include Homosexual Couples," *New York Times*, 7 July 1989.

See also: Arthur S. Leonard, "Legal Recognition of Same-Sex Partners Under US State or Local Law," in Legal Recognition of Same-Sex Partnerships: A Study of National, European and International Law, *ed. Robert Wintemute and Mads Andenæs (Hart, 2001), 133–52.*

192 'a culture where same-sex desire is still structured': Eve Kosofsky Sedgwick, *Epistemology of the Closet* (1990; repr., University of California Press, 2008), 22.

195 'LiFE WiTH FELiX': Ross Laycock to Carl George, 29 July 1988, Carl George/Felix Gonzalez-Torres/Ross Laycock Archive.

196 'one of the greatest and most groundbreaking': "Felix Gonzalez-Torres," *The New Yorker*, 9 June 2016.

196 'The street name literally declares': Miwon Kwon, "The Becoming of a Work of Art: FGT and a Possibility of Renewal, a Chance to Share, a Fragile Truth," in *Felix Gonzalez-Torres*, ed. Julie Ault (Felix Gonzales-Torres Foundation/Steidl, 2006), 309.

196 'JUST REMEMBER—BE BiTCHY': Laycock to George, 1986, George/Gonzalez-Torres/Laycock Archive.

196 'DOLL... BEAVERS EVERYWHERE': Laycock to George, 9 September 1987.

196 'remember to tell them,' etc.: Felix Gonzalez-Torres to George, 12 May 1988, George/Gonzalez-Torres/Laycock Archive.

198 'TiMES OF CONStaNt': Laycock and Gonzalez-Torres to George, 8 August 1988, George/Gonzalez-Torres/Laycock Archive.

198 "SURFS UP!"... 'SUNSETS ARE SO': Laycock to George, 10 March 1989, George/Gonzalez-Torres/Laycock Archive.

198 'Life with La Gonzalez': Laycock to George, 31 March 1990.

198 'the boy': Laycock to George, 3 February 1988.

201 'There's a certain amount of traveling': Langston Hughes, "Same in Blues" (c. 1925), *The Collected Poems of Langston Hughes*, ed. Arnold Rampersad with David Roesell (Alfred A. Knopf, 1994).

201 'my mind meandering through': Carl George, "Gordon Kurtti as murdered by..." *Gordon Kurtti* (Allied Productions, 2013).

10. OTHER PEOPLE'S ISLANDS

Segments previously appeared in a very different form in Little Joe: a magazine about queers and cinema, mostly, *no. 6 (2021); later reprinted in* Little Joe: a book about queers and cinema, mostly *(SPBH, 2024), both edited by Sam Ashby.*

WORKS CITED

208 'Street Light Interference,' Hilary Evans, *SLIders: The Enigma of Streetlight Interference* (Anomalist Books, 2010).

208 *'meaningful cross-connection'*: Carl Jung, *Synchronicity: An Acausal Connecting Principle* (1955; repr., Routledge, 2008), 16.

208 'a certain Slant of light': Emily Dickinson, "There's a certain Slant of light" (c. 1861), *Poems, Series 1* (1890).

208 'gentler than my lover': Walt Whitman, "The Sleeper," *Leaves of Grass* (1855).

208 'The darkest place': Proverb paraphrased by Theodor Reik in

Roland Barthes, *A Lover's Discourse*, trans. Richard Howard (1977; repr., Vintage, 2002), 59.

209 'Cycling,' etc.: Robert Dobkin, interview by Linton Weeks, "Bad Karma? Or Just Bad Lightbulbs?," *Washington Post*, 17 November 2002.

209 'extremely improbable events': Paul Broks, "Are Coincidences Real?," *The Guardian*, 13 April 2023.

210 'I'm nobody!': Emily Dickinson, "I'm nobody! Who are you" (c. 1861), *Poems, Series* 2 (1891).

216 'wholesale slaughter... caution against violence': Tillman Durdin, "Formosa Killings Are Put at 10,000," *New York Times*, 29 March 1947.

216 'much of the island's elite': Michael Forsythe, "Taiwan Turns Light on 1947 Slaughter by Chiang Kai-shek's Troops," *New York Times*, 14 July 2015.

221 'I have to say, I have some': Thomas Miller, dir., *Limited Partnership*, ITVS International/Tesseract Films/Treehouse Moving Images, 2014.

221 'We're more in the closet now': Richard Adams, interview in Miller.

221 'Calls to impose...there is little that is "lax"': Immigration Policy Center/American Immigration Law Foundation, "The Lessons of 9/11: A Failure of Intelligence, Not Immigration Law," *Immigration Policy Focus* 2, no. 3 (December 2003).

12. LOVELAND

For information on the men at the Latin Gate, I drew on Same-Sex Marriage in Renaissance Rome: Sexuality, Identity, and Community in Early Modern Europe *(Cornell University Press, 2016) by Gary Ferguson, affirmed in email correspondence with the author, along with supplemental historical texts. Ferguson worked from fragmented trial transcripts collected by early modern historian Giuseppe Marcocci.*

The survey mentioned is from David P. McWhirter and Andrew M. Mattison, The Male Couple: How Relationships Develop *(Prentice-Hall, 1984). See also: Walt Odets,* Out of the Shadows: The Psychology of Gay Men's Lives *(Penguin, 2019).*

WORKS CITED

242 'put them in "their place" . . . it is worth remembering': Carl F. Stychin, "A Stranger to Its Laws: Sovereign Bodies, Global Sexualities, and Transnational Citizens," *Journal of Law and Society* 27, no. 4 (December 2000).

243 'proclivity for quick and easy sex': Andrew Sullivan, "The Marriage Moment," *The Advocate*, 20 January 1998, cited in Michael Warner, "Normal and Normaller: Beyond Gay Marriage," *GLQ* 5, no. 2 (1999): 149.

243 'Even if gay men did suffer': Warner, 151.

249 'Portugais . . . une estrange confrerie . . . et puis couchoient': Michel de Montaigne, *Journal de voyage de Michel de Montaigne en Italie*, vol. 1 (1774), cited in Gary Ferguson, *Same-Sex Marriage in Renaissance Rome* (Cornell University Press, 2016), 14.

249 'a common euphemism': Ferguson, 27.

249 '*conversos* or so-called New Christians': Ferguson, 55.

250 'enorme, abominevole': Newsletter sent to the Duke of Urbino, Francesco II della Rovere, 9 August 1578, at Biblioteca Apostolica Vaticana, MS Urbinati Latini, Vatican City, cited in Ferguson, 57.

250 'these sharp folk': Montaigne cited in Ferguson, 13.

250 'adhering uncritically': Ferguson, 16.

250 'community molecule': Pavel Florensky, *The Pillar and the Ground of Truth* (1914), trans. Boris Jakim (1997; repr., Princeton University Press, 2004), 301.

250 'general equanimity': John Boswell, *Same-Sex Unions in Premodern Europe* (Villard Books, 1994), cited in Ferguson, *Same-Sex Marriage*, 18.

Note: In the era, adelphopoiesis, no longer in practice in the Roman Catholic Church, continued to be practiced in the Eastern Orthodox Church.

251 '*friends . . . us*': Ferguson, 116.

252 'get married here': Ferguson, 111.

252 'recruitment . . . secret society': Ferguson, 118.

Note: Ferguson continues, 'The idea of forming a secret society is one that has long haunted homosexuals and sexual dissidents more generally, often reflecting a double lived experience: that of a group that needs to hide, to remain invisible, and that of the young or uninitiated who explore and learn from encounters with their elders or the less naive. It also reflects a social anxiety, a homophobic paranoid projection ("they're out to get our children"). In fifteenth and sixteenth-century Italy, the term school *is encountered in other contexts to designate known groups of sodomites' (Ferguson, 118).*

252 'The ancient Romans had no problem': Stephanie Coontz, *Marriage, a History* (Viking, 2005), 11.

252 'a man who allowed himself to be penetrated': Catharine Edwards, 'Unspeakable Professions: Public Performance and Prostitution in Ancient Rome,' in *Roman Sexualities*, ed. Judith P. Hallett and Marilyn B. Skinner (Princeton University Press, 1997), 69.
Note: For information on historical pederastic patterns, Ferguson has shared research from Michael Rocke, Forbidden Friendships: Homosexuality and Male Culture in Renaissance Florence *(Oxford University Press, 1996); and Marina Baldassari,* Bande giovanili e 'vizio nefando': Violenza e sessualità nella Roma barocca *(Viella, 2005).*

253 'a Slav': Ferguson, *Same-Sex Marriage*, 77.

253 'Perhaps not wholly surprisingly': Ferguson, 80.

253 'Pinto ran San Giovanni . . . My lord, my pleasure': Criminal tribunal notes, Archivio di Stato, Rome, cited in Ferguson, 97.

254 'Like the histories': Ferguson, 6–7.
Note: "Comforters" described in Ferguson, 74.

255 'paraded through the streets . . . baked in another batch': Ferguson, 78, 58.

255 'the obscure lives of these early modern immigrants': Ferguson, 82.

256 ' a striking form of polyvalent': Ferguson, 138.

13. JAMES DEAN'S PENIS

For information on Lawrence v. Texas, *I drew on Dale Carpenter,* Flagrant Conduct: The Story of Lawrence v. Texas *(W. W. Norton, 2012), affirmed in email correspondence with the author, along with various news media.*

WORKS CITED

264 'often used to legitimate sexual discrimination': Marc Stein, *Sexual Injustice* (University of North Carolina Press, 2010), 1.

264 'did not reflect sympathy . . . a snarled human story': Dale Carpenter, *Flagrant Conduct* (W. W. Norton, 2012), 12, xii.

265 'murder by automobile . . . a slightly bent': Carpenter, 43, 45.

265 'a Black male going crazy with a gun': Carpenter, 62.

266 'well in excess of a minute . . . I actually saw penis in mouth': Carpenter, 69, 68.

267 'extremely oversized . . . became agitated': Carpenter, 76, 73.

267 'That whole apartment': William Lilly, interviewed by Judge Janice Law, *Sex Appealed: Was the US Supreme Court Fooled?* (Eakins Press, 2005), 18, cited in Carpenter, 78.

268 'Gestapo, . . . a naggy little bitch': Carpenter, 77, 78.

268 'understood that they were being asked': Dahlia Lithwick, "Extreme Makeover," *The New Yorker,* 4 March 2012.

269 'I beg your pardon? . . . Yessir': Charles A. Rosenthal Jr., oral argument, *Lawrence v. Texas,* 539 U.S. 558 (2003).

269 'The sex in the *Lawrence* brief': Carpenter, *Flagrant Conduct*, 193.

270 'not *too* gay': Carpenter, 211.

270 'mere disapproval or hostility': Paul Smith, oral argument, *Lawrence v. Texas.*

270 'So what is the justification for this statute? . . . What about the statute': Justice Stephen G. Breyer, oral argument, *Lawrence v. Texas*.

271 'not correct . . . It is the promise': Justice Anthony Kennedy, opinion announcement, *Lawrence v. Texas*.

271 'protecting themselves and their families . . . Do not believe it': Justice Antonin Scalia, opinion announcement, *Lawrence v. Texas*. *Note: Despite the restraint embedded in Justice Anthony Kennedy's language, Justice Antonin Scalia, in his dissenting opinion, described a court as 'the product of a law-profession culture, that has largely signed on to the so-called homosexual agenda, by which I mean the agenda promoted by some homosexual activists directed at eliminating the moral opprobrium that has traditionally attached to homosexual conduct.' Justice Antonin Scalia, dissenting opinion,* Lawrence v. Texas.

271 'The conduct can be but one element': Kennedy, *Lawrence v. Texas*.

272 'Liberty protects the person,' etc.: Kennedy.

272 'This is actually a step backward': Stephen A. Allen, "Gay Rights: Separate but Equal," *Origins* (July 2003).

272 'not the synonym... Did they even know': Katherine M. Franke, "The Domesticated Liberty of Lawrence v. Texas," *Columbia Law Review* 104, 1399 (2004): 1401, 1415, 1407, 1408.

Note on North Dakota law and Alabama Eleventh Circuit Court: Cited in Stein, Sexual Injustice, *1–2. The Michigan Penal Code confirmed via legislature.mi.gov. The Mississippi Code Title 97: Crimes, Chapter 29: 97–291, confirmed via law.justia.com.*

273 'Kennedy's opinion portrayed the individual': Stein, *Sexual Injustice*, 301.

Note: Justice Sandra Day O'Connor *concurred in the* Lawrence *judgment, but not on whether it overturned* Bowers, *on which she sided with the majority vote.* O'Connor *wrote a separate opinion that it was a matter of equal protection—the Texas law criminalized male-male anal but not male-female anal. 'And because Texas so rarely enforces its sodomy law as applied to private, consensual acts,' she wrote, 'the law serves more as a statement of dislike and disapproval against homosexuals than as a tool to stop criminal behavior.' Apparently omitting previous decisions such as* Boutilier v. Immigration and Naturalization Service*—in which Clive was effectively booted back to Canada for his homosexuality—*O'Connor *described a court that has 'consistently held' that an objective such as the blatant '"desire to harm a politically unpopular group"' cannot be considered a legitimate state interest. This takes language from* Department of Agriculture v. Moreno *(1973), which held that a law preventing a household of unrelated persons from receiving food stamps violated equal protection because of its intention to 'discriminate against hippies.' Justice Sandra Day* O'Connor, *concurring opinion,* Lawrence v. Texas.

273 'From the beginning, *Lawrence*': Carpenter, *Flagrant Conduct*, 125.

273 'We have the law': Carpenter, xv.

274 'Suppose all the States': Scalia, *Lawrence v. Texas*.

274 'your *straight answer*': Breyer, *Lawrence v. Texas*.

274 'as close as one could get': Carpenter, *Flagrant Conduct*, 239–40.

14. WATERFALLS

For information on Clive Boutilier, I referred to the research of Marc Stein, along with that of Joyce Murdoch and Deb Price, as before.

WORKS CITED

276 'the first place on the planet... legally meaningless': Sari Staver, "Award-Winning Journalist Deb Price Dies," *Bay Area Reporter,* 27 November 2020.

Note: The song "Ban Marriage" by the Toronto-formed band the Hidden Cameras, featuring a nuanced narrative of our desires and the systems around them, was released earlier in 2003 on the cusp of the change in law in Ontario.

276 'We watch our siblings': Harrison Smith, "Deb Price, First Nationally Syndicated Columnist on Gay Life, Dies at 62," *Washington Post*, 2 December 2020.

278 'haltingly': Joyce Murdoch and Deb Price, *Courting Justice: Gay Men and Lesbians v. the Supreme Court* (Basic Books, 2001), 132.

278 'For these and many other reasons': Marc Stein, *Sexual Injustice* (University of North Carolina Press, 2010), xii.

279 'Deported from US territorial space': Stein, 243.

279 'According to a reliable source': *Mattachine Society of New York Newsletter*, 1968, cited in Stein, 273.

279 'barely able to speak': Dr. Edward McGovern, memo to INS, 14 July 1967, cited in Stein, 276.

279 'paranoid ideation,' etc.: Dr. Alan E. Joseph, medical certificate for Clive Michael Boutilier, 27 November 1967, cited in Stein, 276.

280 'would have been taking': Stein, 275.

280 'drummed it into his head,' etc.: Stein, 274.

281 'He has the problem too': Stein.

281 'Clive tells her everything': Stein.

281 'the complicated connections': Stein, 278.

281 'memorializing queers... the notion of queering remembrance': Marc Stein, "Crossing the Border to Memory: In Search of Clive Michael Boutilier (1933–2003)," *torquere: Journal of the Canadian Lesbian and Gay Studies Association* 6 (2004): 93.

282 'many holes': Gary Ferguson, *Same-Sex Marriage in Renaissance Rome* (Cornell University Press, 2016), 7.

Note on the Fairview Cemetery headstone: Details and text from image uploaded to findagrave.com.

15. A LITTLE COSMOS

Segments previously appeared in a very different form in Failed States, *no. 3, "Refuge" (March 2019), edited by Jamie Atherton; my text introduced a reprint of my essay "Outlaw Love," first published in* Index, *no. 37 (February 2003), edited by Ariana Speyer and published by Peter Halley.*

WORKS CITED

285 'Mother of Us All': Armistead Maupin, *Tales of the City* (Harper & Row, 1978), 18.

290 'the notion of pure love': Michael Warner, "Normal and Normaller: Beyond Gay Marriage," *GLQ* 5, no. 2 (1999): 134.

293 'If judges insist on forcing their arbitrary will': "Bush: States Shouldn't Change Marriage," CNN, 21 January 2004.

294 'Many happy couples': Deputy marriage commissioner interviewed by Tony De Renzo, "San Francisco Same Sex Marriage 2004," Project Coda Production.

294 'And to think that that is legal': Mark Leno interviewed by Tony De Renzo, "San Francisco Same Sex Marriage 2004."

294 'We really only had problems': Anne Hull, "Just Married, After 51 Years Together," *Washington Post*, 29 February 2004.

295 'the couple understood perfectly': Hull.

295 'spouses for life': Hull.

296 'protect the institution of marriage...kindness and goodwill': George W. Bush, "Same-Sex Marriage Amendment Statement," 24 February 2004, C-SPAN.

296 'Within hours': Hull, "Just Married."

297 'This was all done to victimize': Hull.

300 'Y'better believe it—1849...The end of the day': "Mayor Gavin Newsom," *The Charlie Rose Show*, 25 March 2004.

304 'We are ready to rock and roll': Carl Hulse, "Senate Democrats Offer Early Vote on Gay Marriage," *New York Times,* 10 July 2004.

304 'defenders of traditional marriage . . . We know which senators are for traditional marriage': Carl Hulse, "Senators Block Initiative to Ban Same-Sex Unions," *New York Times,* 15 July 2004.

308 'I believe it did energize': Dean E. Murphy, "Some Democrats Blame One of Their Own," *New York Times,* 5 November 2004.

308 'appeared to stifle a grin': Adam Nagourney, "'Moral Values' Carried Bush, Rove Says," *New York Times,* 10 November 2004.

308 'from the start . . . every state legislator': Murphy, "Some Democrats."

308 'because of the "spectacle weddings"': Murphy.

Note: A helpful thought on the terminology of same-sex marriage *comes from Maggie Nelson: 'One of the most annoying things about hearing the refrain "same-sex marriage" over and over again is that I don't know many—if any—queers who think of their desire's main feature as being "same-sex."' Maggie Nelson,* The Argonauts *(Melville House, 2015), 31.*

315 'Please, can we speak the truth? . . . make a major course correction': John D'Emilio, "The Marriage Fight Is Setting Us Back," *The Gay & Lesbian Review* (November–December 2006).

316 'less socially, economically, and spiritually worthy': Joseph DeFilippis et al., "Beyond Same-Sex Marriage: A New Strategic Vision for All Our Families & Relationships," BeyondMarriage.org (26 July 2006), reprinted in *Monthly Review,* 8 August 2006.

317 'No discussion of the issue': Warner, "Normal and Normaller," 149.

319 'What I want is a little cosmos': Roland Barthes, *A Lover's Discourse,* trans. Richard Howard (1977; repr., Vintage, 2002), 139.

16. RENTERS

Segments previously appeared in a very different form in Little Joe, *as before. The Eileen Myles text mentioned is "To the Class of '92," published in* Maxfield Parrish: Early and New Poems *(Black Sparrow Press, 1995).*

WORKS CITED

336 'For us, this is about . . . have our rights, our civil rights': "First Civil Partnership Ceremony 2005," *BBC News*, 19 December 2005.

Note: Meanwhile in the US on the 16th of December 2005, the House passed the Border Protection, Anti-terrorism and Illegal Immigration Control Act, which would increase penalties for unauthorized residents and those assisting them. Controversially, it would make unlawful presence a felony crime. Following mass protests, the bill died in the Senate. At the time of revising this edition, mere undocumented presence remains a civil violation of immigration law, not a crime under federal law.

17. THE HAPPENING

WORKS CITED

352 'Following legalization of same-sex marriage': David Groff, *Out Facts: Just About Everything You Need to Know About Gay and Lesbian Life* (Universe, 1997), cited in Michael Warner, "Normal and Normaller: Beyond Gay Marriage," *GLQ* 5, no. 2 (1999): 158.

358 'We were surprised at our shock': Maggie Nelson, *The Argonauts* (Melville House, 2015), 28.

Note: Armistead Maupin was first married in Canada in February 2007, then again in California in October 2008.

Note: In Los Angeles County, where nearly seventy percent of voters backed Obama, over half approved Prop 8. According to Sasha Issenberg, spending in the battle totaled eighty-three million dollars, second only nationwide to the presidential election.

358 'I completely believe': Jess Cotton, "Interview with Maggie Nelson," *White Review*, May 2015.

359 'ninety percent of any decision': William O. Douglas, *The Court Years, 1935–1975: The Autobiography of William O. Douglas* (Vintage, 1980), 8.

Note on Justice Anthony Kennedy: While Kennedy was pivotal in the Obergefell *decision, as well as the author of other opinions regarded as advancing gay rights, as noted before, his rulings have been varied. In his final case, announced on the 26th of June 2018 — putting an end to his run of welcome decisions announced on Mom's birthday — Kennedy voted with*

the majority to uphold the president's right to enact a travel ban, even though it smacked of anti-Muslim animus, in Trump v. Hawaii. *Following his resignation, law professor Robert Post wrote that 'the scope of Kennedy's empathies was distinctly limited. He could feel the pain of the devout baker who refused to prepare cakes for same-sex weddings, but he was deaf to the pain of the many Muslims assaulted by Trump's unspeakable rhetoric.' "Did US Justice Anthony Kennedy Just Destroy His Own Legacy?,"* Politico, *28 June 2018.*
Note: In June 2015, shortly before Obergefell, *SCOTUS announced* Kerry v. Din, *with the primary holding that the spouse of a non-citizen who has been deemed inadmissible does not have a due process right to an explanation. In his opinion, Justice Scalia further averred there is no constitutional right to live in the United States with one's spouse.*
Kerry v. Din, 576 U.S. 86 (2015).
Note: In June 2024, as I was revising this book, SCOTUS decided 6-3 in Department of State v. Muñoz *that a US citizen does not have a constitutionally protected 'fundamental liberty interest' in visa petitions filed on behalf of their noncitizen spouse. Representative Linda Sanchez (D-CA) issued a statement including: 'The MAGA majority on the Court today decided the constitutional right to marry, live with a spouse, and raise a family means nothing if a bureaucrat decides to banish a non-citizen spouse from the U.S.' (lindasanchez.house.gov). In her dissenting opinion, Justice Sonia Sotomayor wrote, 'The burden will fall most heavily on same-sex couples and others who lack the ability, for legal or financial reasons, to make a home in the noncitizen spouse's country of origin.'* Department of State v. Muñoz, *602 U.S. 899 (2024).*
Note on Proposition 8: In November 2024, just as I finished editing this book, California voters overturned Prop 8 via Proposition 3, Constitutional Right to Marry, which finally struck out discriminatory language in the California Constitution specifying marriage as between a man and a woman and enshrined the right to marry as 'a fundamental right.'

Jeremy Atherton Lin is the author of the National Book Critics Circle Award winner *Gay Bar.* His essays appear in numerous places, including the *Paris Review,* the *Times Literary Supplement* and the *Yale Review,* for which he was a finalist for the National Magazine Award. His sound programs have been broadcast on NTS Radio. He is based in Los Angeles and East Sussex, England.

GO DEEPER . . .

To listen to the songs in and around *Deep House,* visit **jeremyathertonlin.com/sound**.

RAISING READERS

Books Build Bright Futures

Thank you for reading this book and for being a reader of books in general. We are so grateful to share being part of a community of readers with you, and we hope you will join us in passing our love of books on to the next generation of readers.

Did you know that reading for enjoyment is the single biggest predictor of a child's future happiness and success?

More than family circumstances, parents' educational background, or income, reading impacts a child's future academic performance, emotional well-being, communication skills, economic security, ambition, and happiness.

Studies show that kids reading for enjoyment in the US is in rapid decline:

- In 2012, 53% of 9-year-olds read almost every day. Just 10 years later, in 2022, the number had fallen to 39%.
- In 2012, 27% of 13-year-olds read for fun daily. By 2023, that number was just 14%.

Together, we can commit to **Raising Readers** and change this trend. How?

- Read to children in your life daily.
- Model reading as a fun activity.
- Reduce screen time.
- Start a family, school, or community book club.
- Visit bookstores and libraries regularly.
- Listen to audiobooks.
- Read the book before you see the movie.
- Encourage your child to read aloud to a pet or stuffed animal.
- Give books as gifts.
- Donate books to families and communities in need.

BOB1217

Books build bright futures, and **Raising Readers** is our shared responsibility.

For more information, visit **JoinRaisingReaders.com**

Sources: National Endowment for the Arts, National Assessment of Educational Progress, WorldBookDay.com, Nielsen BookData's 2023 "Understanding the Children's Book Consumer"